AF801410

Contributions to Economics

The series *Contributions to Economics* provides an outlet for innovative research in all areas of economics. Books published in the series are primarily monographs and multiple author works that present new research results on a clearly defined topic, but contributed volumes and conference proceedings are also considered. All books are published in print and ebook and disseminated and promoted globally. The series and the volumes published in it are indexed by Scopus and ISI (selected volumes).

Jörg J. Dötsch

Economic Policy in the Digital Age

How Technology is Challenging the Principles of the Market Economy

Springer

Jörg J. Dötsch
Andrássy University Budapest
Budapest, Hungary

ISSN 1431-1933 ISSN 2197-7178 (electronic)
Contributions to Economics
ISBN 978-3-031-53046-3 ISBN 978-3-031-53047-0 (eBook)
https://doi.org/10.1007/978-3-031-53047-0

© The Editor(s) (if applicable) and The Author(s), under exclusive license to Springer Nature Switzerland AG 2024

This work is subject to copyright. All rights are solely and exclusively licensed by the Publisher, whether the whole or part of the material is concerned, specifically the rights of translation, reprinting, reuse of illustrations, recitation, broadcasting, reproduction on microfilms or in any other physical way, and transmission or information storage and retrieval, electronic adaptation, computer software, or by similar or dissimilar methodology now known or hereafter developed.
The use of general descriptive names, registered names, trademarks, service marks, etc. in this publication does not imply, even in the absence of a specific statement, that such names are exempt from the relevant protective laws and regulations and therefore free for general use.
The publisher, the authors and the editors are safe to assume that the advice and information in this book are believed to be true and accurate at the date of publication. Neither the publisher nor the authors or the editors give a warranty, expressed or implied, with respect to the material contained herein or for any errors or omissions that may have been made. The publisher remains neutral with regard to jurisdictional claims in published maps and institutional affiliations.

This Springer imprint is published by the registered company Springer Nature Switzerland AG
The registered company address is: Gewerbestrasse 11, 6330 Cham, Switzerland

Paper in this product is recyclable.

I do not know why it is that just when I was hoping to come to the end of our inquiry, I see instead other questions arising, as though sprouting forth from the roots of the questions we have felled.

Anselm of Canterbury (The Fall of the Devil, 227)

Preface

The idea for this book goes back to a lecture on competition policy I gave at Andrássy University in Budapest, in the 2021 spring term. Originally, I had planned to "simply add" a chapter on digitalisation at the end of the semester. "Simply add"—of course… It soon became clear that many aspects had to be taken into account in order to be able to describe the problems in a reasonably adequate way and to present them meaningfully. Moreover, the scope of the changes everywhere also extended beyond the narrow topic of the lecture. So, without further ado, I decided to approach the problem from a more general perspective and resorted to Eucken's principles as a heuristic structure. Each principle seemed challenged by digitalisation.

I then developed this approach further in seminars and lectures with the students, partly in the context of my courses at Andrássy University, Budapest, and also in my courses at the Budapest University of Technology and Economics. I owe a lot to the lively discussions with students at both universities and have received valuable inspiration and suggestions from them. I especially remember the fruitful discussions with Patrícia Kalafut, Xinzhi Zhong, Derique Mikhail Cidro Casio, and of course the discourse about various online platforms with Ákos Vörös and Dinara Sungatullina.

Likewise, I am very grateful for the support of my dear colleagues. First and foremost Dietmar Meyer, with whom I had the opportunity to discuss the initial versions of each chapter in a very lively manner. I learned a lot, especially how little I know. I am also very grateful to Stefan Okruch for his help and, as always, constructive criticism. I would like to thank also my much esteemed colleague Tim Alexander Herberger for his support.

I would also like to take this opportunity to thank my research assistants. To Katharina Wilke for her preliminary research, which ultimately encouraged me to enter the project, and especially to Karin Widmann for her thorough work, input and, above all, her very clear and valid criticism during the creation of this volume. She has particularly encouraged me to keep the book in a tone that is understandable and is easy to follow, especially for interested students. Last but not least I would like to thank Andrew Mile for the proof-reading and his kind help.

Since I had to write this book within half a year alongside other commitments, its completion meant not only a whole series of night shifts but also my unavailability for my family. Therefore, I thank my wife for her motivation, support and understanding. She'll probably know that I've given myself this task mainly to impress her anyway. I hope it works.

Budapest, Hungary
Autumn 2023

Jörg J. Dötsch

Contents

Part I
Theoretical Outline

Chapter 1
Introduction

> Especially so far as economic policy is concerned, principles are practically all that we have to contribute. (Hayek 1963, 227)

1.1 The Impact of Digitalisation

This chapter treats the question of what changes are being brought about by digital technology and what consequences this has for the economy and society.

It is intuitively comprehensible to everyone that digitalisation has a massive impact on all areas of life. Perhaps the answer to the question of which individual and social areas are *not* affected and changed by digitalisation says more than the attempt to rank all areas covered by digitalisation: This answer will be very brief in any case.

The umbrella term "digitalisation" includes a wide range of phenomena. It is simply comprehensible that this is not just another new technology like the four-wheel drive, the Teflon coating or the microwave oven. Digital technology can not only improve existing products. It changes products and services as well as the processes necessary to create them. Digital technology has made entirely new goods and services possible. It connects people and things. It is, formulated in everyday language, able to learn. If cycles of social and economic development based on certain technologies can be identified, then digital technology is certainly the new leading technology after steam and electricity. It is, as will be discussed, a new *general purpose technology* (Bresnahan and Trajtenberg 1995).

At first glance, this is obvious to everyone. However, we still know very little about what this actually means for our society and economy. As with all leading technologies, one has to admit that the long-term consequences of their application are initially unpredictable. Perhaps this is today truer than ever.

Much about the current change is indeed radical and remarkable. Fundamentally its speed; the extent to which it encompasses the most diverse areas of technology, science and the social sphere in general. The interplay of actors and devices in

© The Author(s), under exclusive license to Springer Nature Switzerland AG 2024

J. J. Dötsch, *Economic Policy in the Digital Age*, Contributions to Economics,
https://doi.org/10.1007/978-3-031-53047-0_1

complex networks with increasing dynamism repeatedly produces surprising developments. Digital technology has radically changed existing markets and also given rise to new ones. Wherever one looks, the extent of change exceeds anything that has gone before. Y. N. Harari rightly discusses the separation of intelligence and consciousness as an unprecedented revolutionary event—"intelligence is mandatory but consciousness is optional" (Harari 2017, 183); the revolution of communication via social networks has a disproportionately greater social impact than the use of the telephone; the economy of the internet suspends economic "laws" such as falling marginal costs. It would be easy to continue the list of examples.

1.2 The Task for Economic Policy

The following section outlines the extent to which the changes brought about by digitalisation pose particular challenges for economic policy.

Where is this development leading? In what ways can it be influenced or controlled? Or do we now simply have to resign ourselves to the "VUCA world" often discussed in management literature (see, e.g., Jankowska et al. 2020; Nandram and Bindlish 2017 or Mack et al. 2016)? For the individual, this may be partially true. For those responsible for economic policy, which must set the framework for sustainable and balanced development, as enshrined in numerous constitutions today, this cannot and must not apply. The question raised by the economist Walter Eucken,

> How to give the modern industrialised economy a functioning and humane order? (Eucken 2004, 14, own translation)

seems to be very topical today. All those responsible for economic policy in democratic societies have to ask themselves again and again. Yes indeed, this is an old question. And there have never been simple answers. But, remarkably, the question seems more relevant today than ever. It is the leading question of this book.

That this question has lost none of its relevance is confirmed by even a brief glance at the economic policy agendas of developed economies today, all over the world. The focus seems to be on competitiveness, efficiency and innovation; and digital technology—or, more generally, "digitalisation"—seems to be a suitable means of achieving this. At the same time, policymakers seem to be both the driving force behind the phenomenon and the driven by it. Without exception, they are currently struggling to keep pace with the changes of the digital age. The urge to act is omnipresent. Digitalisation in all areas of life is seen as the key to prosperity. *Prima facie*, there are several reasons that suggest this assumption to the responsible politicians. For example, companies are more than ever exposed to global competitive pressure. Digital technology can be a key to countering this. Be it by understanding customers better, by using data from them. Be it by being able to offer customised products and services via digital technology. Individualised products are increasingly becoming a requirement of customers in developed economies. Be it that one can offer the same product at a lower price through a more precise control of the value creation processes and/or by robotisation.

Digitalisation as a potential competitive advantage pushes companies as well as politicians interested in the competitiveness of their economies to invest in digital technology. Moreover, this technology is a way to counter the shortage of qualified labour, because jobs can be robotised. This is all the more imperative as the demographic trend in the developed economies is not making the situation on the labour markets any easier. And so on.

1.3 The Approach of This Book

This chapter briefly presents the most important questions and the corresponding analytical focus of this book.

This book does not presume to provide a simple, clear-cut and definite answers. The aim is different. The aim is to present in a comprehensive way the extent to which the economic policy objective posed with this central question—"How to provide a functioning and humane order for the economy?"—*has come under new conditions in the age of digitalisation.*

Regarding its object area, this book follows a twofold approach. First and foremost, it tackles the economy and asks what digitalisation changes in principle. On the other hand, this book takes the position that the economy as a whole has a technical or, in other words, *instrumental character*. What does this mean?

The economy is a social technique for reducing the problem of scarcity.[1] Admittedly, this first of all concerns individuals who value something as scarce. Through their behaviour, however, they bring about a phenomenon, which is peculiar enough to occupy a separate science and treated under the term "economy". This area of the social realm can be seen as a kind of its own and that is of public interest. And accordingly, this area of reality is also an object of normative criticism. In this respect, the economy must satisfy more than just economic criteria. The core question can also be asked the other way round: Does the economy help to reproduce a social whole that can be described as a "humane" order?

Of course, what is "humane" has always been the subject of debate based on social and cultural conditions. It is discussed differently by economic ministers in the Far East than in Northern Europe, for example. There can be no single, one-size-fits-all recipe for dealing successfully with the phenomenon of economy. And in this respect, to stay with the term "humane", it would be wrong to go into detail about what this means exactly, or what, for example, the derived term "social market economy" should mean. There are different ideas about that, too (see Goldschmidt and Wolgemuth 2008).

[1] Here and in the following, in the sense of Walras (2014, 41): "(...) all things, material or immaterial (...) that is to say, that are both useful and limited in quantity (...) all scarce things and only such things have value and are exchangeable".

But whichever way you look at it, the very assumption of an *instrumental character of the economy* as a whole is normative per se. This assumption is the starting point of this book, because it will have to be shown that it is precisely with a view to this instrumental character that far-reaching changes are currently taking place. Before this happens in the following, however, it is important to make the normative presuppositions that signify the preconditions of the instrumental character in developed economies explicit. These are typically Western presuppositions that underlie the Occident's conception of man and society. We limit ourselves, it must be said, explicitly to these presuppositions.

Firstly, with regard to the individual level, this book is based on a liberal concept of man.[2] Each person and ence economic actors should be able to make decisions at his or her own discretion and take responsibility and behave accordingly. Secondly, with regard to the level of society, material inequalities should be avoided to the extent that this could lead to destructive tendencies for the whole and endanger peaceful coexistence. Thirdly, in the sense of linking the second condition back to the first, the amount of material goods that individuals acquire should, as far as possible, be based on their performance and not on their status.

The economy, as the sphere of social activity concerned with the reduction of scarcity, must be able to meet or to approximate these goals in a sustainable manner. As will be demonstrated, normativity and economic law are two sides of the same coin called "market economy". This connection becomes explosive insofar as an economy that follows these principles always produces unpredictable changes and innovations, not least technical ones. Digitalisation is one of them.

The fact that the economy is of public interest and therefore always instrumental is anything but trivial against the background of endogenous technological change. It has already been mentioned above that the scope of the changes brought about by digitalisation is perceived by many social groups as well as by numerous scientific disciplines. Sometimes the impression emerges that people, and also the responsible politicians, are no more than mere spectators of what is happening. Is that a bad thing? Should not the economy be left to act independently? Here it is worth taking a closer look.[3]

The nuclear physicist and philosopher Carl Friedrich von Weizsäcker described this problem area in connection with the threats of the nuclear age in such a way that man is therefore both a technical actor and merely an observer of technological development, since modern technology is in many respects "untechnical". One would not sufficiently understand what technology actually is, namely a *means to an end*. Modern technology, however, was partly an end in itself and partly an instrument

[2] The question of what a "liberal conception of man" is might also fill shelves. For the purposes of the following considerations, it must suffice at this point to first make the role of the individual and his relationship to the economy and society partially explicit, and which must be assigned to him within the framework of such a concept of society in which the economy has an instrumental character.

[3] Here we cannot avoid at least touching on the area of important anthropological, philosophical or sociological questions. Admittedly, this is not the actual subject of these considerations, but it is precisely the scope of the current technological change that makes it unavoidable—here and also later—to at least point out such perspectives.

of particular interests, more precisely, economic or political power. He assessed this constellation as potentially destructive and derived from it a demand for acquiring knowledge: "A culture cannot be robust whose means are by a scale better developed than the consciousness of their ends" (Weizsäcker 1977, 104, own translation). For the subject of this book, this means an important message. If we assume that we live and want to live in a free society that makes use of the market economy and the division of labour, then it is necessary to understand to what extent digitalisation challenges the principles of our previous way of doing so.

Admittedly, this desideratum is very complex and, yes, at first glance too complex. It should only be mentioned here that Friedrich August von Hayek (1979, 164) already pointed out that we have "(…) never designed our economic system. We were not intelligent enough for that. We have stumbled into it (…)" and ultimately have little idea of the unspoken rules—strictly speaking, therefore, also techniques—on which it is based. Moreover, the quotation from Weizsäcker should not mislead us into thinking that a cultural-theoretical investigation is being undertaken here.

No, the intention is more modest. The book wants to make clear the extent to which the technology digitalisation poses *new* challenges to the principles of the free-market economy, a market economy that is supposed to serve people and society as a technique, i.e. instrumentally. Digitalisation is also a technique, and even a deliberately created, constructed one, this distinguishes it from "mere" culture.[4] It should therefore at least be possible to show where the effect of this technology comes in, what it sets in motion, and what it means for the economic order and an appropriate economic policy. If the economy serves the public interest, i.e. its character is instrumental, and if it is accordingly the task of the respective policy to ensure that the economy is a prosperous affair for our society as a whole, then it must be clear where opportunities lie and where dangers lurk. This book would like to contribute to the better understanding of these issues.

---

[4] An exhaustive discussion of this problem area would be longer than this book alone, even without a focus on digitalisation, and already fills shelf metres in libraries. It would be more a contribution to the philosophy of technology than to the problems of economic policy. Be that as it may, it is no coincidence that the problem of the very nature of technology, i.e. instrumentality, appears in the discourse associated with questions of economic policy at the technological level of digitalisation in the narrower sense (e.g. ERP systems, business models, robotisation and its impact), at the level of its significance for long-term, economic-social change processes (e.g. digital transition and transformation) and also at the level of the economy in relation to society (e.g. the impact of digitalisation on wealth and employment). All three levels will be touched upon in the course of the book, without committing to only one. Fernández-Macías (2018, 5) has broken down this crucial element of instrumentality in the context of digitalisation to a minimum: "Analysed in greater detail, a technology can be understood as a domesticated natural phenomenon: a device that allows the reproduction and control of a mechanism observed in nature". This attempt at explanation points very nicely to the problem of complexity that we encounter with digitalisation, namely ibid: "The more technologies that become available, the more the possibilities for the recombination and discovery of new phenomena and, therefore, the possibility for further technological development". It is precisely this complexity, among other things, that is the danger to which Hayek (1979, 164) referred when he continues his argument cited in the text above as follows: for our modern economy "(…) has carried us to unforeseen heights and given rise to ambitions which may yet lead us to destroy it".

A technique, i.e. a means to an end, will only be handled appropriately if one understands the laws according to which it functions and which one cannot change. While von Weizsäcker, from whom we have borrowed this thought here, was thinking of laws of nature, here, by focusing on the realm of the social, we must focus on the conditions under which, by people acting freely, an economy can unfold freely, which then in turn meets our normative expectations. This is quite a high level of abstraction. Böhm-Bawerk (1914) may have summed up the problem of the acceptance of preconditions and the feasibility of normatively motivated desires in the most succinct and prominent way: "Power or economic law?".

1.4 Heuristical Access

The following section explains the extent to which the central principles of the market economy, as formulated by Walter Eucken, can be used as a heuristic access structure in order to better understand the challenges which digitalisation poses for economic policy.

The present considerations enter an explosive area. Namely, the question arises as to what an economic perspective can achieve with regard to a new phenomenon such as digitalisation. In view of the scope and complexity of current developments and the challenges they pose for economic policy, the quotation that precedes this introduction seems to express a highly topical and appropriately modest desideratum: "Especially so far as economic policy is concerned, principles are practically all that we have to contribute" (Hayek 1963, 227).

It is the merit of the economist Walter Eucken, in whose work the position of the Freiburg School crystallises to a certain extent,[5] to have summarised the prerequisites for the emergence of a modern, industrialised economy in the form of a few principles in his work "Principles of Economic Policy".[6] He compiled a group of seven basic prerequisites, which he summarised under the term *constitutive principles*[7]:

(1) A functioning price system
(2) Primacy of monetary policy
(3) Open markets
(4) Private property
(5) Freedom of contract
(6) Liability
(7) Continuity of economic policy.

---

[5] See Chapter 3.

[6] Eucken died while still working on this work during his stay at the London School of Economics; it was later published by his wife and K.P. Hensel. At this point, the principles—which, of course, also triggered an extensive and still ongoing academic discussion, see later on—are briefly mentioned; Eucken's approach and its background are dealt with in due brevity in the next chapter.

[7] See Eucken (2004), 254–291. The principles were originally formulated in German, which is why there are slight variations in the translations commonly used in the corresponding discourse.

Since, on this basis, a market economy would be able to develop, but would probably not be able to secure itself in the long run, Eucken supplemented these principles with four so-called *regulative principles*,[8] which represent categories of potential state intervention that have the purpose of securing the very constitutive principles:

(1) Competition policy
(2) Income policy
(3) Correction of externalities
(4) Correction of anomalous labour supply.

It can be argued that the basic arguments of the "Freiburg School" are laid down in concentrated form in these principles.

On the one hand, this book is based on the conviction that these principles are still valid today. And on the other hand, precisely the perspective of these principles is an *excellent heuristic* to illustrate where the effects of digitalisation challenge the market economy, and that this is a qualitatively new process.

There is no doubt that the literature on the topic of digitalisation in economics alone is literally almost endless. What is lacking, however, are presentations that attempt to describe in an overarching way the extent to which the change actually represents an enormous challenge for the *instrumental character* of our economy as a whole. The principles mentioned, as a heuristical access structure at a sufficiently general but differentiated level, are suitable for that. One might argue that it is more topical than ever. Thus, the level of observation of this book is relatively abstract. But it is by no means remote or lacking pragmatism. Hence the approach of the Freiburg School is a *pragmatic* approach and offers an instructive way to assess the scope of the digital transformation and provide guidance for sensible, responsible economic policy. The analytical approach of the "constitutive" and "regulative" principles of the market economy is comprehensive and clear and offers the necessary flexibility to adequately categorise specific situations.

This book does not aim at a strictly "Freiburg School" or "Euckenian" interpretation of current events. The principles will be used as a starting point and serve as an *access structure* to make clear, where the effects of digitalisation come in and where they change the actual functioning of the economy and its relation to individuals, firms and society. To this end, they will also be partially summarised, specifically in relation to the focused problem of digitalisation. In the application of this access structure or heuristic, more modern economic approaches will also be used, such as transaction cost theory, the property rights approach or the perspective of institutional economics among others.

[8] See ibid., 291–304.

1.5 Chapter Structure

This chapter briefly introduces the structure of the book.

The first part briefly introduces the theoretical basis and explains in a first step what is meant here by digital transformation. In a second step, the background and the most important arguments, such as those of the proponents of the Freiburg School, are presented. Then Eucken's principles are discussed in detail, and the way in which they are to be used as an organising structure for the present study is explained. The second part then goes into detail on the problem areas resulting from the structure of the principles with regard to digitalisation.

The chapters are written in such a way that, on the one hand, they should enable independent reading, and on the other hand, they should also be accessible to a readership that has not yet dealt with this tradition of economic thinking and/or is not familiar with the discussion in the relevant areas. Each chapter therefore endeavours to disclose basic thoughts and facts at the beginning—which is sometimes also necessary because facts that have long been considered basic, and are covered in every textbook, have now come under new conditions. This approach to presentation inevitably leads to overlaps in individual areas, but this is also due to the high complexity of the phenomenon of digitalisation, which is to be examined from different perspectives. A summary and an outlook conclude these reflections.

This book is a theoretical enterprise positing that it is necessary to develop an appropriate view to adequately understand the current practical challenges of those economic policy actors who are committed to sustainable policies for the populations of liberal and democratically constituted societies. This is precisely why the book strives for a holistic perspective and does not focus on singular economic phenomena such as the problem of marginal costs in the age of digital goods or the extent to which evidence-based policy is or is not more important today. In this respect, this book takes a position that has gone out of fashion in the field of economics. With its subject matter—namely the change in the conditions of economic activity through technological development and the effects of this on society—it is dedicated to a highly abstract question. However, it cannot be denied that such questions are timely and must be asked today. This book is therefore aimed at a wide audience, at all those who are interested in the extent to which the way in which the modern, industrialised economy changes under digital conditions.

On the one hand, I have therefore endeavoured to use a tone that is as generally comprehensible as possible and at times also intentionally provocative, which certainly differs in some cases from the standard style of academic literature, without thereby compromising the actual argumentation. On the other hand, in view of the multitude of topics addressed and the interdependence that exists in some cases, it was necessary to deal with the references to the corresponding academic discussion with a sometimes extensive footnote apparatus to help the flow of reading in the main text.

References

Böhm-Bawerk, Eugen v. (1914): Macht oder ökonomisches Gesetz? Zeitschrift für Volkswirtschaft, Sozialpolitik und Verwaltung 23, 205–271.

Bresnahan, Timothy F. / Trajtenberg, M. (1995): General purpose technologies 'Enginges of growth'? Journal of Econometrics 65 (1), 83–108.

Canterbury, Anselm of (2007): The Fall of the Devil. Complete Theological and Philosophical Treatises. Translated by Jasper Hopkins and Herbert Richardson. Minneapolis: The Arthur J. Banning Press.

Eucken, Walter (2004): Grundsätze der Wirtschaftspolitik. Herausgegeben von Edith Eucken und K. Paul Hensel. Tübingen: Mohr Siebeck.

Fernández-Macías, Enrique (2018): Automation, digitalisation and platforms: Implications for work and employment. Eurofound, Publications Office of the European Union, Luxembourg.

Goldschmidt, Nils / Wohlgemuth, Michael (2008): Social Market Economy: origins, meanings and interpretations. Constitutional Political Economy 19 (3), 261–276.

Harari, Yuval Noah (2017): Homo Deus. A brief history of tomorrow. New York: HarperCollins.

Hayek, Friedrich August von (1963): The Economy, Science and Politics. The Collected Works of F.A. Hayek. Volume XV. Market and other Orders. Edited by Bruce Caldwell. Chicago, London (2014): The University of Chicago Press, 217–231.

Hayek, Friedrich August von (1979): Law, Legislation and Liberty, vol 3: The Political Order of a Free People. London: Routledge & Kegan Paul.

Jankowska, Barbara / Tulder, Rob van / Verbeke, Alain (2020): International business in a VUCA world: the changing role of states and firms. Bingley, England: Emerald Publishing.

Mack, Oliver / Khare, Anshuman / Kraemer, Andreas / Burgartz, Thomas (2016): Managing in a VUCA World. Cham: Springer.

Nandram, Sharda S. / Bindlish, Puneet K. (2017): Managing VUCA Through Integrative Self-Management: How to Cope with Volatility, Uncertainty, Complexity and Ambiguity in Organizational Behavior. Cham: Springer.

Walras, Léon (2014): Elements of Theoretical Economics. Or, the Theory of Social Wealth. Edited and translated by Donald A. Walker and Jan van Daal. Cambridge: Cambridge University Press.

Weizsäcker, Carl F. v. (1977): Der Naturwissenschaftler, Mittler zwischen Kultur und Natur, in: Idem: Der Garten des Menschlichen. Beiträge zur geschichtlichen Anthropologie. München, Wien: Carl Hanser, 91–106.

Chapter 2
The Digital Transformation as a Starting Point

2.1 Basic Distinctions

The following chapter presents the basic decisions on the subject of digitalisation and the chosen approach.

Section 2.1.1 introduces the topic and addresses the question of how the generally perceived phenomenon of digitalisation poses a challenge, especially regarding economic considerations.

Section 2.1.2 deals with some technical aspects that are relevant for the purposes of this contribution.

Section 2.1.3 is devoted to the decisive drivers of the particular dynamics of change that the phenomenon of digitalisation unfolds in the economy and society.

Section 2.1.4 treats the phenomenon of connectivity, a particularly salient characteristic of digitalisation, which will also be taken up again in later sections.

2.1.1 Preliminary Considerations

The following section is devoted to the question of how the phenomenon of digitalisation challenges the scientific discipline of economics and from which position this book aims to address this challenge.

First of all, digitalisation is a phenomenon of unprecedented scope. It is no coincidence that people usually speak of "transformation" in the same breath (see, e.g., Baker 2015). Accordingly, this transformation is taking over many sciences, including economics.

No one could deny that digital technology has a very significant impact on all areas of the economy, from consumers consulting a digital menu to Industry 4.0 and Fintech. What do these profound changes mean for the "wealth of nations"? A plethora of questions arise. Has digitalisation fundamentally changed the way we do

© The Author(s), under exclusive license to Springer Nature Switzerland AG 2024

J. J. Dötsch, *Economic Policy in the Digital Age*, Contributions to Economics,
https://doi.org/10.1007/978-3-031-53047-0_2

business? Is the way of coordination in markets different from the pre-digital era? Has a paradigm shift in economics and economic policy become necessary? There are studies on a wealth of aspects that follow different approaches. If one understands economics not only as the community of those who follow a certain method, but defines this science from its subject matter, then it has an extremely diverse set of methodological tools to offer.[1]

The fact that there is no such thing as one unified theoretical edifice in this field, but that there are disagreements among academics, theoretical strands and schools, does not detract from the scientific nature of the attempts to understand economic reality. After all, disagreement among scientists of one discipline belongs to all sciences, and even within recognised disciplines there are incompatibilities among watertight theoretical approaches. In physics, one aspect of this problem has gained some attention under the term complementarity (see, seminal, Bohr 1937). Perhaps precisely because it was formulated at the time of unprecedented successes of the perhaps most acknowledged of all sciences, physics.[2]

In fact, methods must always be measured by the quality of the answers they provide. It is, therefore first of all the question that relates to a specific subject area that then determines the methods. This perspective illuminates the fact that we are still at the beginning of the search for answers. For the situation with regard to digitalisation is still anything but clear. Many pixels, but no clear picture yet. On the one hand, there is an enormous output of research on the remarkable facets of the phenomenon and, on the other, there is an actually relatively manageable number of overarching presentations (most recently, for example, Hornuf 2022; Liu 2022; Brauweiler et al. 2020; Goldfarb et al. 2015; Vogelsang 2010).

This situation forms the starting point of this contribution. Its subject is both practical and fundamental. The question to which the following chapters are devoted is: To what extent have economic policy objectives come under new conditions in the age of digitalisation? It is important to note that this question is fundamental

[1] Of course, this understanding has always been controversial per se. And the opposite view is undoubtedly the one that dominates the academic course of thought. The list of its proponents would be long and famous; the claim to be able to treat simply everything with instruments of mainstream economics, i.e. the neoclassical strand, has become known as "economic imperialism" (a term coined by Ralph William Souter in 1933), of which Gary Becker is a good example: "I am saying that the economic approach provides a valuable unified framework for understanding 'all' human behaviour" (Becker 1990, 14). Hirshleifer (1985, 53) even speaks of "the universal grammar of social science". Now, one should not belittle the intellectual achievement of economic imperialists, but one should by no means share their confidence. From a serious scientific-theoretical point of view, the situation is unfortunately less clear (the fact that the no less "successful" and no less high-sounding linguistic universal grammar—to stay with the image Hirshleifer chose—is considered obsolete should give pause for thought). I have discussed this problem in detail in another contribution with regard to a specific methodological question (Dötsch 2022). This book takes a different standpoint: namely that *the problem determines the method, not* vice versa. This should—in order to avoid a detailed discussion of methodology, which would take up a book of its own for a comprehensive presentation—become plausible in the course of this chapter.

[2] Not only is physics well acknowledged, but the attitude of some of its representatives is similar to that of certain economists, e.g. well expressed in Rutherford's famous quote: "All science is either physics or stamp collecting" (quoted after Ratcliffe 2016).

because digitalisation has brought about a change of such magnitude that *the object of economic policy has changed.* For when we speak of "the economy" today, the social events that are commonly understood by it take place under different conditions than in the pre-digital age. An appropriate economic policy must be aware of what exactly is different. The following chapters will accordingly focus on developing an appropriate understanding.

In order for the sub-questions to be posed reasonably and the answers to be satisfactory, it is necessary to disclose the most important basic assumptions as well as some limitations. If one understands economic policy as all those measures with which the state both sets the rules of the game for economic activity and intervenes with a view to certain results of economic activity, this results in a division, in a double perspective: *positive economics* on the one hand, which must adequately describe economic facts,[3] and *normative economics*, which can provide recommendations for action for policy on the basis of clear goal-means relationships. Furthermore, economic policy can be differentiated with regard to its areas of impact. *Structural policy* can relate to various sectors, but also specifically to infrastructure and is thus directly addressed with the technical aspect of digitalisation. *Process policy* is dedicated to the challenge of continuous economic change and can be applied in various fields, e.g. monetary policy, trade or labour markets. There is no common English equivalent for the term "*Ordnungspolitik*", which expresses the approach of the Freiburg School. It refers to the sum of institutional conditions within which a market economy can develop (Schnellenbach 2021): It is rule-based economic policymaking. A basic assumption of this study is that digitalisation poses new challenges for both positive and normative economics and in all areas of economic policy named here. The aim is to clearly elaborate these challenges in each case.

The following section explains what is meant by the phenomenon of digitalisation here and makes some heuristic delimitations. There are different ways to segment the phenomenon of digitalisation analytically. Mostly, technical, economic and social aspects are distinguished. The crucial thing is that they interact. The following sections attempt to clarify this in more detail.

[3] For the sake of completeness, it must be mentioned here that the problem mentioned in the first footnote also applies to this statement. For it could be critically objected that no one describes any "facts", but rather interprets something on the basis of certain methods—no "facts" without a method! This problem of scientific theory will not be solved here. But it is part of every science and every discipline that with every further step in the specification of its abstractions it must at some point arrive at a level of general comprehensibility. The facts about which one can speak in two languages (to use Hirshleifer's metaphor again)—or not—remain unaffected by this, however. Those who deny this get bogged down in an endless constructivist regress that is not particularly fruitful.

2.1.2 Technical Aspects

This section briefly discusses the character of the new technology as such, since the broad phenomenon of digitalisation and digital transformation is the consequence of a technological innovation.

For the purposes of this study, only a few brief remarks on the technical side in the narrower sense should suffice. From a technical point of view, digitalisation means, to put it succinctly, a transfer from an analogue value into a format of binary strings of numbers. The still instructive and extremely thorough account by Vogelsang (2010) therefore names Gottfried Wilhelm Leibniz, who first represented multi-digit Arabic numbers with binary numbers, as the inventor of digitalisation (!).[4]

This "transfer" is the basic principle. The historical stages of technical development via Morse code technology to the development of the first computers do not need to be discussed in detail here (see also Vogelsang 2010, 7f.), especially since chip-based modern IT represents a technological quantum leap compared to the previous techniques. For our purposes, it is now decisive that the state of technology today makes it possible that, on the basis of the principle of those binary number strings, information about basically any facts can be encoded into such formats that can be stored and further processed by IT systems.

Of course, not "any facts" can be coded, but only what is recognisable, i.e. observable behaviours, certain observable properties of entities. The causes of such behaviours themselves—e.g. the sight of an attractive individual leading to higher heart rate, the cause of business success—can, of course, *not* be coded. This book will return to this explosive connection several times. For two reasons: firstly, because in many contexts digital technology "recognises" faster and better than human observers. On the other hand, because the technology is capable of *learning*, i.e. it can certainly deduce causes and does so increasingly well, even if it does so in a different way than humans with their brains. To clarify this exactly, one would have to enter the fields of epistemology and also artificial intelligence research in equal measure, which cannot be done here. So let us content ourselves for the time being with the statement that *digital technology means the possibility of digital reproduction, storage, modification and duplication of non-digital facts*, which is extremely far-reaching and develops—partly independently—so dynamically that in the following we will rather emphasise what digital technology cannot do.

The almost arbitrariness of being able to code is an indication of the large computer capacity behind this process, which was still a technical hurdle in the early days of digital technology. Just remember the gigantic size of the first computers. This hurdle has eroded in many respects and very quickly. From this technical point of view, the revolutionary development in this field is made clear by "Moore's Law" (originally Moore 1965), which is actually not a law, but "(…) the prediction that

---

[4] I owe Dietmar Meyer the hint that this is perhaps not to be taken entirely seriously, because even the Latin number system represented different digits with differently inclined strokes. Either way, it is certainly not the case that the more precisely one describes the origin of the way of coding, the better one would understand today's digitalisation or the "digital transformation".

transistor densities of semiconductor chips will double, speeds double, and prices drop by half approximately every eighteen months to two years" (Baldwin 2021). The technological basis of digitalisation, or more precisely, its capacity for encoding and processing the encoded, is thus growing exponentially. The greater the capacity, the more facts, *in principle of any kind*, can be recorded in this way.

This basically exceedingly astonishing technical capacity is the basis for the unfolding of a quite extraordinary dynamic of change, which is generally discussed under the term "digital transformation". Of course, for the purposes of these considerations, not all factors that have an impact here can be fully covered. However, for the chosen focus on the economy of society, different dimensions of digital technology that provide a kind of categorical grid for orientation will be given special attention. These are discussed in the following paragraphs.

Firstly, there is the dimension of *data*. Of course, data is not an invention of the digital age, but the latter has led to a completely new quality in both its extraction and processing, so that there is currently also talk of data as a new "raw material". Digital technology creates both a huge and growing amount of data and, on the basis of this, an undreamt-of wealth of (economic) opportunities arise through the same technology. It is therefore not without reason that we often encounter word combinations such as "data economy" (e.g. Schweidel 2015), "data-driven economy" (e.g. Cavanillas 2016), "data-capitalism" (e.g. Myers West 2017) and similar. We will not engage here in narrowing down certain conceptual meanings or definitional problems, but will try to understand the role of data with a view to the functioning of the market economy. This important dimension, the significance of the generation and use of different types of data, will therefore have to be discussed from several perspectives on a whole range of aspects and is not tied to a specific concept, such as that of a "data economy".

Secondly, there is the dimension of what the given computing capacity can actually do with this data and the dimension of *artificial intelligence and machine learning*. This, too, is a highly complex field of research, the technical aspects of which can only be dealt with comparatively superficially. We will therefore use these terms in a rather general sense and differentiate in detail when the corresponding research question requires it. This dimension is of the greatest importance for the present considerations because *knowledge* plays a central role in processes of social coordination, and thus also in all facets of the economy: knowledge about customer wishes, knowledge about procedures, knowledge about competitors, knowledge about all those factors that are components of economic decisions and those processes that create value. The capacity of digital technology to process data, mentioned above with regard to data, already contained an indication of the fact that it can absorb such knowledge. Digitalisation in the economy thus creates a *new dimension* that will be encountered everywhere, especially with regard to questions of coordination.

Thirdly, a certain aspect of the latter dimension will be treated as a separate dimension on another level, namely that digital technology is entering into direct *competition with human labour*. This is widely discussed, especially under the heading of robotisation. The effects are partly immediately visible and perhaps hardly surprising where a relatively complex machine replaces manual labour, but the potential to absorb human cognition mentioned in the previous section has extraordinary cross-cutting effects, which will therefore be examined from several perspectives.

It is easy to see from this brief overview that current developments are massively driven by technology, but of course the observable dynamics result from an *interplay* between technology and the economy. What are the driving forces behind this process are dealt with in the following chapter.

2.1.3 Drivers of Transformation

The following section explains which driving factors have led to the unimagined change that has taken place in recent years, which is generally and aptly discussed under the term *digital transformation.*

Firstly, the rapidly growing capacity of the new technology—"(…) (s)ince 1949, computing power increased, on average, by 45% per year" (Arntz et al. 2019, 1)—cannot be explained by technical arguments alone. It is inextricably linked to economic aspects. First of all, it is important to emphasise that the necessary technology can be provided cheaply—and increasingly cheaply—today. Rapid technical development is therefore accompanied by corresponding economic development.

Accordingly, economics also links "(…) faster innovation in semiconductor manufacturing to rapidly improving price-performance for semiconductors, to larger price declines for information technology" (Flamm 2018, 39). The capacity of the crucial technical basis is growing, while its price is falling in relative terms. This partly explains the dynamics of the development. Certainly, digital technology would spread even if it were relatively more expensive, partly due to the reasons mentioned in the previous paragraph. However, because it is cheaper and easier to use everywhere, it enables the phenomenon of an increasing degree of connectivity. This in turn leads to a self-reinforcing process of acceleration and dynamisation.

This is hence a diffusion process that is extraordinarily dynamic. Diffusion processes have been studied very thoroughly in innovation research (e.g. Morone 2010, on IT see, generally, OECD 2016); the dynamics and scope associated with digitalisation derive precisely from the fact that in principle everything can be coded. And therefore, it is possible today that almost without exception all individuals in modern industrial societies are now—directly and indirectly—in contact with phenomena of digitalisation and/or are interconnected via them. This even applies to hermits (see Diamond and Hoeller 2020) and even the Church of England has its "digital lab", in order to practice "digital evangelism" (see Church of England 2022). This whole process is most clearly illustrated by the use of smartphones, which are also becoming cheaper and cheaper (see Feng and Yu 2019).

The important fact of a growing degree of connectivity through the means of digital technology is very much a technical prerequisite for the special phenomena that digitalisation then produces on a further level. However, the fact of interconnectedness is not purely technical, but also a result of both market processes and social processes. Such processes have been thoroughly analysed. To what extent is the current process of change something special?

Let us first clarify the basic mechanisms and then focus on digital technologies in detail. The principle of such a process was already described by Schumpeter (2003, first published in 1942) as a process of "creative destruction", in which a new, innovative combination of possibilities destroys industries and market structures in order to then advance technical progress as a whole in a diffusion process carried out by imitators who follow suit and make it accessible to more demanders. This phenomenon is known in various forms.

In the most extreme form, technical innovations also give rise to completely new industries and induce waves of economic development. Such technologies are referred to as *general purpose technologies*, a term coined by Bresnahan and Trajtenberg (1995). These are the types of technical innovations from which a number of other innovations originate and which thus change entire industries. Bresnahan and Trajtenberg proposed three main characteristics of such general purpose technologies: firstly, their widespread distribution; secondly, their technological dynamics; and thirdly, their complementarity with application sectors. These are technologies that hence affect the entire economy and that change and have far-reaching consequences for all participants, even in the private sphere (see generally Helpman 1998) and hence the whole society.

Such waves of long-term economic development, explained by the change of technological paradigms—such as steam power (see Rosenberg and Trajtenberg 2001), the combustion engine or electricity—are also known as Kondratieff cycles (see Mager 1987).[5] It is more than obvious that the new, decisive technological paradigm is digital technology and the internet is commonly recognised as such a technology (see, e.g., Field 2008). However, how one then classifies their role against the background of other, epoch-making technological upheavals is quite different. Brynjolfsson and McAfee (2015) aptly title "The Second Machine Age", Freeman and Louçã (2001) interpreted the digital Revolution as the *fifth* technological revolution of capitalism (likewise Pérez 2003), Schwab (2017) and Mariniello (2022, 5) as a *fourth*, and Rifkin (2011) as a *third* kind of industrial revolution.

It is therefore understandable that the scientific discourse not only addresses digital technology in general as a general purpose technology, but that this is also attributed to different manifestations of digital technology, as their impact has a very considerable and sometimes hardly assessable scope. Fernández-Macías (2018, 1) starts with the microprocessor, Kane (2017) or Ozcan and Unalan (2020) write specifically about blockchain as a general purpose technology, Goldfarb et al. (2022) see such a technology in machine learning, Crafts (2021) or Klinger et al. (2021) categorise

---

[5] Admittedly, the discussion about the cyclicality of economic and social developments is extremely broad and cannot be reproduced here. The scope and duration of such patterns of change, which are perceived as cycles, are assessed differently. A general purpose technology is not a necessary prerequisite for such cycles and they are not always associated with the name of the pioneer Kondratieff, whose name is used to describe long-term patterns of great significance. Shorter cycles are discussed, for example, under the name of the Juglar cycles, which can again be treated in the context of longer-term developments. See, for example, Grinin/Korotayev (2014).

artificial intelligence as such, and Thompson and Spanuth (2021) already write about "(...) the decline of computers as a general purpose technology". These are only a few examples and the list could easily be extended. For the purpose of this study, it does not seem necessary to follow a specific categorisation or to make a category of one's own in order to then work economic policy issues through this grid. Rather, the concern in the next part of this book will be to confront fundamental principles of economic policy with the new phenomena of the digital world.

In the following, we will not deal with the theoretical question of where we stand today in an assumed development, nor will we think about periodisation or duration, but we will familiarise ourselves with the character of this change and its economic and social relevance. However, present time seems indeed a new age, because the economic and social impact of digital technology is particularly far-reaching: "artificial intelligence and machine learning are increasingly pervasive, embedded in people's everyday life (consider the use of smartphones, for example), and are therefore reshaping much of the economy and society" (Mariniello 2022, 286). This is a change of certainly a greater scope than that caused by the use of the steam engine or electricity.

In addition, there are other characteristics of modern economies that can be seen as drivers of digitalisation, because obviously self-reinforcing effects also play a role. The more developed an economy is, the stronger the incentives to use digital technology in more and more areas. This is because many companies in developed economies face (international) competition, which exposes them to considerable pressure to innovate in terms of products and production technology. Digital technology offers opportunities to increase competitiveness across the entire value chain, from the possibilities to customise a wide range of products, to the potential efficiency gains in manufacturing via better control, to sales via marketing channels that reach every potential customer on their smartphone. Moreover, in a highly competitive labour market for skilled workers and against the background of an ageing society in the developed world, companies have significant incentives to replace workers with robots in production and artificial intelligence in other areas.

One could argue that this has always been the case with new technologies. But digitalisation, as the next sections will discuss in more detail, goes further. For it is already a commonplace that *knowledge* is the decisive competitive advantage in the modern global economy (see, e.g., Westeren et al. 2020, 61f; Kaur 2019). But it is precisely this immaterial component in the economic process that can be absorbed by digital technology. To stay with the aforementioned scarcity on the labour markets: Digital technology can take on increasingly complex cognitive tasks, but it does not need social security, it does not get sick and it never has any other grievances.

Based on the concept of general purpose technologies, Fernández-Macías (2018, 1) speaks of the "digital age" and offers a general but for our purposes quite useful working definition:

> "The digital age can be defined as a historical period marked by the widespread use of digital technologies in different aspects of human activity, including the economy, politics and most forms of human interaction."

And he also points out the consequences: "This widespread use of digital technologies implies a profound transformation of social, economic and political systems, in the same way as the steam engine or electricity transformed past societies" (ibid.). We tend to think that the present transformation goes even further, as will become clear in the further chapters.

2.1.4 Connectivity

This chapter is dedicated to perhaps the most important element of digitalisation, namely the potential *connection* of a wide variety of things. This phenomenon is referred to in this context as *connectivity*.

For it has already become clear from what has been said so far that digital transformation represents a situation in which (1) technology (the growing capacity for coding), (2) market phenomena (technology that is rapidly becoming cheaper and rapidly diffusing through markets) and (3) social processes—the multiplication of the effect of (1) and (2) precisely through the networking of individual actors and also things (!)—mesh. Moreover, they *reinforce* each other. It is precisely this mixture that leads to the revolutionary character of the digital paradigm shift, to transformation. The digital transformation is indeed an all-encompassing, an exponentially spreading process of change.

The technological basis of this connectivity—which brings us back to the technical starting point—is the internet. Ultimately, it represents a network of computer networks and can, in principle, connect all computers with all computers (for its technical structure, see, just as clearly, Vogelsang 2010, 8f.) For this reason, of course, the internet can also be seen as a general purpose technology (e.g. Quiang and Xu 2017). The connection of any number of computers and any number of users produces a highly complex network that generates or permits new kinds of phenomena.

This connectivity raises a wealth of economic and also legal questions in connection with its technological realisation in detail. At this point, it should only be pointed out that digital technology made this phenomenon possible in the first place; what this means for the instrumental character of the economy in detail will be examined more closely from various perspectives in the following chapters of this book.

However, it is already clear at this rather general level that a process of change with a high cross-sectional impact and self-reinforcing effects has been triggered here, a change of a new character, which also means a new challenge for economic policy in particular. This aspect will be considered in more detail in the following chapter.

2.2 Social Relevance as a Challenge for Economic Policy

This chapter deals with the important connection between social change through new technologies and the role of economic policy.

The few remarks in the previous section illuminate that digitalisation is having effects that are obviously even more profound than those of the previous evolutionary leaps by other general purpose technologies. The phenomena that occur together with the new technology, on the one hand being able to encode in principle any circumstance, i.e. *to absorb knowledge* technically in a completely unprecedented way, and on the other hand the *connectivity* of any desired entities, are a new dimension of change. The following sections illuminate the extent to which this is problematic and the extent to which this represents a new challenge, also and especially for economic policy.

Section 2.2.1 outlines the novel character of the current change in more detail.

Section 2.2.2 describes an important element for the perspective of the present considerations, namely the basic assumption that the economy is the result of a social technique and has hence an instrumental or technical character.

Section 2.2.3 focuses on the element of normativity, because economic questions, in the end, are always social questions.

2.2.1 The Novel Character of Change

In the following section, we will briefly outline why the digital transformation is a process that is at least as far-reaching as the industrial revolution, and possibly even more so.

Though tragic for many individuals, it is at the same time an unavoidable part of economic progress that in the course of industrialisation some traditional crafts have given way to modern production machines. This has given rise to the role of the luddites (Caprettini and Voth 2020; Horn 2005)—a historical figure that seems to be booming again (Donelly 1986; Amies 2022).

This process, increasing productivity and production through innovation, is in principle desired today and forms an important element of any economic and competition policy. To want this in terms of economic policy presupposes on the one hand that the necessary adjustment costs on the part of the working individuals are regarded as unavoidable, even necessary pain in a market economy. And on the other hand it is proposed that adjustment costs can be absorbed in the long term either through further forms of division of labour, i.e. specialisation, or through clever adaptation of the individuals, e.g. through individual learning. For hopeless cases, the market economy, as the most efficient form of economic coordination, can generate a relatively high level of wealth, part of which can then be redistributed.

Now, however, things are a little different with digitalisation. For one thing, the *speed* of change is new (Marieniello 2022, 286). Secondly, on the basis of the phenomena outlined in the previous chapter, the *scope* is far greater than anything previously known. Thirdly, and strictly speaking this is one of the reasons for the enormous scope, today not only are machines optimised or physical work replaced, digital technology replaces human *intelligence*. The central ethical problem today is no longer the extent to which a worker replaced by technology can be helped, whether he or she can train, change location or industry, etc., but the fundamental problem of the technical possibility of separating intelligence from consciousness as prominently summed up by Harari (2017).

Now, in principle, a theoretical excursion would be appropriate at this point, namely on the question of what exactly is to be understood by intelligence.[6] On the one hand, it cannot be denied that computers today play chess better than humans, compose excellently or interpret documents more quickly and thoroughly with a view to specific questions, but on the other hand, computers can hardly be said to have emotional intelligence, for example.[7] This is certainly a remarkable discussion but does not have to concern us in detail in the context of this work.[8] Without having to theorise here about what intelligence is, it is obvious that fewer and fewer people tend to be needed for even intangible services that can now be replaced by computing capacity. Digitalisation therefore goes one step further than the replacement of an "employee" by a "machine". If one takes a broad view of the concept of intelligence, one could formulate in economic terms that the resource intelligence is less scarce, i.e. it becomes cheaper (otherwise it would not make sense to replace work steps previously carried out by employees with algorithms).

This is a novel phenomenon that points us to fundamental questions about the function of economy in our society. This is also of particular relevance to economic policy. The circumstances are now explosive, to say the least.

[6] This is a problem area that will be touched on several times. With regard to the possibility of substituting human labour, see above all Chapter 8.3.1 and the footnotes there.

[7] Even if this is probably less relevant in practice than one might like. The author of this book posed the following question to the artificial intelligence CHATGPT on 18.05.2023: "Can you help lonely people overcome their problems, because these people believe that you can empathise with them?" One sentence of the answer read: "I can certainly empathize with people and provide guidance based on the information and knowledge I have been trained on". The reaction on the human side doesn't seem to make much difference either, at least this is what CHATGPT has registered as follows: "People often express their gratitude to the developers and creators who have designed and built AI systems like me. (…) It's heartening to know that people find the interactions with AI helpful and meaningful in their own ways". It depends from one's point of view whether this is rather disheartening or not.

[8] Of course, the extent to which digital technology can imitate human intelligence and thus absorb the economic factor of human intelligence will be discussed in more detail later. This problem will be encountered several times, but in the chosen perspective of this contribution it is particularly virulent in the area of labour markets and will therefore be focussed on in Chap. 8, especially in its third sub-chapter.

2.2.2 The Technical Character of the Economy

The following paragraph introduces a normative element that is important for the considerations in this book, namely that the economy, although it should not be centrally steered or planned, should serve people and society.

Markets are a social technique for reducing scarcity. It probably sounds a little too narrow to say that the economy is technology. Nonetheless, it has *a technical character*.

As we have seen above, this becomes problematic from time to time when the economy endogenously generates novelty through new technologies. The resulting changes can vary in scope. We have already briefly discussed the extreme scope of change brought about by digital technology. Under the given conditions, there seems to be neither reason nor means to restrict the use of digital technology itself. At best, efforts to achieve at least minor control are discernible in certain areas (see, e.g., the case of GDPR Europe; on this, e.g. Houser and Voss 2018).

Even if the scope of the transformation through digital technology is certainly perceived by many, there are apparently major problems in adequately understanding the situation or even somehow controlling it. As the above example should make clear, this goes beyond the lack of controllability of development processes that are *deliberately* kept open. Who would want a planned economy today?[9] However, a better understanding of the most significant driving forces is necessary so that appropriate goal-means constellations can be formulated and appropriately negotiated in economic policy in the first place.

At this point, let us once again take up the problem emphasised by Carl Friedrich von Weizsäcker mentioned in the introduction: "A culture cannot be robust whose means are by a scale better developed than the consciousness of their ends" (1977, 104, own translation). Now, one can endlessly argue philosophically about the role of consciousness of such "means". But if one allows oneself to replace "culture" with "economy" in this quotation, one will not want to deny its validity in terms of economic policy.

[9] The calls for this in the public sphere in the Western world seem to be getting louder at times, and the state quotas in the developed countries also seem to offer an indication that the public sector already steers considerable parts of the economy. A discussion of how much central steering and planning is still justifiable would go beyond the scope and is also not the subject of this contribution. We assume here that no better form of social coordination than markets has been found so far to solve the problem of scarcity. The extent to which digitalisation influences the forms of coordination in detail is the subject of this examination. On the fact that digitalisation sometimes leads to very optimistic assessments with regard to the central possibilities for central planning, see Sect. 4.3.

2.2.3 *Normativity of Economic Policy*

This section focuses on the connection between values, economic order and the task of economic policy.

The concept of technology problematised by Weizsäcker can help in this context. For on the one hand we have digital technology, designed by man, which then, like so many other things, apparently is becoming astonishingly independent. And on the other hand, markets, accordingly, and the market economy based on the division of labour are a cultural technique that was by no means invented by man, but into which he "stumbled" (Hayek 1979, 164). This seems to apply no less to digitalisation.

The explosive phenomenon of artificial intelligence without consciousness (or without people) has already been pointed out above. Another indication of the scope of the digital transformation also arises at this point, namely that no market can manage without individual actors. Cultures, too, are not completely independent of people; they always require individuals and their interaction, even if the assertion is correct that these interactions produce emergent social systems, i.e. entities of their own order. Artificial intelligence, however, is capable of learning, it programmes itself and different entities equipped with artificial intelligence communicate with each other. Depending on which system level one looks, one can also manage completely without human individuals.

In this context, it becomes clear that economic policy considerations cannot do without normative elements (see, e.g., Okruch 2006). For it is an activity carried out by people who are responsible to people, to their voters. It must be based on normative positions that are constitutionally secured in developed economies today, e.g. freedom of the individual, securing property rights, etc. These are normative positions on the basis of which it is possible to discuss specific goals. However, such goals, no matter what they are, can only be realised under the condition that the laws of the real world are recognised (no parliament can unanimously decide on sunshine) and it is also necessary that the laws of the social world are recognised too.

There are economic laws that no political power can escape (see, classical, Böhm-Bawerk 1914). And just as the power of water can only be harnessed by recognising physical laws, the economy can also only be made serve a political purpose by recognising economic laws. The economy follows its own laws, but it is not an end in itself—this is the normative element that requires economic policy action. And under normative conditions, the economy has a technical character in Weizsäcker's sense: It is a social technique for reducing scarcity which, when combined with other social techniques and technologies in the narrower sense, generates an extremely high degree of complexity that the state must keep in check with rules so that it remains true to its technical character. It should have become clear here that digitalisation raises completely new questions in this context, because digitalisation increases the complexity exponentially.

This outlines the field of tension in which this book will move. On the one hand, the economy as an independent realm and the laws of which must be known and accepted. On the other hand, there is the regulator, the state, which, obliged to its people, has to ensure that this economy maintains it *instrumental character*. For the state, the central question is both normative and economic:

> How to give the modern industrialised economy a functioning and humane order? (Eucken 2004, 14, own translation)

Digitalisation, by creating an unimagined level of complexity, has given this question a whole new relevance.

References

Amies, Nick (2022): A growing movement is advocating the rejection of our digital society. The Brussels Times, Saturday, 31. December. Online: https://www.brusselstimes.com/343996/a-growing-movement-is-advocating-the-rejection-of-our-digital-society (last access: 16.05.2023).

Arntz, Melanie / Gregory, Terry / Zierahn, Ulrich (2019): Digitalization and the future of work: Macroeconomic consequences. ZEW Discussion Papers 19–24.

Baker, Mark (2015): Digital Transformation. Charleston: CreateSpace Independent Publishing Platform.

Baldwin, Carliss Y. (2021): Design Rules Volume 2: Chapter 12—The Planar Process and Moore's Law (June 16, 2021). Design Rules Volume 2: How Technology Shapes Organizations. Available at SSRN: https://ssrn.com/abstract=3868964 or https://doi.org/10.2139/ssrn.3868964 (last access: 24.09.2022).

Becker, Gary. S. (1990): The Economic Approach to Human Behavior. Chicago, London: The University of Chicago Press.

Böhm-Bawerk, Eugen v. (1914): Macht oder ökonomisches Gesetz? Zeitschrift für Volkswirtschaft, Sozialpolitik und Verwaltung 23, 205–271.

Bohr, Niels (1937): Causality and Complementarity. Philosophy of Science 4 (3), 289–298.

Brauweiler, Hans-Christian / Kurchenkov, Vladimir V. / Abilov, Serik / Zirkler, Bernd (eds) (2020): Digitalization and Industry 4.0: Economic and Societal Development. An International and Interdisciplinary Exchange of Views and Ideas. Wiesbaden: Springer Gabler.

Bresnahan, Timothy F. / Trajtenberg, M. (1995): General purpose technologies 'Engines of growth'? Journal of Econometrics 65 (1), 83–108.

Brynjolfsson, Erik / McAfee, Andrew (2015): The Second Machine Age. Wie die nächste digitale Revolution unserer aller Leben verändern wird. Kulmbach: Börsenmedien AG.

Caprettini, Bruno / Voth, Hans-Joachim (2020): Rage against the machines: Labor-saving technology and unrest in England, 1830–32. American Economic Review: Insights 2 (3), 305–320.

Cavanillas, José María (2016): New Horizons for a Data-Driven Economy: A Roadmap for Usage and Exploitation of Big Data in Europe. Cham: Springer.

Church of England (2022): Church of England Digital Labs. Online: https://www.churchofengland.org/resources/church-england-digital-labs (last access: 17.09.2022).

Crafts, Nicholas (2021): Artificial intelligence as a general-purpose technology: An historical perspective. Oxford Review of Economic Policy, 37 (3), autumn, 521–536.

Diamond, Madeline / Hoeller, Sophie-Claire (2020): Intimate photos of ghost-town dwellers and modern-day hermits show what a life lived in solitude is really like, Insider, Updated Oct 14, 2020, 6:53 PM, online: https://www.insider.com/inside-the-lives-of-modern-day-hermits-intimate-photos-2018-12 (last access: 17.09.2022).

Donelly, F. K. (1986): Luddites Past and Present. Labour / Le Travail 18 (Fall), 217–221.

Dötsch, Jörg J. (2022): The role of emergence for a complexity approach in economics. Limits, problems and opportunities. A reply. Acta Oeconomica 72 (2), 249–269.

Eucken, Walter (2004): Grundsätze der Wirtschaftspolitik. Herausgegeben von Edith Eucken und K. Paul Hensel. Tübingen: Mohr Siebeck.

Feng, Juhong / Yu, Kam (2019): Moore's Law and Price Trends of Digital Products: The Case of Smartphones. Economics of Innovation and New Technology, July, DOI https://doi.org/10.1080/10438599.2019.1628509, Available at SSRN: https://ssrn.com/abstract=3424363 (last access: 24.09.2022).

Fernández-Macías, Enrique (2018): Automation, digitalisation and platforms: Implications for work and employment. Luxembourg: Eurofound, Publications Office of the European Union.

Flamm, Kenneth (2018): Measuring Moore's Law: Evidence from price, cost, and quality indexes. NBER Working Paper No. 24553. Cambridge: National Bureau of Economic Research.

Freeman, Chris / Louçã, Francisco (2001): As time goes by: From the industrial revolutions to the information revolution. Oxford, New York: Oxford University Press.

Goldfarb, Avi / Greenstein, Shane M. / Tucker, Catherine E. (eds) (2015): Economic Analysis of the Digital Economy. Chicago, London: University of Chicago Press.

Goldfarb, Avi / Taska, Bledi / Teodoridis, Teodora (2022): Could Machine Learning Be a General Purpose Technology? A Comparison of Emerging Technologies Using Data from Online Job Postings. NBER Working Paper No. 29767. Cambridge, MA: National Bureau of Economic Research.

Grinin, Leonid / Korotayev, Andrey (2014): Interaction between Kondratieff Waves and Juglar Cycles, in: Leonid E. Grinin, Tessaleno C. Devezas, Andrey V. Korotayev (eds): Kondratieff Waves. Juglar–Kuznets–Kondratieff. Yearbook. Volgograd: Uchitel Publishing House, 25–95.

Harari, Yuval Noah (2017): Homo Deus. A brief history of tomorrow. New York: HarperCollins.

Hayek, Friedrich August von (1979): Law, Legislation and Liberty, vol 3: The Political Order of a Free People. London: Routledge & Kegan Paul.

Helpman, Elhanan (1998): General purpose technologies and economic growth. Cambridge, Mass: MIT Press.

Hirshleifer, Jack (1985): The Expanding Domain of Economics. American Economic Review 75 (6), 53–68.

Horn, Jeff (2005): Machine-breaking in England and France during the Age of Revolution. Labour / Le Travail 55 (Spring), 143–166.

Hornuf, Lars (2022): Diginomics Research Perspectives. The Role of Digitalization in Business and Society. Cham: Springer Publishing.

Houser, Kimberly A. / Voss, Gregory W. (2018): GDPR: The End of Google and Facebook or a New Paradigm in Data Privacy? Richmond Journal of Law & Technology (1).

Kane, Ethan (2017): Is Blockchain a General Purpose Technology? Economics of networks eJournal.

Kaur, Vaneet (2019): Knowledge-Based Dynamic Capabilities. The Road Ahead in Gaining Organizational Competitiveness. Cham: Springer.

Klinger, Joel / Mateos-Garcia, Juan / Stathoulopoulo, Konstantinos (2021): Deep learning, deep change? Mapping the evolution and geography of a general purpose technology, in: Scientometrics 126, 5589–5621.

Liu, Zhiyi (2022): Principles of Digital Economics. Innovation Theory in the Age of Intelligence. Singapore: Springer Nature.

Mager, Nathan (1987): The Kondratieff waves. New York: Praeger.

Mariniello, Mario (2022): Digital Economic Policy. The Economics of Digital Markets from a European Union Perspective. Oxford: University Press.

Moore, Gordon E. (1965): Cramming more components onto integrated circuits. Electronics 38 (8), April 19.

Morone, Piergiuseppe (2010): Knowledge diffusion and innovation: modelling complex entrepreneurial behaviours. Cheltenham, Northampton, Mass.: Edward Elgar.

Myers West, Sarah (2017): Data Capitalism: Redefining the Logics of Surveillance and Privacy. Business & Society 58 (1), 20–41.

OECD (2016): Stimulating digital innovation for growth and inclusiveness: The role of policies for the successful diffusion of ICT. Organisation for Economic Co-operation and Development. Paris: OECD Publishing.

Okuch, Stefan (2006): Vaules and Ecoomic Order: In Search of Legitimacy. Andrássy Working Paper Series No. XVIII. Online: https://www.andrassyuni.eu/pubfile/de-29-okruch-values-and-economic-order-in-search-of-legitimacy.pdf (last access: 30.4.2023).

Ozcan, Sercan / Unalan, Serhan (2020): Blockchain as a General-Purpose Technology: Patentometric Evidence of Science, Technologies, and Actors. IEEE Transactions on Engineering Management 69 (3), June.

Pérez, Carlota (2003): Technological revolutions and financial capital: The dynamics of bubbles and golden ages. Cheltenham, UK: Edward Elgar.

Quiang, Christine Zhenwei / Xu, Lixin Colin (2017): The Internet as a General-Purpose Technology: Firm-Level Evidence from Around the World. World Bank Policy Research Working Paper No. 7192.

Ratcliffe, Susan (ed.) (2016): Oxford Essential Quotations. Oxford University Press. Online: https://www.oxfordreference.com/display/10.1093/acref/9780191826719.001.0001/q-oro-ed4-00009051 (last access: 05.08.2023).

Rifkin, Jeremy (2011): The third industrial revolution: How lateral power is transforming energy, the economy, and the world. New York: Palgrave Macmillan.

Rosenberg, Nathan / Trajtenberg, Manuel (2001): A General Purpose Technology at Work: The Corliss Steam Engine in the late 19th Century US. NBER Working Paper No. 8485.

Schnellenbach, Jan (2021): The Concept of Ordnungspolitik: Rule-Based Economic Policy-Making from the Perspective of the Freiburg School. Freiburg Discussion papers on Constitutional Economics 21/7. Freiburg: Walter Eucken Institut.

Schumpeter, Joseph (2003): Capitalism, Socialism, and Democracy. London, New York: Routledge.

Schwab, Klaus (2017): The fourth industrial revolution. New York: Crown Publishing.

Schweidel, David A. (2015): Profiting from the data economy: understanding the roles of consumers, innovators, and regulators in a data-driven world. Upper Saddle River, NJ: Pearson Education.

Thompson, Neil C. / Spanuth, Svenja (2021): The decline of computers as a general purpose technology. Communications of the Association for Computing Machinery 64 (3), 64–72.

Vogelsang, Michael (2010): Digitalization in open economies: theory and policy implications. Heidelberg: Physica.

Weizsäcker, Carl F. v. (1977): Der Naturwissenschaftler, Mittler zwischen Kultur und Natur, in: Idem: Der Garten des Menschlichen. Beiträge zur geschichtlichen Anthropologie. München, Wien: Carl Hanser, 91–106.

Westeren, Knut Ingar / Cader, Hanas / de Fátima Sales, Maria / Similä, Jan Ole / Staduto, Jefferson (2020): Competitiveness and Knowledge. An International Comparison of Traditional Firms. London, New York: Routledge.

Chapter 3
The Approach of the Freiburg School and Why It is Particularly Useful Now

3.1 Background

This chapter introduces the approach of the Freiburg School and explains its particular relevance to the focus of this book.

As we have seen, digitalisation is affecting the most diverse areas of the economy and society. As will be shown in the following chapters, the relationship between the two is also changing. Which argumentative approach could then be chosen to describe the relationship between the economy, society and individuals to show to what extent economic policy is facing new challenges?

An appropriate approach requires a sufficient degree of generality that covers the phenomena in question, which here concern both positive and normative economics, and is acknowledged by what is considered a scientific community. In view of the subject matter chosen here, the approach of the Freiburg School seems more relevant than ever. Why?

It seems appropriate at this point to once again refer to the technical, i.e. *instrumental character* of the economy and to take this as a starting point. This view in fact opens up a complex field of tension characteristic of economic policy. With a little courage to simplify and reduce, one can say that it is characterised by three poles. Firstly, there is the necessity to accept economic laws. Secondly, there is a normative component to every economic policy decision that has to weigh up between *is* and *ought*. Thirdly, a particular difficulty arises from the fact that the economy produces novelty endogenously and it is always dynamic. The latter means that every economic policy must also allow for an appropriate degree of openness.

It is the approach of the Freiburg School, as formulated in particular by Walter Eucken, which explicitly attempts to depict this field of tension with a pragmatic intention. The term for this approach is "Ordnungspolitik". Its aim is,

> ... to shape the forms of economic activity or to influence the conditions under which they arise. But it leaves planning and action of households and enterprises free in these forms. ...the economic policy making (takes place) on the basis of knowledge of the individual

© The Author(s), under exclusive license to Springer Nature Switzerland AG 2024
J. J. Dötsch, *Economic Policy in the Digital Age*, Contributions to Economics,
https://doi.org/10.1007/978-3-031-53047-0_3

> forms of order, the interrelationships of the economic process and the interdependence of the orders. It is not ideologies about capitalism, socialism, etc., but orderly thinking that guides regulatory action (Eucken 2004, 242, own translation).

In this respect, the approach of the Freiburg School has the necessary degree of generality to catch the economic significance of digitalisation in its full scope. Moreover, the chosen perspective sheds light on the challenges posed by novelty. And precisely by recognising the necessity of both novelty and economic laws, the limits of what is pragmatically feasible can also be made clear.

So, what exactly is the approach of the Freiburg School and what distinguishes it? This is what the following sections are about.

3.2 "Ordnungsökonomik"—"Ordnungspolitik": About the Concept in a Narrower Sense

The following chapter provides a brief overview of the concept of "Ordnungsökonomik" or "Ordnungspolitik", focusing on three key aspects.

Section 3.2.1 gives a brief overview of the historical origins and background and provides some references to the key representatives.

Section 3.2.2 endeavours to provide a concise summary of the most important arguments of the Freiburg School.

Section 3.2.3 focuses on an aspect that is particularly important for the purposes of these considerations, namely the relationship between the rules constituting an order and its openness to development.

3.2.1 Origin

This section categorises the approach of the Freiburg School in terms of the history of economics and explains the background to its development.

First of all, the Freiburg School and its concept is by no means a one-size-fits-all theory either. Its approach was developed in the first half of the twentieth century and its basic arguments were and are shared by different scholars (Schnellenbach 2021, 1). The historical background of this concept is a time of upheaval. Thus, it represents a part of the response to the economic—and thereby social—problems of the nineteenth century and the dramatic economic crises of the early twentieth century (see Schnellenbach 2021, 7 or Feld et al. 2021, 1). This background of upheaval, which made fundamental reflection necessary, seems quite related to ours.

An important thrust was to consider how to turn away from the classical laissez-faire liberalism, which was obviously some sort of threat to the "greater good" as well as to individuals, without abandoning the central postulate of freedom (Vanberg 2017, 10). Chicago, London, Vienna and finally Freiburg were the epicentres of these reflections, a current that also went by the name of "neoliberalism", which today admittedly carries a new and different meaning (see in more detail, e.g., Vanberg 2004 or, more recently, Kolev 2020).

The German-speaking variant of this current has also become known as "Ordoliberalism" or "Ordo-liberal School", which can be traced back to the Freiburg School of Law and Economics founded by Walter Eucken, Franz Böhm and Hans Großmann-Doerth. Interestingly, and possibly to a greater extent than could be explained by the native German language of its most important proponents—Nobel Prize winner F.A. Hayek also achieved great prominence and can certainly be read as an "ordo-liberal" (see Kolev 2010)—this approach has actually become known primarily as a kind of German Sonderweg. It has again come into focus in the recent past, which has been marked by crisis developments, especially in the euro zone (see, for example, Dullien and Guérot (2012); or even, quite prominently, in the Economist, 9 May 2015, 21–22), and one can even attest to a certain degree of alienation here. Denord et al. (2015) even saw it as "Germany's iron cage" (!), while Beck and Kotz (2017) entitled their instructive volume on the topic, no less quaintly, "A German oddity"; Bofinger (2016), for three periods one of Germany's "Five Sages of Economy" (an honourable designation for the members of the German Council of Economic experts), even speaks of the "long shadow of Walter Eucken". Where the light comes from, he does not say.

Without being able to go into the historical background of the theory in more detail here (see, e.g., Sally 1996, also Vanberg 2014a, and briefly the latter 2017), it should be mentioned for the sake of completeness that two other currents can be distinguished from the most prominent strand of ordoliberalism, the Freiburg School, which formulated a kind of founding manifesto in 1936 with "Our Task" and which is also at the centre of the considerations presented here. On the one hand, the concept of "social market economy", primarily known through Ludwig Erhard, known as the father of the German "Wirtschaftswunder"—economic miracle—after World War II, and Alfred Müller-Armack; and on the other hand, "sociological liberalism", best known through Alexander Rüstow and Wilhelm Röpke.

Although these three currents differ in certain aspects, they share a core of common convictions (see in nuce Feld et al. 2021; Vanberg 2017). These were most clearly formulated by Walter Eucken (see below).

3.2.2 Main Arguments

This chapter briefly presents the central arguments of the Freiburg School.

What was the mission of the "Freiburg School"—and why does it also bear the designation "ordoliberalism"?

A good starting point is what it does *not* want. As indicated above, it does join the liberal tradition, but in view of the experience of serious economic as well as social upheavals, it turns against laissez-faire liberalism. What does this mean? From the perspective of the Freiburg School, markets or a market economy does not develop in a sustainable manner when the actors are left completely to their own. Market and market economy are, as Vanberg once aptly put it, "(...) not a natural event but a political-cultural product" (Vanberg 2014a, b, 5). Both require preconditions. Freedom is a necessary but not sufficient one. On the one hand, it is a matter of limiting the destructive and/or freedom-restricting potential of forces unfolding in markets; on the other hand, it is a matter of preventing the state from such interventions, which in turn would result in losses of freedom or prosperity. At the centre of the considerations are thus the complex conditions for a free-market economy.

The Latin first compound of the word suggests precisely this: Under the varieties of "ordo-liberal" or "ordo-economic", there is a strand of theoretical considerations on the question of what order or what framework of *order*—"ordo"—must be guaranteed so that economic activity unfolds as a market economy. This is desirable because, on the one hand, the greatest possible degree of prosperity can be realised through the system of markets. Smith's "invisible hand"[1] works through the market; here the Freiburg School seamlessly follows classical liberalism. On the other hand, this is desirable because citizens should be granted the greatest possible degree of freedom, hence the second compound of the word "-liberalism".

Freedom and prosperity are mutually dependent. But because they are open in their concrete results, it therefore depends on a framework that makes them possible. Only under the prerequisite of individual freedom will "competition on performance" come about, which will be able to deliver the best possible results for consumers (see Vanberg 2014a, 5). The state being responsible for the framework must thereby first recognise the inherent lawfulness of the market and then do no more than provide the rules for the game. It is not to force any desired results! This means two things. Firstly, the state acts primarily only with the aim of protecting the framework of rules within which the coordination principle of the market economy unfolds. A state that intervenes in economic activity too easily makes itself the agent of particular interests and thus enables tendencies that Franz Böhm has called "re-feudalisation" (Vanberg 2014b, 8; Zweynert 2015, 5). For the time being, a rich literature deals with this phenomenon under the term "rent seeking" (see, e.g., very short, Seekamm 2022; Tullock 1994). Secondly, the state has to intervene beyond the sheer rules, if—possibly precisely because of the market's inherent lawfulness—tendencies of monopolisation occur.

Accordingly, the concept of order is at the same time both an analytical and a normative umbrella term for a social constellation that enables a life that is as prosperous and as humane as possible (Eucken, 2004, 14). The question of order

[1] Smith's—incidentally rare—use of the term leaves room for different interpretations and it would be too much to say that Smith actually "knew" what this mechanism actually is. The discussion on this term seems never-ending (see, e.g., for overview Kennedy (2009), most recently, Torr (2022)); more recent contributions also refer to Smith's deistic worldview (see, for example, Oslington 2012; Long 2022). This discussion cannot be adequately reproduced here. With a view to the problem of *coordination* in markets, its *costs* and the *freedom* of the participants, which is the focus here, we limit ourselves to a simple emergence-theoretical interpretation of this metaphor, best known under the phrase "the whole is more than the sum of its parts".

thus posed is also a constitutional question: "the treatment of all practical politico-legal and politico-economic questions must be keyed to the idea of the economic constitution" (Böhm 1989, 23, cited after Vanberg 2001, 39).

Because of this tension between the mutual conditionality of individual freedom, the market and "society", the approach of the Freiburg School has always required a combination of several perspectives. In analytical terms, it combines the economic perspective with the perspective of law in an obvious way. The home of the Freiburg School at the "Faculty of Law and Political Science" already suggests this, and this guided the view of the founding fathers. Vanberg (2014a, b, 2) draws on Böhm, who emphasised as a common feature of the founders of the Freiburg School "(…) their common concern with the question of the constitutional foundations of a free economy and society". The normative component can be inferred from the second part of the quotation. The humanly possible is to be achieved under the recognition of economic laws. It is this mutual conditionality of several elements that makes this approach, on the one hand, really "basic research" of economic reality. On the other hand, compared to other economic approaches, it has a relatively wide object area.

One might object that such fundamental questions probably extend too far into the realm of other disciplines. The Freiburg School, however, explicitly opposed the "historical school" of German national economics by claiming systematicity beyond mere descriptiveness. It was Walter Eucken who, in his fundamental works "Foundations of Economics" and "Principles of Economic Policy", attempted to provide a theoretically consistent, systematic approach that combined the market-theoretical perspective with the constitutional question—together: the question of economic constitution—while taking into account the interrelationships of society as a whole.

This is where the core principles and most important argumentative or analytical building blocks for understanding an economic order can be found. Indeed, it is not without reason that Schnellenbach (2021, 1) chose the formulation that despite the diversity of implications of this concept, "the main thrust of the School's theoretical research program can be extracted from the works of its most prominent proponent, Walter Eucken". Accordingly, his principles, which are commented on below for the purpose of introduction, provide the leading perspective in this book.

3.2.3 Rules and Openness

This chapter explains the apparent contradiction between the central role of clear rules on the one hand and openness to development on the other.

Neither can nor should this be the place to delve further into specific theoretical aspects of this school. In this context, it is important to emphasise that it is not only a theoretical stance, but one that provides an approach for practical economic policy: "Regulatory policy" is directly linked to the "theory of order". After all, it is about the best possible design of a framework given the possibilities, within which unpredictable results may, indeed should, come about. Feld et al. (2021, 3) put it clearly: "Instead of describing the interactions of economic agents within existing rules (e.g. on markets), the Freiburg School focuses on describing the effects of different rule frameworks". As long as certain basic principles are preserved, this approach then trusts in the forces of the market, which will then, indeed, produce the best of all possible worlds. *Nota bene*: This may turn out to be much more modest than some politicians would like to promise their voters and interest groups.

The state sets the rules of the game and adjusts them if necessary. In doing so, he must perform a demanding balancing act, because the order as a whole must—while taking into account the real possibilities—enable a humane life for society as a whole. An ideal order is "functioning and humane" (Eucken 2004, 14, own translation). It is therefore a demanding but realistic approach. Its realism lies precisely in the fact that it focuses on preserving order among and for agents, but otherwise does not strive for concrete results.

Both the openness of the approach—the market and society spontaneously produce unforeseen results and formations—and the scope of its object area—the individual and society, wealth and distribution—are reasons for its realism. Admittedly, the field of tension that is fundamentally set up between the individual, the market and the state is a drastic simplification, because for all three there must admittedly also be a more differentiated picture in each case.[2] All "theory of order" is therefore also always social theory oriented towards certain core questions.

A milestone of the approach discussed here is Walter Eucken's posthumously published work "Principles of Economic Policy", which captures the described context by means of a typology of "economic orders" that move in the field of tension between centrally planned economy and free-market economy. Programmatically, he refers to the economic policy described above, which is limited to providing and ensuring the rules of the game. It is opposed to interventionist policy—using Eucken's term "process policy".

3.3 Eucken's Principles in the Light of Digitalisation: Recombinations and Additions

This chapter will present the principles of the market economy formulated by Walter Eucken and explain why it makes sense to recombine and supplement them for the purposes of our study.

Eucken's normative commitment to individual freedom, the market and humanity is reflected in the corresponding type of order, the "competitive order" (Vanberg 2004, 15). To this end, Eucken formulated principles, so-called *constitutive principles* that are intended to be the basic prerequisites for such an order to come into being. They

[2] This is a field of tension among different categories of *actors*. At this point, however, it is also worth mentioning again the field of tension in economic policy action, which is presented as three-pole, as mentioned in the introduction, namely the necessity to accept economic laws, the normative component to every economic policy decision and endogenous novelty.

can be understood as a set of minimal but necessary prerequisites for the functioning of markets. These must be fulfilled simultaneously both so that a competitive order can come into being at all and so that it is sustainable. In concrete terms, these principles are the pillars of the regulatory framework that the public regulator must set so that a competitive order or, in other words a free-market economy in the instrumental sense can emerge.

In addition, Eucken formulated so-called *regulative principles*, which provide a category for how the public regulator can specifically intervene in a rule-based manner when the functioning of the competitive order is endangered. These principles together provide the structure, the heuristic perspectives of this book. Why?

Firstly, because these principles describe the inevitable prerequisites of a market economy. If digitalisation is such a technology that brings about a far-reaching, epochal change, then it seems worthwhile to look at the extent to which these very principles may come under new conditions.

Secondly, it is worthwhile to choose these principles as a heuristic access structure, as it can map the necessary degree of *openness* of the developments,

Thirdly, this access structure opens up a perspective that can *integrate* otherwise separate aspects. This is particularly important in view of the complexity caused by digitalisation.

Fourthly, these principles offer a proven starting point for *pragmatic* considerations which, in view of the increased complexity of economic and social events, must be holistic and should be sustainable.

This access structure is therefore ideally suited to demonstrating the challenges for economic policy. Because Eucken's principles can be read as a minimalist blueprint of state activity and intervention competence. Particularly important for our purposes is the fact that this minimalism is not only the result of the normative basis—individuals as free as possible, as much prosperity as possible, an order as humane as possible—but formulates in a pragmatic perspective the foundations of an economic policy that recognises *economic laws*.

And it is precisely from this last perspective that we see how explosive the current transformation through digitalisation actually is. For it seems to have become much more difficult to follow these fundamental principles of economic policy. This is the reason why this book is oriented towards these principles, also with regard to its chapter structure. At this point, only a few brief references will suffice.

3.3.1 Constitutive Principles

The following section explains Eucken's first group of principles, the so-called *constitutive principles*.

Eucken formulated seven "constitutive principles" that sum up the most important convictions of the Freiburg School. He described them in his posthumously published work "Principles of Economic Policy" (see Eucken 2004, 254f.). Let us name these principles in turn and briefly outline the extent to which digitalisation poses new challenges for these principles. In a sense, this then briefly reflects the detailed procedure of the main chapters.

The first constitutive principle is a *functioning price system*. Prices are a kind of neural system of the market economy, as they express individual scarcity ratios in a countable unit of measurement and make them anonymously communicable. The price system enables the coordination of the conduct of any number of actors in markets. The other way round: Without functioning prices, there is no division of labour and no adequate information about scarcity. In the view of F.A. Hayek, prices are the social technique that enables economic competition as a discovery procedure and thus the greatest possible use of dispersed knowledge and thus greater prosperity. Digital technology can challenge this social technique and changes the coordination among actors by encoding facts *without* using prices; by enabling perfect price discrimination; by observing the prices not through the observation of entrepreneurs and critical customers, but by price-bots. Thus, both the way prices are formed and what they express are to be interpreted differently today than in the pre-digital age. Chapter 4 is devoted to this problem.

The second constitutive principle is the *primacy of monetary policy*. The core claim is to ensure monetary stability. It is essentially justified by the fact that the "functioning" prices addressed with the first principle can only fulfil their very function if the value scale in which prices are counted is stable. Now the discussion about the devaluation of money is by no means new. However, digitalisation, firstly, may have new effects on inflatory developments and open new possibilities for monetary policy. Secondly, the traditional central banks now face competition in the form of "cryptocurrencies". Thirdly, and directly related to the latter new form of currency competition, digital technology is enabling the "unbundling" of traditional money functions that were previously bundled in central bank currencies (see Fiedler et al. 2019). Fourthly, central banks around the world are planning to introduce a new complement to cash, namely digital central bank money. These are all completely new challenges for the claim for stable money. Chapter 5 deals with these issues.

The third constitutive principle is *open markets*. This has two main meanings. On the one hand, this principle is to be understood in the sense of open economies, i.e. it has a significance for trade policy, which aims to make optimal use of the effects of the division of labour through free trade. On the other hand, an open market must also be understood in terms of competition policy, namely that even within a national economy, undertakings must be exposed to competition from others at all times, and new players should be able to enter markets. Even though ensuring this has never been a trivial task, the age of the internet brings with it completely new challenges. For example: What does it mean when marginal costs no longer play a role for digital goods? Can markets really be kept open on the internet when indirect network externalities and snowball effects have taken on an unimagined dimension? Or does the internet even enable more competition in certain areas—because competition is "just one click away"? These questions will be addressed in Chap. 6.

The fourth principle concerns *private property*. Securing private ownership of the means of production meant an important aspect for Eucken and the Freiburg School, since the idea of collective ownership in combination with corresponding centralised planning competence was relevant as a solution to problems in the economy at the time of the approach's emergence. The debate about centrally directed or market-based economy seems to be over and with it the question of ownership of the means of production. However, digitalisation has also opened up revolutionary possibilities in this respect. Everyone has been saying for a long time that data is the key to success, and that data is the "oil of the twenty-first century" (The Economic Times 2018). However, it is neither clear who should own what data, when and why and how, nor is it trivial how it should be technically possible to enforce respective regulations. Moreover, the platform-based "collaborative economy" and, to use the more common and widely discussed expression, the "sharing economy" are new phenomena, so that the issue of private property in the context of economic policy requires a new, more differentiated assessment. Chapter 7 discusses these questions.

The fifth principle is *freedom of contract*. Now, it is clear that all participants should have the freedom to draw up and conclude contracts independently, and it is equally unambiguous that this freedom of action must not be used to the detriment of the other principles. For example, the establishment of a monopoly is obviously not one of them. In the digital world, however, this principle is not unproblematic with regard to the principle of property rights, because it is precisely the disposal of these that is subject to contracts. It therefore seems worthwhile to treat both principles, i.e. the fourth and the fifth, in Chap. 7 together.

The same applies to the sixth principle, *liability*. This principle emphasises that each individual actor should be liable for the risks he takes. In the present study and its focus on economic policy challenges, no separate chapter will be devoted to liability. Questions of the respective responsibility will be dealt with accordingly in connection with the other sub-questions.

The principles mentioned so far already shed light on the fact that the sixth principle, an overarching demand for economic policy, faces new challenges. This is the *continuity of economic policy*. It is therefore necessary for actors to be able to make long-term decisions, to plan safely and to cooperate and compete with each other at their own risk. The predictability of economic policy is a significant prerequisite for participants to dare to innovate. Digitalisation, however, obviously sparks a completely new development dynamic in the economy. It cannot be appropriate for economic policy to lag behind developments and expose citizens to dangers, nor can it be appropriate for excessive restrictions to deny citizens the potential of digitalisation. A new balance must be found.

In today's usual language, one would probably rather use the—admittedly somewhat strained—umbrella term *sustainable* economic policy. Now, the fundamental problem of democratic governments is a short-term focus, interest in votes, and thus long-term problems and costs that will be passed on to the next generation will probably neither be solved by digitalisation, nor be exacerbated to such an extent that it would be worth a chapter of its own. Instead, each chapter focuses on the possible long-term implications of the new challenges posed by digitalisation.

3.3.2 Regulative Principles

The following section describes the second group of Eucken's principles, the so-called *regulative principles.*

Eucken complemented the constitutive principles in his "Principles of economic policy" with four so-called regulative principles (Eucken 2004, 291f), those that categorise the possibilities of state intervention in the economic system, which should serve to safeguard the constitutive principles.

The first is *antitrust* or *competition policy.* In fact, digitalisation has confronted competition policy and competition theory with completely new challenges. To put it optimistically, the situation is quite diffuse. "It's not easy to know how those changes affect competition—or even, in some cases, exactly what has changed. But we need to understand them, to do our job properly", Margerete Vestager said at Harvard University in 2018, referring to digitalisation and competition policy. And indeed, the assessment of platforms, search engines and the variety of digital business models poses major challenges for competition policy. Problems such as the relationship between concentration, efficiency and (potential) competition appear in a new light.

Now, it would undoubtedly require another book to give a halfway adequate account of the challenges of digitalisation to competition policy. For the purposes of the present considerations, namely, to present the basic, overarching challenges of a basic nature, it makes sense to treat this regulatory principle together with the constitutive principle of *open markets.* This already implied a competition policy dimension and provides the corresponding opportunity to show where anti-competitive tendencies can unfold through digitalisation.

Just as the combination of one of the constitutive principles with one of the regulative principles seems to make sense, the problem of digitalisation suggests that two further regulative principles should be considered in combination: the so-called principle of the *correction of anomalous labour supply* on the one hand and the *income policy* on the other. This is necessary because digitalisation, with its potential for robotisation and the possibility of replacing human labour with artificial intelligence, has a characteristic effect on labour markets as well as on the distribution of income. To separate this heuristically would hardly make the essential interrelations comprehensible. Accordingly, Chap. 8 will look at both, *labour and incomes*, together and will show where the effects of digitalisation come in.

This leaves only one of Eucken's regulative principles, that of the *correction of externalities.* Eucken thus proved to be extremely far-sighted, as he already had the problem of environmental pollution in mind. As topical as this problem is today, the possibilities that digitalisation offers for better management of potential environmental problems are more technical in nature—i.e. in the sense of prognostics, control, sensor technology, etc.—and do not in themselves, from our point of view, represent a qualitative leap in such a way that it would be worthwhile to deal with them individually with regard to the central question of this book—how to give the modern industrialised economy a functioning and humane order. Individual aspects relevant in this context, such as the high energy consumption of crypto-mining or social networks, are appropriately referred to where appropriate.

3.3.3 Additional Perspectives

This section concisely demonstrates the extent to which the perspectives of the principles must be supplemented by further relevant approaches for the considerations of this book.

As already noted in the introduction, the basic convictions of the Freiburg School laid down in Eucken's principles will be used as a guiding heuristic for the following considerations in order to adequately portray the extent to which digitalisation is changing the social phenomenon of the economy and thus also challenging economic policy. Two aspects that do not have a structural expression in the composition of this book should be briefly pointed out here.

The first aspect concerns the approach of the Freiburg School itself. On the one hand, Eucken had supplemented his principles, briefly outlined above, with further principles, namely those explicitly related to public policy—hardly adequately translatable as "state policy principles", "staatspolitische Prinzipien"—in order to be able to adequately represent the role of the state. For certainly the order outlined here does not require a weak state, but a strong state, strong with regard to the enforcement of the rules and equally strong with regard to its own self-restraint. On the one hand, this demand referred to the possibility of "neo-feudalisation" through the interaction of interest groups and the bodies of the state, and on the other hand to avoid steering the economy concretely in favour of merely shaping the forms of order. The power of private actors is to be limited by the pressure of competition, the power of public actors by rules. Now this is an area that poses different problems in different policy areas, but in the end it is always illuminated by reference to the constituting or regulating principles. Accordingly, it should become clear in these considerations that digitalisation places various policy areas under new conditions, but separate sub-chapters will not be devoted to this.

The second aspect concerns the concrete method of presentation in detail. Admittedly, this cannot mean that more recent analytical tools in economic science developed since then are not also used for an appropriate understanding of the phenomena covered by this heuristic. Accordingly, the structure of the chapters is based on the components outlined in the previous sub-chapter, which result from the partial combination of Eucken's principles. In order to describe the problems encountered in each case appropriately and clearly, other methodological instruments will have to be used, depending on the focus. Therefore, methods of institutional economics, transaction cost economics, property rights theory, but also price and competition theory, among others, will be consulted.

This methodological plurality is on the one hand the result of the conviction that the problems determine the methods, not vice versa; on the other hand, however, it is also a necessity that arises from the claim to develop a comprehensive account of fundamental problems that guarantees the interested reader an understanding of the scope of current changes, but also an appropriate initial access to the broad arsenal of methods.

This will undoubtedly lead to pragmatic reductions in some cases, which cannot reflect the current discussion in the respective sub-fields of economics in its breadth. Where this seems appropriate, the theoretical background, aspects of the history of theory and current discussions are referred to mainly in the footnotes. This also applies in detail to the use of some terms, which—such as "artificial intelligence", "scarcity" and "price"—are sometimes used and understood in different ways and are therefore respectively specified for the purposes of this contribution.

References

Beck, Thorsten / Kotz, Hans-Helmut (2017): Ordoliberalism: A German oddity? London: CEPR Press.

Bofinger, Peter (2016): German macroeconomics: the long shadow of Walter Eucken. VOX EU, 7 Jun. online: https://cepr.org/voxeu/columns/german-macroeconomics-long-shadow-walter-eucken (last access: 11.09.2022).

Böhm, Franz (1989): Rule of law in a market economy, in: Peacock, A. / Willgerodt, H. (eds): Germany's Social Market Economy: Origins and Evolution. Basingstoke: Macmillan, 46–67.

Denord, Francois / Knaebel, Rachel / Rimbert, Pierre (2015): Germany's iron cage. Le Monde diplomatique, August. Online: https://mondediplo.com/2015/08/03ordoliberalism (last access: 25.09.2023).

Dullien, Sebastian / Guérot, Ulrike (2012): The Long Shadow of Ordoliberalism: Germany's Appoach to the Euro Crisis. European Council on Foreign Relations. Policy Brief, February.

Eucken, Walter (2004): Grundsätze der Wirtschaftspolitik. Herausgegeben von Edith Eucken und K. Paul Hensel. Tübingen: Mohr Siebeck.

Feld, Lars / Köhler, Ekkehard A. / Nientiedt, Daniel (2021): Ordoliberalism and the Social Market Economy. Freiburg Discussionpapers on Constitutional Economics 21/05, Freiburg: Walter Eucken Institut.

Fiedler, Salomon / Gern, Klaus-Jürgen / Stolzenburg, Ulrich (2019): The impact of digitalisation on the monetary system, in: European Parliament: The Future of Money. Compilation of papers. Study requested by the ECON committee. Monetary dialogue, December, 5–29.

Kennedy, Gavin (2009): Adam Smith and the Invisible Hand: From Metaphor to Myth. Econ Journal Watch 6 (2), 239–263.

Kolev, Stefan (2010): F. A. Hayek as an ordo-liberal. HWWI Research Paper 5–11. Hamburg: Hamburg Institute of International Economics.

Kolev, Stefan (2020): Ordoliberalism's embeddedness in the neoliberalisms of the 1930s and 1940s, in: Dold, M. / Krieger, T. (eds): Ordoliberalism and European economic policy: Between Realpolitik and economic utopia, London: Routledge, 22–28.

Long, Brenadan (2022): Adam Smith and the Invisible Hand of God. London: Routledge.

Oslington, Paul (2012): God and the market: Adam Smith's invisible hand. Journal of business ethics 108 (4), 429–438.

Sally, Razeen (1996): Ordoliberalism and the Social Market: Classical Political Economy from Germany. New Political Economy 1 (2), 233-257.

Schnellenbach, Jan (2021): The Concept of Ordnungspolitik: Rule-Based Economic Policy-Making from the Perspective of the Freiburg School. Freiburg Discussionpapers on Constitutional Economics 21/7. Freiburg: Walter Eucken Institut.

Seekamm Jr., Kurt von (2022): Rent Seeking and Human Capital: How the Hunt for Rents Is Changing Our Economic and Political Landscape. London: Taylor & Francis.

The Economist (2015): Automation angst. Three new papers examine fears that machines will put humans out of work. Online: https://www.economist.com/finance-and-economics/2015/08/13/automation-angst (last access: 10.06.2023).

The Economic Times (2018): Data is the 21st century's oil, says Siemens CEO Joe Kaeser. ET Bureau. Last Updated: May 24, 2018, 08:50 AM IST. Online: https://economictimes.indiatimes.com/magazines/panache/data-is-the-21st-centurys-oil-says-siemens-ceo-joe-kaeser/articleshow/64298125.cms?from=mdr (last access: 11.06.2023).

Torr, Christopher (2022): The conditions under which Adam Smith's invisible hand operates. In: Ioana Negru, Penelope Hawkins (eds): Economic methodology, history and pluralism: expanding economic thought to meet contemporary challenges. London: Routledge, 185–194.

Tullock, Gordon (1994): Rent Seeking. Aldershot: Elgar.

Vanberg, Viktor J. (2001): The Constitution of Markets. Essays in political economy. New York: Routledge.

Vanberg, Viktor J. (2004): The Freiburg School: Walter Eucken and Ordoliberalism. Freiburg Discussion Papers on Constitutional Economics 04/11. Freiburg: Walter Eucken Institut.

Vanberg, Viktor J. (2014a): Ordnungspolitik, the Freiburg School and the Reason of Rules. Freiburg Discussionpapers on Constitutional Economics 14/01. Freiburg: Walter Eucken Institut.

Vanberg, Viktor J. (2014b): Liberalismus und Demokratie: Zu einer vernachlässigten Seite der liberalen Denktradition. Freiburg Discussionpapers on Constitutional Economics 14/04. Freiburg: Walter Eucken Institut.

Vanberg, Viktor J. (2017): Ordoliberalism and Ordnungspolitik. A Brief Explanation. Freiburg i. Br.: Aktionskreis Freiburger Schule – Initiative für Ordnungspolitik e.V.

Zweynert, Joachim (2015): The concept of *Ordnungspolitik* through the lens of the theory of limited and open access orders. Constitutional Political Economy 26, 4–18.

Part II
An Order Challenged

Chapter 4
A Functioning Price System

> The market has become completely adjusted to a system of money; all economic calculation is carried out in terms of money values, all prices are money prices, and all market transactions are exchanges of goods or services against money. (Kirzner 2011, 16)

4.1 The Centrepiece Principle

This chapter deals with two different perspectives. On the one hand, it demonstrates the crucial role of a functioning price system for the economy. On the other hand, it explains, how the principle of a functioning price system is interrelated with the other principles. These interrelationships are fundamental. They will be discussed thoroughly because digitalisation does indeed influence and change these fundamental interrelationships. The remainder of this chapter is structured as follows.

The first Sect. 4.1.1 presents the prerequisites for a functioning price system and demonstrates the relevance of this principle. The second part, Sect. 4.1.2 discusses the role of prices for the coordination on markets and finally presents those aspects of digitalisation that shall be discussed in more detail in the following chapters.

4.1.1 Prerequisites, References and Complements

This chapter outlines the reasons for the outstanding importance of the price system and briefly discusses the corresponding conditions.

Each of Eucken's principles complements a particular aspect of the market economy. They must be realised simultaneously together, and in this respect the order of presentation is not strictly relevant. For one of the principles, however, this applies with certain restrictions, namely that of a functioning price system. It is the perhaps most important and called "centrepiece principle" by Eucken. In his "Principles of Economic Policy", Eucken even quotes Napoleon in this regard: "Here lies

© The Author(s), under exclusive license to Springer Nature Switzerland AG 2024

J. J. Dötsch, *Economic Policy in the Digital Age*, Contributions to Economics,
https://doi.org/10.1007/978-3-031-53047-0_4

our 'Toulon'" (Eucken 2004, 255, own translation).[1] A functioning price system is *the* starting point of his considerations, the explicit "common centre" (ibid., own translation) of the other principles.

This requires a few words of explanation. Before the next sections deal in detail with those aspects of the functioning price system that are influenced by digitalisation, a few basic considerations should therefore first be made in order to be able to meaningfully place the aspects related to this "basic principle" in the overall considerations of this book. In doing so, the relationship to the other principles, which presuppose each other in a complementary way—including the basic principle—should be made clear. The following sections highlight four aspects in this regard.

First, one must bear in mind that Eucken had a *reference situation* in mind when considering the functioning of the market economy. In his view, a functioning price system is fully realised in the situation of perfect competition (Eucken 2004, 254f.). The meaning of this reference is, essentially, an *undisturbed* price system. Accordingly, this has implications with regard to the market structure that does not necessarily coincide with considerations on the dynamics of markets (Suntum et al. 2011, 7). However, it can be assumed that perfect competition cannot be realised on planet Earth. We hence make the assumption here that the core of the argument is aimed at the operating principle of competition rather than the structure of the market. Competition as the operating principle of the market economy should take place as undisturbed *as possible*[2] and this, first and foremost, requires undisturbed price signals. Accordingly, the following sections also focus on the *function of prices in the competitive process*. Remarkably, as will be shown, it is precisely at this point that the change brought about by digitalisation comes in.

Secondly, there is a striking overlap between this basic principle and questions of the role of money, i.e. the second principle, the "primacy of monetary policy". This is because prices admittedly only work undisturbed if the medium that in which prices are expressed accordingly is stable. Otherwise, the relations of supply and demand could no longer be adequately reflected. Accordingly, Eucken himself names as dangers to the basic principle of a functioning price system not only price policy instruments in the narrower sense such as price caps (Eucken 2004, 254), but also monetary policy instruments such as a low interest rate policy or currency rationing

[1] Even at the time of the publication of the "Principles of Economic Policy", this quotation needed explanation. The corresponding footnote read: "'Here lies Toulon!' Napoleon obstinately repeated, pointing—instead of to the town Toulon—to the estuary which formed the key position for the conquest of Toulon. And thus he won his first great victory" (Eucken 2004, 255, footnote 1, own translation).

[2] Of course, real competition is also bound to a whole series of institutional preconditions; what is meant here in principle is not the closest possible approximation of real conditions to the ideal-typical situation of perfect competition, but that the economic actors can compete with each other to the greatest possible extent by being able to orient their conduct to real conditions. Since the conditions for this are not only economic, but also social, spatial, etc., the complexity of the environment of the economic system is so high that it will in principle not function completely without interference, and this also applies to prices themselves. Here we focus on the exact function of prices and the extent to which they can be largely preserved from disturbances and why.

(ibid.). The latter two examples, however, belong to the field of monetary policy, which will be dealt with in the next main chapter. Following the differentiation of the principles, we concentrate in this chapter on the way in which *prices are formed and how they work* in the narrower sense. We, therefore, are not dealing with the precondition of monetary stability in this chapter.

Third, beyond the price policy interventions mentioned above, it should be clear that, of course, all forms of monetary policy or discretionary economic policy also have an impact on the functioning of the price system too, because in the overall economic context all actions are interconnected by the price system without exception—and were so even before the age of digitalisation. All kinds of interventions hence deviate the economic reality from the reference situation, more exactly, from the principle of competition realised as far as possible and without distortions. Accordingly, the later chapters that focus on other principles will also refer back to the core of the functioning price system. This chapter focuses on the question of how digitalisation influences the formation and function of prices in the narrower sense.

Fourthly—and this is the "Toulon" of this book!—the preconditions of the basis on which the formation of prices in the narrower sense actually takes place have changed in a completely unforeseeable way due to digitalisation. The aim of the following sub-chapters is to work this out.

4.1.2 Prices and Economic Coordination

This chapter is dedicated to the question of what role exactly prices play in the context of economic coordination.

The starting point of all economic considerations is, even if unspoken, the well-known saying "There is no free lunch", that is, all things have their price. For all things there is more or less supply and more or less demand. Demand and supply are coordinated on markets.

Sure, this coordination can be realised in different forms. Marriage markets work (e.g. Anderberg et al. 2019; Holmlund 2022), but they work differently than, for example, markets for consumer goods (e.g. Darougheh 2021). But prices for goods and services, whatever they are made of and however they are expressed, are ultimately and always the result and means of coordination between supply and demand in markets. Here we exclusively deal with those markets where prices are expressed in monetary units, markets in developed, industrialised economies.[3]

Prices are always both, at the same time a *means* of coordination and a *result* of the process in which both quantities are aggregated on a market depending on

---

[3] Of course, there are also studies on price formation in general and on payment or different forms of money in particular, which need not be discussed here. As far as the *coordinative capacity* and the *potential for the development of productivity* are concerned, the modern economy based on a modern money system (on this in the next chapter) makes a qualitative difference to all other forms. See the extensive as well as instructive account concerning the use of money by Einzig (1966).

individually determined demand and individually determined supply. Then prices arise on the basis of the relation of market supply and demand. Prices, in that sense, are signals according to which the individual actors can direct their individual activities. Individual activities are coordinated by relating to each other by the means of prices. It is useful to remember this fundamental interrelation, even if one has become accustomed to the fact that prices in developed economies today are comprehensively expressed in monetary units. The monetary units, as a measure, express signals for individual conduct. The economic term for the fact that is expressed by prices in a form as countable units is *scarcity*.

Scarcity is an individual category and, basically, assessed by individuals.[4] It is first of all a normative (a modern and liberal) claim that for no individual and for no community or society should it be prescribed what they should and should not consider scarce. However, it is also an economically compelling prerequisite for economic activity based on the division of labour to leave it to the individuals to assess what they find scarce. All these individuals can in this way contribute their individual knowledge of specific circumstances without having to be aware of the specific circumstances under which their anonymous coordination partners act. Money plays the role as a unit of account that enables a kind of communication—by prices—similar to a common language (Brunnermeier 2019, 7; Issing 1999).[5]

In a developed economy based on the division of labour, prices accordingly have the function of behavioural signals that indicate to individuals how they can adapt best to continuously changing circumstances. Prices incorporate these, they *encode the knowledge* of those involved in the process of value creation based on the division of labour.[6] By encoding scarcity, high prices signal to individual actors when it is

[4] "(…) Scarcity of means to satisfy given ends is an almost ubiquitous condition of human behaviour" as Robbins (1932, 15) put it. With reference to Menger, Mises, Fetter and Strigl, he accordingly makes this phenomenon the subject of economics: "Economics is the science which studies human behaviour as a relationship between ends and scarce means which have alternative uses" (ibid). A detailed theoretical-historical account of the meaning of scarcity is not the subject of this chapter; for the purposes of this book, we can leave it at this reference and assume the term to be common and sufficient in its generality here. See also footnote 4 in Chap. 1.

[5] This connection is also crucial with regard to another dimension, because similar to languages, one reason for the use of a certain currency is the network effects relevant here. This issue is addressed in more detail later. Interestingly, Auer et al. (2021, 2) mention money as "society's 'memory'", referring to Kocherlakota and Wallace (1998).

[6] With the view that prices fulfil a kind of epistemological function that is crucial for the success of economic endeavours, this study follows the view of F.A. Hayek. Hayek, in order to explain the productive coordination performance of markets, had gone beyond the original conception of the economics as the science of the "relationship between ends and scarce means" and focused on the problem of the "division of knowledge" (see Hayek 1948): The core problem of the economy, the "economic order", which is also the topic here, was for him correspondingly "(…) determined precisely by the fact that the knowledge of the circumstances of which we must make use never exists in concentrated or integrated form but solely as the dispersed bits of incomplete and frequently contradictory knowledge which all the separate individuals possess" (Hayek 1945, 519). Now, one can justifiably object that this "price theory" has also been disputed in detail [see, for example, the extremely lucid critical account by Bronk (2013), who, while attesting "serious flaws" (ibid., 82), nevertheless calls it "peerless" (ibid. 102)], for the purposes of this book, however, the perspective is

worth making an effort and for what. In an economy based on the division of labour with complex value chains, prices accordingly incorporate knowledge about various forms of scarcity, about whose local, temporal and personal context actors no longer need to know anything. The corresponding knowledge is sufficiently codified (see, seminal, Hayek 1948). The more complex value chains are, the more important it is that prices can fulfil their function appropriately.[7] However, until recently, prices ensured coordination and the usage of knowledge superior to any other man-made coordination system.

This connection has been treated thoroughly by Friedrich August von Hayek, since he was concerned with the connection between the use of knowledge in society and prosperity (see especially Hayek 1945).

Economic actors can also, quasi like a researcher, use their presumptive knowledge and put energies into risky ventures to discover or create new knowledge that can subsequently be offered for money on markets. As others observe this, the process of competition in markets always leads to a diffusion of knowledge. This diffusion process is the main factor enhancing economic and societal progress, famously described in terms of market theory by Schumpeter as a process of "creative destruction". Thus, economic competition using price signals is, as F.A. Hayek put it, first and foremost a "discovery procedure" for discovering new knowledge (see Hayek 1968), which helps the risk-taking, competent entrepreneur to gain an edge. Other, less competent entrepreneurs, who are nevertheless good observers of what is offered in exchange for money, follow suit as imitators. Competition can hence be viewed as a knowledge machine which brings about an allocation of factors that is efficient in reality and without alternative—provided that money fulfils its function of expressing price signals.

This function of prices enables a normative element as well. Because in an economy based on money and prices only that which is scarce is expensive in terms of prices, and this makes it possible to pay for performance, not status. Remuneration according to performance, not rents according to status, is a basic principle of a free society. Even companies whose brand represents a certain "status" had to work for it first and they had to know in some way what was necessary to achieve it. Since all actors in this competitive situation have to fear that their gains in advantage will be competed away, all other actors will also strive to be preferred by the demand side by performing as well as possible.

In summary, then, we can say that prices primarily have a role as behavioural signals. These behavioural signals fulfil a kind of epistemological function by encoding knowledge about scarcity. They enable the division of labour and progress and ensure that the knowledge dispersed in different forms and also among individuals is used to the greatest possible extent.

---

quite decisive, *since digital technology is so successful precisely because it can absorb knowledge.* This will be discussed in detail in the following chapters. In this section, we will content ourselves with adopting Hayek's core argument, albeit in a condensed form.

[7] This points ahead to the topic of the chapter treating monetary stability: complex value chains can only come about under the condition that prices (i.e., from another perspective: money) are relatively stable and they can also only be sustained under this condition.

4.1.3 Where Digitalisation Comes in

The following section examines the extent to which the presence of digital technology makes a difference with regard to the role of prices.

Concerning the question where does digitalisation actually come in, two aspects are equally important. On the one hand, it is obviously a question of the stability of money (the next chapter is devoted to this). And on the other hand—presupposing stable money—a question of *how prices are actually formed*. As will be shown, digitalisation has created new conditions in this respect. Based on the general considerations presented in the previous sections, three aspects stand out. Before the following Sect. 4.2 differentiates these individually, they will now be briefly introduced.

Firstly, digitalisation has increased *transparency*. The internet provides a couple of ways to monitor and compare qualities, quantities and prices (see Kostetskyi 2021). With so much more information available to all participants, one could say that the market is actually approaching a state of perfect competition. The extent to which this is the case and what consequences can be observed is dealt with in Sect. 4.2.1.

Secondly, *data* has gained an important influence on the *formation of prices* itself. In extreme cases, many goods and services are now free in monetary terms—think of a video or a piece of music on the internet— they are de facto "paid for" with data. A process that the user sometimes knows about, sometimes not.[8] Other goods or services will be offered at reduced prices to the customer if the customer makes data available for the provider, for example via more or less extensive registration; and in other cases, higher prices will be offered to the potential customer if the provider already has data on the respective person. It is not always clear who has what data and what the data given away is ultimately worth to whom and when (see Acquisti et al. 2013). This is an extremely explosive relationship, which is also described as a "privacy paradox" (see Norberg 2007; Solove 2021; see also Schreiner and Hess 2015).[9] So how does data interfere with the formation of prices exactly? This is the topic of Sect. 4.2.2.

Thirdly, prices expressed in monetary units and accessible via digital technology are no longer necessarily observed and set by customers in person but are observed and optimised by *price bots* through the possibilities of digital technology. In some circumstances, algorithms may observe algorithms. In addition, one aspect of the previously mentioned challenge must be taken into account. Namely, through dense connectivity, almost any amount of data on behaviour, preferences and plans can now be collected, so that those who have the technology to analyse this data can not only

---

[8] One can indeed speak of "paying" in the case of monetarily free offers, because an *exchange* takes place. While in the case of payment with money, the good or service can be weighted against the demanded amount of money formulated with the price, this relationship is much more complex in the case of an exchange for data. See Chap. 7 for more details.

[9] In this area of phenomena, quite typical for the digital economy, various elements interact, which for heuristic reasons are considered separately and presented from different perspectives in this book. This chapter is primarily concerned with how digital technology influences the process of *price formation*. In Chap. 7 on property, the focus will be on the data itself and, accordingly, on property rights and information asymmetries.

individualise their products and services but also realise forms of price discrimination that would have been a purely theoretical option just a few years ago.[10] Thus, the question arises whether this technology-based emergence of prices corresponds to what we would expect from a free-market competition of goods and services. This problem is discussed in Sect. 4.2.3.

4.2 Prices Under the Conditions of Digitalisation

This chapter focuses on how prices are formed in concrete terms and to what extent digitalisation has a transformational effect in this context.

The first Sect. 4.2.1 is devoted to the phenomenon of a new level of *transparency* created by digitalisation and its impact on price formation.

Section 4.2.2 discusses prices in a broader context with regard to the new possibilities of both *bartering with data and gaining knowledge* outside the system of prices, which is then also worth money again.

Section 4.2.3 takes these ideas further and focuses on the process of *price formation* in the digital age in the narrower sense, namely prices set by algorithms.

4.2.1 Effects of Transparency

The following section explains the effects of the new degree of transparency provided by the internet in particular.

In the theoretical world of perfect competition, players both on the demand side and the supply side are perfectly informed. Until the age of digitalisation, the lack of perfect information was one of the core problems of economic coordination in reality. Without any doubt digitalisation creates greater transparency, especially through the possibilities of the internet. The internet can, for example, significantly expand the possibilities of turning experience purchases into search purchases and thus reduce information asymmetries. From a perspective of transaction cost economics, this can reduce search costs (Stigler 1961).[11] The greater opportunities on the demand

[10] One may make restrictions here, because since ever the possession of capital, the existence of production capacities has generated power and dependencies and sometimes also made price discrimination, etc. possible. Digitalisation, however, enables a completely new scope of these phenomena, since the penetration of wide areas of reality is incomparably deeper; borders of nations, of the private realm, even of the natural and the artificial lose significance in the face of the processing capacity of digital technology, while the capacity for commodification grows. This is exactly what we will try to shed light on from different angles in the following chapters.

[11] However, the possibility to expand and refine the search can also increase the effort of the search. See, e.g., Hanna et al. (2019).

side to obtain adequate information correspondingly reduce the potential for adverse selection.[12]

The *theoretical* model of perfect competition does not take transaction costs into account at all. Consequently, greater transparency should lead to better approximation to the reference situation of perfect competition. This cost reduction can accordingly result in corresponding welfare gains. This potential is limited by the fact that it is of course expensive to adequately process more information. And insofar as digital technology, which may be expensive, can help to acquire this information, the opportunities to use transparency may be unequally distributed. So how high the net welfare gain will be at the end of the day is hard to assess precisely. Of course, it is not only the possibilities of *obtaining* information that are cheaper on the demand side. It is also cheaper for sellers to *disseminate* information.[13]

Accordingly, transparency itself also has an important effect on competition, because it increases the competitive pressure on market participants, who are accordingly forced to reduce their profit margins and/or lower production costs. At the same time, transparency may also lead to the elimination of risks that were previously factored into business decisions. Transparency in this context leads to an *acceleration* of the competitive process and markets becoming more like the situation of perfect competition. Players on both sides of the market are much better informed in a much shorter time at much lower costs and also the exchange acts in the narrower sense are processed within a shorter time at lower expense.[14] Accordingly, it would in principle be expected that the profit margins of the suppliers be cut down much faster and further. One has to add, of course, that this transparency also concerns transparency for the comparison of the quality of products and services, the speed of delivery, etc. and not only the visibility and comparability of prices.

All this may lead to the possible assumption whether prices *converge* more than before, especially in the virtual space. Empirically, the situation is not clear-cut. Galewski (2015) has already pointed out that, contrary to the assumptions of neoclassical theory, prices for homogeneous goods do *not* become increasingly similar on the internet. However, Cavallo (2017) was able to show in his first empirical, international large-scale comparison of prices simultaneously collected from the websites and physical stores that the differences between online and offline prices at large, multi-channel retailers are by no means large: "Prices are identical about 72% of the time, and while price changes are not synchronized, they have similar frequencies

[12] Information asymmetries between both market sides can potentially lead to worse market outcomes, a phenomenon noted most famously by Akerlof (1970) which has become well known under the label of the "market for lemons".

[13] This, of course, also creates the possibility for influence, which is not the same as better information. Is not for instance, that "fake news" is one of the most burning issues of the digital age? See for example Kshetri and Voas (2017). In the digital economy, several aspects are important here, which will be discussed in more detail in the next chapter. This section is limited to the function of prices.

[14] Menu costs are also much lower in terms of time and money. Outside the internet, this can also be tracked in everyday life, e.g. in the form of e-shelf labels. See, e.g., European Central Bank (2021a), 93.

and sizes" (ibid., 300). If physical shops were also available, the parallel offer on the internet seemed to have provided more of an incentive to simply price the same (ibid., 301). Charbonneau et al. (2017) also note the parallelism of offline and online prices.[15]

Thus, it can be assumed that digitalisation, on the one hand, does intensify competition and thereby brings about an overall acceleration. Namely, in this specific context, through a tendency to shift from experience purchases to search purchases and the easier comparability of prices.[16] However, this does not make competition perfect, because obviously companies still have the possibility to set their prices tactically and strategically (see Marburger 2015; Morris and de Vincent-Humphreys 2019). Thus, based on the above-mentioned empirical considerations, it would also be a possibility to e.g. maintain offline trade, precisely in order to sell at higher prices there by means of cross-subsidising particularly low prices on the internet.

Generalisations are of course subject to restrictions such as the particularities of industry, the role of the traded goods in a specific value chain, the internationality of the markets and the distribution of the shares of goods traded and availability online and offline, and also the extent to which they are offered simultaneously online and offline by the same or different agents on the supply side to name just a few (see, e.g., Brynjolfsson and Smith 2020; Dumitru and Wieland 2020). In the latter case in particular, other effects such as the impact of brands will have to be taken into account for an appropriate assessment. In this respect, the picture is not clear. Another question would be to what extent longer or shorter periods are considered. In their empirical study throughout the years 2014–2017, Goolsbee and Klenow (2018) find that inflation[17] for goods traded online was over one per cent lower than offline in the corresponding period.

All in all, the new transparency does not seem to fundamentally change anything about the well-known mechanisms on markets; at most, the processes that take place on their basis seem to be strengthened. Overall, it can be said that a trend can be identified for which three elements are decisive. Firstly, an *acceleration* of market activity, secondly, an *intensification of competitive pressure* and both together, thirdly, a *self-reinforcing effect*, namely the process that all market sides exploit the possibilities of digitalisation as far as possible in order to remain competitive. This leads us to another level. For it has always been those who *knew* the most who were the most competitive. Here, too, digitalisation plays a new role, which is the subject of the following section.

---

[15] A large amount of relevant literature is devoted to the topic of e-commerce, of course also beyond the narrower topic of pricing. See, for example, Lacuesta et al (2020), Goolsbee and Klenow (2018), Gorodnichenko and Talavera (2017) or Laudon (2009).

[16] One of the most important drivers of this trend is to be seen in the platforms that use the corresponding tools, namely signalling and screening techniques. See Chap. 7 for more details.

[17] See for the inflation topic Sect. 5.3.

4.2.2 Prices, Knowledge and Data

This section addresses the problem that economically relevant knowledge is encoded by prices, but that the same can also be achieved without prices using modern digital technology.

Let us go back to the starting point. Markets are a social technique coordinated via price signals to solve the problem of scarcity. On the one hand, they work because of the normative postulate that economic actors should be free to act. On the other hand, this postulate is supported by the economic argument which presupposes that markets have so far been superior to other forms of coordination because prices make it possible to generate and disseminate more knowledge overall without a better alternative. In this respect, a functioning price system is at the heart of the complementary principles presented here, because the creation, discovery and dissemination of knowledge with the help of price signals can only function adequately as long as economic actors are free and the price signals are not distorted.

All knowledge spoken of here is always knowledge related to scarcity, otherwise it would not be encoded in prices. What is assessed as scarce can be anything: a microchip, a hideously fashionable dress or a relatively better technical solution, i.e. even knowledge itself. In the end, what counts, literally in monetary units, is always the knowledge of this scarcity. Bluntly said, scarcity is an abstraction that pays off. Seen in this light, knowledge about the preferences of potential customers is also scarce. Whoever knows these best clears the market.

As long as individual actors were not interconnected with each other via digital technology, prices were a much more essential means of communication. Until the widespread use of digital technology, the starting point for all participants in markets was what Stigler had formulated:

> Prices change with varying frequency in all markets, and, unless a market is completely centralized, no one will know all the prices which various sellers (or buyers) quote at any given time. A buyer (or seller) who wishes to ascertain the most favorable price must canvass various sellers (or buyers) – a phenomenon I shall term 'search.' (Stigler 1961, 213)

Artificial intelligence and the varieties of machine learning or deep learning are, however, completely new elements in this context, i.e. the connectivity of any number of actors with any number of things and the possibility of collecting, analysing and using data in a technically practically unrestricted way. Have we arrived where, half a century ago, Lange claimed, "(l)et us put the simultaneous equations in an electronic computer and we shall obtain the solution in less than a second. *The market process may be considered as a computing device of the pre-electronic age*" (Lange 1967, 401f., cited after Huerta de Soto 2010, 265)? What does this actually change with regard to the role of prices and the price system, on the one hand, and with regard to the normative claim that individuals should be individually free, on the other?

First of all, one of the main features of the economy in the digital age is that some goods and services are no longer or only partially offered against money, but voluntarily and/or involuntarily against data. The respective goods and services are thus only "free" in terms of the nominal monetary value that applies to the respective transaction, but the data serves as a medium of exchange. What are these situations? To answer this question, it is necessary to understand why, and under what circumstances, it is worthwhile for at least one of the parties involved in an exchange to accept or give data instead of money.[18] Of course, only if it is, at the end of the day, also worthwhile in monetary terms. Data must be worth its money, so it functions accordingly as an economic good. Raw data are not yet that; they only become an economic good when information is generated of them or if one hopes to be able to generate information on the basis of that data.

Data can indeed be the new "oil" (The Economist 2017) if supply can be improved by a clever evaluation of certain data—by improving quality or functionality or personalisation of products and services (see OECD 2020b, 19)—and thus a competitive advantage can be achieved. Or, once obtained in any way, data can be resold to third parties. A third possibility is to drive up or reduce prices due to exact knowledge of the demand side.[19] The first situation, the improvement of goods and services by an increase of knowledge based on data, is a complement to the traditional competitive discovery process on markets and a reaction to the higher competitive pressure described in the previous section. Selling data to third parties is a direct monetisation in a downstream market. The possibility to use data to shape prices is discussed in the next section of this chapter.

In any case, a situation of bartering with data arises in circumstances that were previously handled on the market and coordinated by monetary prices. The explosive aspect of this barter trade, however, is that it is essentially characterised by asymmetrical information. While in an exchange for monetary units the value of the transaction is clearly expressed by the numéraire, this cannot be said of data at all. Data is not money, but can only be turned into money, i.e. monetised. There is also a fundamental problem in that the data per se is not worth anything.[20] Data storage may even incur costs. Its value is only created by turning it into information and digital technology can do this even more efficiently than humans (see Macías 2018, 16). The many problems associated with the phenomenon of big data will be discussed in other contexts. Let us first stay with the creation of prices themselves.

---

[18] Chapter 7 is devoted in detail to this extremely complex issue. Here we focus exclusively on the question of the extent to which the use of data has an influence on price formation in the narrower sense. Here, as elsewhere, this focus is a heuristic approach that inevitably leads to partial thematic overlaps of sections.

[19] Data, or rather the collection, processing and, if necessary, sale of data, is of course the core of the digital economy. In the form of artificial intelligence, the dynamics unfolding here have already taken on a life of their own in some areas. Kemp (2020, 10) has summed this up well with reference to Cannataci (2018) and Mayer-Schönberger and Ramge (2018): "Machine learning is data hungry". This connection will be examined again and again from different perspectives in the following chapters.

[20] Sticking to the wording, one might object that even a banknote "is not worth anything per se"; but the banknote is the official documentation of a claim.

As for the common usage of the term, it is a bit misleading to talk about *paying* with data.[21] Data is something different than money. Even if, for example, certain services become cheaper in monetary terms through the transfer of data, consumers cannot arbitrarily substitute money for data when using services or buying goods. This possibility, namely that the medium of exchange is universally recognised, is what makes money.[22] It can never be *generally* determined what data is worth in monetary units, because for that there would first have to be a market for data—and market means: coordinated by prices, expressed in money.

This reveals a connection that is quite decisive for our considerations. The value of data lies in the value of the information that can be extracted or constructed from it, information that is relevant in a market where money can be paid. Hardly anything illustrates this more clearly than the fact that goods or services can become *both*, cheaper and more expensive in a given act of exchange if the supply side has data from the demand side. This topic will be dealt with separately in the next section.

Does this use of data then interfere with the functioning of the price system? This becomes clear when one considers a famous Hayekian argument: "(…) (I)t is useful to remember that wherever we make use of competition, this can only be justified by the fact that we do not know the essential circumstances that determine the actions of those in competition" (Hayek 1968, 9). With this assumption from the pre-digital age, the price system is relevant because of its superiority in discovering, generating and distributing knowledge. Of course, there are also costs involved in using markets. This is the core argument of the approach of transaction costs: "the distinguishing mark of the firm is the supersession of the price mechanism" (Coase 1937, 389). If the capacities of artificial intelligence exceed those of humans, then this must also mean that the boundaries of the market are shifting now in favour of those who master the digital possibilities best. *The price system becomes less relevant* in the digital age for the discovery, processing and distribution of knowledge as a whole! The opportunities to monetise data are greater on the side of the owners of the digital technology, and it is not in their interest to inform those by and with whom data is generated how much monetised exchange value arises from the processing. This is one element of the explanation of the sheer breath-taking success of the big platform providers. This is dealt with in depth in Chap. 6.

The "discovery procedure" of competition therefore, indeed, still functions. However, the function of the market controlled by price signals is crowded out by the use of artificial intelligence and the use of big data. This leads to the somewhat

---

[21] This formulation is very often used in scientific discourse (see, e.g., among many others Rockenbach et al. 2021; Palinski 2022, etc.). This connection, which is characteristic and crucial for the age of digitalisation, will be examined in more detail in Chap. 7.

[22] Admittedly, it may be that a girl gets her ice cream for free from the lucky seller in exchange for her phone number. But this situation cannot be generalised—and, as mentioned above, we are not interested in marriage markets here. Data may have exchange value in some circumstances, but it will be of limited use and often quite cumbersome to exchange certain data for certain data, whereas currencies can usually be exchanged readily. And the exchange of telephone numbers not only follows a different logic, but even becomes quite unlikely in general under the premise that one could only be exchanged for the other.

paradoxical situation that, on the one hand, the greater degree of transparency seems to lead to a reduction of transaction costs, especially on the demand side, and thus makes welfare gains possible. On the other hand, due to the now relatively high transaction costs of using the price system, a new form of information asymmetry is emerging: The market mechanism based on price signals—enabling the emerging of a *market*, on which individual actors make their own decisions—is being pushed back in favour of *organisations*, i.e. entities within which decisions can be prescribed to others. With the help of digital technology, they control the discovery, generation and distribution of knowledge more cheaply than the market. At the end of the day, this obviously pays off in monetary units—and obviously pretty well.

However, the information asymmetry underlying this situation also directly affects the normative postulate mentioned at the beginning of this section. The function of prices shows that the digital age is developing a tendency that threatens freedom. If one wants to take this to a provocative extreme, then, if one takes Coase seriously—"(...) the distinguishing mark of the firm is the supersession of the price mechanism" (Coase 1937, 389)—one could say that the price of individual freedom is equal to the amount of the opportunity cost of using prices instead of data.

4.2.3 *Blame the Algorithm!*

The following section focuses on the question of how prices are created and to what extent digital technology brings about fundamental changes.

The previous paragraph has illustrated how the use of data shifts the role of prices as signals that encode information about scarcity in favour of those who have the technology to do so. The following section takes a narrower focus and discusses the concrete *formation* of prices in the digital age and draws on some further aspects.

Let us first stay at the level of observing markets where goods and services are offered and demanded in exchange for money. Here, as mentioned above, the internet enables greater transparency. However, this transparency is not only available to customers, nor is it solely available to human observers. The accessibility of prices can also be used with the help of artificial intelligence. If the use of data in certain situations represents a possible influence on prices, the formation of prices in the narrower sense can also be managed by algorithms. These take into account both the relevant data and the pricing behaviour of the respective competitors. "Price bots" interpret market information and set prices at the same time.[23] What does this mean for the function of prices?

[23] This is a quite complex issue especially for competition law, here only a general overview of the problem can be offered. The areas of application of such bots are of course very broad and there is an impressive variety just in this area, such as arbitrage bots (see Angerer et al. 2022), online shopping bots (already Sadeddin et al. 2007; Serenko and Hayes 2010), or for manipulating ticket prices (Courty 2019) and so on. The imagination knows no bounds as long as money can be made with it. "May the bots with you!" (Malik et al. 2022).

In principle, the use of digital technology to optimise processes is not new, e.g. in the area of corporate finance. Software for yield management has long been common in some industries, such as the aviation industry (Calvano et al. 2020, 2). It is therefore not surprising that the use of this technology for coordination problems outside the company boundaries, i.e. directly on the markets, was also immediately observable when the business model of platforms on the internet spread. For example, Chen et al. (2016) already showed that a third of the sellers on Amazon Marketplace used price algorithms. As networking through digital technology has advanced considerably and the capacities of artificial intelligence have grown rapidly, this phenomenon is no longer limited to certain platforms on the internet, but now encompasses almost everything: "Why do gas station prices constantly change? Blame the algorithm" (Bam Schechner in The Wall Street Journal, 8. May 2017) potentially fits a plethora of markets.

Basically, two types of algorithms can be used for pricing. In one variant, the price for a good or service changes rapidly over time, and it becomes more volatile.[24] The respective price applies to all customers. This is referred to as "dynamic pricing". Blaudow and Burg (2018, 79) define dynamic pricing as "(…) the use of automatic algorithms to change prices at short notice due to changes in market conditions or due to parameters indicating a consumer's willingness to pay". This means that, in addition to observing the prices of all other suppliers in real time, other data can also additionally be used for pricing.

Another, technically obvious possibility is the *personalisation* of prices at the same point in time based on the use of data.[25] This means that the case of perfect price discrimination, which, since the discipline's inception, could only be found in textbooks, has become a reality. The use of big data thus creates a new type of information asymmetry by making it possible to determine individuals' willingness to pay.[26]

Moreover, it is remarkable that digital technology does not merely observe prices and pricing behaviour, but "(…) algorithms consistently learn to charge supra-competitive prices, without communicating with one another. The high prices are sustained by collusive strategies with a finite phase of punishment followed by a gradual return to cooperation" (Calvano et al. 2020, abstract). This, of course, creates a remarkable competition policy problem, because "Q-learning pricing algorithms systematically learn to collude. (…) The algorithms learn to play these strategies by

[24] A remarkable phenomenon insofar as volatility actually has to be priced into the long term, which theoretically leads, in the long term, to a higher price level.

[25] The academic discussion on this is quite broad and it is obviously connected mainly in the context of competition theory or competition theory issues. Accordingly, remarkable problems also arise for the legal sciences in this context. See, for example, Ezrachi and Stucke (2016), Harrington (2018), Kühn and Tadelis (2018), and also Schwalbe (2018).

[26] An aspect directly related to this and perceptible in everyday life is the use of personalised advertising. However, this does not directly belong to the problem area of the function of prices and money, but is, as presented in the previous section, an element of the monetisation of data along the value chain. The same applies to the possibilities of a—correspondingly personalised—bundling of product or service offers, which is a more competition-theoretical problem.

trial and error, requiring no prior knowledge of the operating environment" (ibid., 35). Apart from the problems of competition policy, the possibilities of digitalisation also give rise to a fairness problem (see Cavallo 2018), because goods and services may be sold at a price level that does not actually correspond to the *real* conditions of demand.—Or does it?

If there were only two groups of intelligent actors in the market, namely human suppliers and human consumers, then the transparency gained through the internet would probably lead to a price for a certain good in a relatively short period of time, which would remain relatively stable until either innovations in production technology on the supplier side or an expansion of the supply quantity make a further reduction in the price possible, or if, on the other side of the market, demand increases or decreases. This is not the case, however, because it can be empirically demonstrated that prices for a certain good can vary greatly within short periods of time. This is because it is not simply two intelligent groups that determine the game, but artificial intelligence used by players in complex networks.

Overall, it cannot be denied that the use of artificial intelligence—"price bots"—has an impact on the process of price formation in the narrower sense. However, it is difficult to assess to what extent this in turn has an impact on the higher-level context, namely the market process as a whole and its functioning as a discovery procedure. In view of the still rather fragmented theoretical situation and still pending long-term and broad empirical studies, all that remains is conjecture.

However, it seems feasible that this change within the elementary process of pricing is a factor for the phenomenon of *acceleration* already discussed in the previous chapter. To what extent the original informative value or the meaningfulness of prices is damaged by the fact that they were created by artificial intelligence remains to be seen. In any case, it is not necessarily so. However, this technology opens up the possibility of deliberate or even involuntary manipulation—and is thus relevant in terms of competition theory and competition law.

4.3 Conclusions

This chapter summarises the aspects presented in the previous sections on the subject of prices and provides further thoughts on the topic.

What conclusions can be drawn from the three aspects presented above? As has been shown, digitalisation means changes in the possibilities for actors in markets. It is not always easy to separate the original function of prices from the role of other phenomena such as data, or algorithms.

While for a classic market theorist like Friedrich August von Hayek it was precisely prices that made coordination among individually independent, "free" decision-makers possible and thus allowed a phenomenon of its own order to emerge, a market that was the product and prerequisite of a freely constituted society, prominent tech giants today may see things quite differently: "Because we have access to all kinds of data, we may be able to find the invisible hand of the market" (Jack Ma, quoted from Yue 2017).

This addresses an important aspect, namely that the current technological revolution also raises normative questions in the context of market coordination. The following subsections therefore endeavour to provide a structured summary that deliberately makes fundamental problem areas explicit once again.

The first Sect., 4.3.1, highlights the connection between normativity and economic law in a structured form.

The second Sect., 4.3.2, relates this to the area of the price system and the consequences of digitalisation.

Section 4.3.3 gives some indications of the consequences for economic policy.

4.3.1 Two Sides of the Same Coin: Normativity and Economic Law

This section explains the extent to which there is a crucial link between the price system and the normative foundations of the economy.

The fact that the price system is a kind of neural system of the economy has always been undisputed by economists. In the perspective chosen here, two complementary economic and two normative arguments were used to justify the importance of the price system as the "centrepiece" of the market economy. The remainder of this section names all four again explicitly. The next subsection then goes into the effects of digitalisation. However, this does not mean that they have different weights. They are interdependent and complementary.

The first economic argument is a market-theoretic one. The original basic assumption was that the more the economy would approach the state of perfect competition, the more efficient it would be in delivering favourable outcomes to people. At the centre of this assumption is not so much the idea of an atomistic market structure and other theoretical properties, as offered by the model world of neoclassics, but, in an explicitly application-oriented perspective, the prevailing *functional principle of competition*. This should be realised in the most undisturbed way possible. For this to be the case, prices must also be able to be formed undisturbed.

The second economic argument refers to the function of prices in the competitive process in a narrower sense. In this context, prices have the role of *encoding scarcity* and, like a language, making coordinative relationships possible among all participants in the market process (see Brunnermeier 2019, 7; Issing 1999). If the signals are distorted, the individual adjustments led by price-sensitive conduct can only be less appropriate than in the case of undistorted signals. The market economy then performs below its potential.

The first normative argument is the *postulate of prosperity*. This postulate is closely linked to the operating principle of competition. It is useful to read this operating principle in this context with Hayek's interpretation of competition as a "discovery procedure" for knowledge. At the micro-level, the discovery or utilisation of knowledge means to find better solutions and technological progress in order to reduce scarcity. This leads to a higher degree and a wider dispersion of used knowledge as well as to a higher degree of prosperity at the micro- *and* the macro-level.[27] Those who want the greatest possible prosperity for a society must engage in the discovery procedure of competition. However, this can only function on the basis of a functioning price system.

The second normative argument is the *postulate for freedom*. This argument actually has two dimensions. First of all, it is a purely ethical postulate. It is presupposed that economic actors, people, should be free. Therefore, the social technique that people use to solve their problems of scarcity—e.g. markets—should also respect this postulate of freedom. Of course, one can have quite different opinions about this, because different cultures have very different concepts of freedom as well as of what scarcity means. However, this normative postulate also has an economic flip side, because, on the one hand, actors decide individually what is scarce for them, and on the other hand, the price signals, abstract and aggregate, indicate what is scarce for others. This means that individuals can only act and adapt freely to the greatest possible extent if prices really reflect the extent of scarcity.

An intervention, of whatever kind, on the free formation of prices is therefore always also an intervention in people's freedom, it is a kind of reduction of their epistemological possibilities. It is irrelevant whether prices are distorted due to a directly comprehensible intervention (such as a price cap) or an only indirectly comprehensible intervention (such as an excessively lax monetary policy, see the next chapter on monetary issues). To the extent that prices no longer reflect the real scarcity conditions, the freedom of individuals to adapt to the real conditions is restricted.

These are no new insights, and one will still agree both that the economy should be such a social technique serving a humane life and society, and that a functioning price system is crucial for the realisation of such an economy. Nor is the insight new that the price system can be realised everywhere completely undisturbed. How are the specific effects of digitalisation to be assessed? These are new, however, and they are not clear-cut and they are highly complex. We remain of the opinion that normative and economic aspects are two sides of the same coin, and on this basis we highlight four problems in particular in the following section.

4.3.2 Increasing Dynamics and Change

In the following, we will now focus on the effects of digitalisation, referring to the aspects highlighted in the previous section.

[27] This means that through the better solution at the micro-level, the dividend, i.e. according to the Latin origin of the word "that which is to be distributed", is greater overall at the macro-level, a connection that Hayek (1945) also pointed out.

Firstly, digitalisation at the level of the price system contributes to an increasing *acceleration* of the whole competitive process along the time axis. At first glance, this is understandable due to a higher degree of transparency, which at first appears to make the market more similar to the state of perfect competition and enables welfare gains through a reduction of transaction costs. Digitalisation is thus a technology in the sense of the first and the third argument of the previous section. This transparency increases the competitive pressure and is self-enforcing, because it is also a massive incentive to digitalise products and processes.

However, such an increase in pressure is *prima facie* nothing new in the sense of the argument that a higher degree of transparency of scarcity relations enables a more cost-effective reduction of scarcity, since competition now functions better. This is a self-reinforcing process which, because digital technology is a new form of general purpose technology, leads to more and more areas of life being digitalised. So, there are spill-over effects of a whole new magnitude. Here, as in other problem areas dealt with in this book, it is not always easy to say that there is a specific reason for increasing dynamics or a self-reinforcing effect; there are several that are interrelated, the degree of transparency as an essential factor in the formation of prices being one of them.

This raises the normative question, which no longer belongs to the narrower object area of the price system, to what degree digitalisation of all areas of life is desirable, if the economy has an instrumental character. On the one hand, the spill-overs triggered by digitalisation are of a much more far-reaching nature than those of electricity, for example. For another, this question can no longer be answered clearly in 2023. An indication of possibilities to stop this dynamic can be gained for the problem area dealt with in this chapter via the way of price formation, on the one hand, and via the costs of the application of the social technology "economy", on the other hand, which the next two subsections briefly discuss. Both then lead back to the postulate of freedom and the problem of the costs of freedom.

Secondly, digitalisation changes price formation in the narrower sense. Whereas until the digital age it could be assumed that prices encoded scarcity ratios to which all actors in the market had to orient themselves, this situation has changed radically with digital technology. Today, (some) prices are formed, among other things, on the basis of price algorithms that take the algorithms of other suppliers into account and can potentially be linked to the data of the demanders. In principle, this situation is paradoxical, since, on the one hand, it can lead to collusion among price bots, but, on the other hand, it is able to express the real scarcity conditions relatively better, e.g. in the case of individual price formation. Both are problematic. The phenomenon of "digital collusion" would have to be prohibited in the sense of the postulate that competition should be a discovery procedure, and individual price formation would be a violation of fairness. While with regard to the formation of prices in the narrower sense, violations of the principle of competition or fairness can still be reasonably well understood, there is, however, a general phenomenon with regard to the use of data in the context of price formation.

Thirdly, if the market is based on the principle of the "discovery procedure", given the new digital capacity to process data, which can also relate to prices, but not only to prices, the use of the price system itself under certain conditions becomes relatively costly in the sense of transaction costs. If, with regard to the individualisation of products and services, the possibilities for processing data can be understood as progress in the sense of encoding scarcity and an increase of the potential for prosperity, this process is quite problematic with regard to the role of the price system. First of all, the boundaries between the sphere of the private and the commercial become blurred. Because digital technology can codify potentially any circumstance and because of the digital penetration of all areas of life described in the previous section, knowledge can be gained outside of the price system as well as knowledge being used that only a short time ago could only have been acquired through sophisticated secret service observation. One must bear in mind that, at least on the part of the state, no one may be observed without suspicion, even today. Of course, private actors are now observing, but they are achieving a potential commercialisation that is akin to a quantum leap. Here, too, the question would have to be asked whether this form of data-based business is conducive to a humane way of life or not.

Fourthly, beyond this relationship between demanders and suppliers, which today can certainly be judged as problematic, data-based coordination outside the price system creates yet another problem. Because today it is not only the price system that enables the Hayekian "discovery procedure". It is partially absorbed by the possibility of processing data, in that specialised knowledge can be internalised even before it would need to be communicated in prices. Hence the productivity gains due to division of labour can be exceeded by a central, digitally coordinated mode of production. However, the problem arises that precisely this leads to a monopolisation tendency, which is more efficient on the one hand, but under certain circumstances may have a negative impact on freedom. Deploying this argument in an extreme form means that the relatively higher transaction costs of using the price system are the cost of protecting individual freedom.[28] Thus, with the digital solution, a new problem arises.

4.3.3 *Consequences for Economic Policy*

This chapter discusses the consequences for economic policy arising from the areas of tension described in the previous sections.

There will be no one-size-fits-all-recipe for economic policy to deal with these problems. What is indeed disturbing about the opinion of Jack Ma—"Because we have access to all kinds of data, we may be able to find the invisible hand of the

[28] The argument is exaggerated in the sense that it makes a fundamental fact clear by generously simplifying it. The simplification here is that the underlying concept of freedom has not been discussed. This discussion was extensive even before digitalisation, even within the discourse on economic policy. For the purposes of the considerations presented here, it must suffice to point out that the possibilities of digitalisation have made an appropriate conception of precisely this concept of freedom more complicated than ever.

market" (Jack Ma, quoted from Yue 2017)—is that the "invisible hand"[29] has, in fact, always been seen as the guarantee that individuals pursuing their individual self-interest would, due to the coordinative performance of the market system, produce an unplanned whole whose overall economic output would be greater than that of all other attempted solutions, while guaranteeing the maximum freedom of all participants.

This is why it is not at all the invisible hand that Mr Ma pretends to be able to find. For, firstly, what can be achieved through the processing of data is not a phenomenon of its own kind, as is the market, but an organisation that—unlike the market—is in the hands of very specific interests. This hand may then be de facto invisible, but it is then nevertheless a hand that is guided by concrete interests of people and/or an organisation, and it is no longer a metaphor for a phenomenon of its own, whose advantage is precisely that it does *not* obey the interests of some.

Now it may well be the case, and this is obviously what Mr Ma is after, that the social use of knowledge for economic purposes can be achieved more cheaply, if not today, then soon, with digital technology than with the help of prices. But to put it bluntly: Freedom has its price. Taking this exaggeration further, one could say that this price corresponds to the extent to which the processing of big data by artificial intelligence internalises the function of prices to encode individual scarcity ratios. In principle, this is certainly the case, but in practice the relationships are very complex and difficult to assess adequately.

For while in the act of paying with monetary units before the digital age, the process relevant to the invisible hand in question was completed, this is no longer the case in the digital age, since knowledge that is worth money only emerges from the linking of data, i.e. through generating information based on data. As with the act of paying in the pre-digital age, it would have to be possible to define clear property rights and their transition in this context. However, against the background of complex value chains, this is a highly complex task, even within national borders, especially since it may not even be possible to clearly specify which criteria should be used to determine who should participate with which shares of the proceeds. The problem of property rights thus becomes a new kind of "centrepiece" of the digital economy. Chap. 7 of this book is dedicated to this topic.

Other important consequences from the changes in the price system arise directly for competition policy. While some phenomena of competition can clearly be recorded as anti-competitive under digital conditions, such as price discrimination or collusion, new complex problems arise due to the new role of data and the possibilities of intelligent processing of data.

---

[29] See footnote 1 in Chap. 3 .

References

Acquisti, Alessandro / John, Leslie K. / Loewenstein, George (2013): What Is Privacy Worth? The Journal of Legal Studies 42 (2), 249–274.

Akerlof, George A. (1970): The Market for "Lemons": Quality Uncertainty and the Market Mechanism. The Quarterly Journal of Economics 84 (3), 488–500.

Anderberg, Dan / Bagger, Jesper / Bhaskar, V. / Wilson, Tanya (2019): Marriage Market Equilibrium, Qualifications, and Ability. ZA Discussion Papers, No. 12210. Bonn: Institute of Labor Economics.

Angerer, Martin / Neugebauer, Tibor / Shachat, Jason (2022): Arbitrage Bots in Experimental Asset Markets. Available at SSRN: https://ssrn.com/abstract=4010055 or https://doi.org/10.2139/ssrn.4010055 (last access: 30.5.2023).

Auer, Raphael / Frost, Jon / Gambacorta, Leonardo / Monnet Cyril / Rice, Tara / Shin, Hyon Song (2021): Central bank digital currencies: motives, economic implications and the research frontier. BIS Working Papers No 976.

Blaudow, Christian / Burg, Florian (2018): Dynamic pricing as a challenge for consumer price statistics. EURONA (1): Eurostat, 79–93.

Bronk, Richard (2013): Hayek on the wisdom of prices: a reassessment. Erasmus journal for philosophy and economics 6 (1), 82–107.

Brunnermeier, Markus K. / James, Harold / Landau, Jean-Pierre (2019): The Digitalization of Money. National Bureau of Economic Research Working Paper 26300, September.

Brynjolfsson, Erik / Smith, Michael. D. (2020): Frictionless Commerce? A Comparison of Internet and Conventional Retailers. Management Science 46 (4), 563–585.

Calvano, Emilio. / Calzolari, Giacomo / Denicolò, Vincenzo / Pastorello, Sergio (2020): Artificial Intelligence, Algorithmic Pricing, and Collusion. American Economic Review 110 (10), 3267–3297.

Cannataci, Joseph A. (2018): Report of the Special Rapporteur on the Right to Privacy to the General Assembly of the United Nations (Advanced Unedited Report, A/73/45712, 17 October), 91–97.

Cavallo, Alberto (2017): Are Online and Offline Prices Similar? Evidence from Large Multi-Channel Retailers. American Economic Review 107 (1), 283–303.

Cavallo, Alberto (2018): More Amazon Effects: Online Competition and Pricing Behaviour. NBER Working Paper 25138.

Charbonneau, Karyne / Evans, Alexa / Sarker, Subrata / Suchanek, Lena (2017): Digitalization and Inflation: A Review of the Literature. Bank of Canada Staff Analytical Note. Ontario.

Chen, Le / Mislove, Alan / Wilson, Christo (2016): An Empirical Analysis of Algorithmic Pricing on Amazon Marketplace, in: Proceedings of the 25th International Conference on World Wide Web, WWW16, 1339–1349, International World Wide Web Conferences Steering Committee.

Coase, Ronald Harry (1937): The Nature of the Firm. Economica 4 (16), 386–405.

Courty, Pascal (2019): Ticket resale, bots, and the fair price ticketing curse. Journal of Cultural Economics 43, 345–363.

Darougheh, Saman (2021): Consumer good search: Theory and evidence. Danmarks Nationalbank Working Papers, No. 176, Copenhagen: Danmarks Nationalbank.

Dumitru, Ana-Maria / Wieland, Elisabeth (2020): Online vs. Offline Prices: Evidence from German CPI micro data. Presentation at the 11 November meeting of the ESCB research network PRISMA.

Einzig, Paul (1966): Primitive Money: In Its Ethnological, Historical and Economic Aspects. Oxford i.a.: Pergamon Press.

Eucken, Walter (2004): Grundsätze der Wirtschaftspolitik. Herausgegeben von Edith Eucken und K. Paul Hensel. Tübingen: Mohr Siebeck.

European Central Bank (2021a): Work stream on digitalisation: Digitalisation: Channels, impacts and implications for monetary policy in the euro area. ECB Occasional Paper 266, Frankfurt a. M.: European Central Bank.

Ezrachi, Ariel / Stucke, Maurice (2016): Virtual Competition. The Promise and Perils oft he Algorithm-driven Economy. Cambridge: Harvard University Press.

Fernández-Macías, Enrique (2018): Automation, digitalisation and platforms: Implications for work and employment. Luxembourg: Eurofound, Publications Office of the European Union.

Galewski, Tomasz (2015): Problems in measuring price dispersion in e-commerce. Institute of Economic Research Working Papers No. 50/2015. Toruń: Institute of Economic Research (IER).

Goolsbee, Austan / Klenow, Peter (2018): Internet Rising, Prices Falling: Measuring Inflation in a World of E-Commerce. AEA Papers and Proceedings 108, 488–492.

Gorodnichenko, Yuriy / Talavera, O. (2017): Price Setting in Online Markets: Basic facts. International Comparisons, and Cross-Border Integration. American Economic Review 107 (1), 249–282.

Hanna, Richard C. / Lemon, Katherine N. / Smith, Gerald E. (2019): Is transparency a good thing? How online price transparency and variability can benefit firms and influence consumer decision making. Business Horizons 62 (2), 227–236.

Harrington, Joseph E. Jr (2018): Developing Competition Law for Collusion by Autonomous Artificial Agents. Journal of Competition Law and Economics 14 (3), 331–363.

Hayek, Friedrich August von (1945): The Use of Knowledge in Society. The American Economic Review 35 (4), 519–530.

Hayek, Friedrich August von (1948): Economics and knowledge. In: idem: Individualism and the economic order. Chicago: Chicago University Press, 33–56.

Hayek, Friedrich August von (1968): Competition as a Discovery Procedure. Translated by Marcellus S. Snow from German of F.A. Hayek's "Der Wettbewerb als Entdeckungsverfahren," a 1968 lecture sponsored by the Institut für Weltwirtschaft at the University of Kiel, published as No. 56 in the series Kieler Vorträge. The Quarterly Jornal of Austrian Economics (3) (Fall 2002), 9–23.

Holmlund, Helena (2022): Preferences and opportunities in the marriage market: How comprehensive schooling made the wealthy marry down. Working Paper, No. 2022:11. Uppsala: Institute for Evaluation of Labour Market and Education Policy (IFAU).

Huerta de Soto, Jesús (2010): Oskar Lange and the 'Competitive Solution', in: Huerta de Soto, Jesús (ed.): Socialism, Economic Calculation and Entrepreneurship. New Thinking in Political Economy series. Cheltenham: Edward Elgar, 198–268.

Issing, Ottmar (1999): Hayek—Currency Competition and European Monetary Union. BIS Review.

Kemp, Katharine (2020): Concealed data practices and competition law: why privacy matters. European Competition Journal, online: https://papers.ssrn.com/sol3/papers.cfm?abstract_id=3432769 (last access: 10.06.2023).

Kirzner, Israel (2011): Market theory and the price system. Indianapolis: Liberty Fund.

Kocherlakota, Narayana / Wallace, Neil (1998): Incomplete record-keeping and optimal payment arrangements. Journal of Economic Theory 81 (2), 272–289.

Kostetskyi, Pavlo (2021): Does Digitalization Lead to Better Transparency: Bibliometric Approach. Business Ethics and Leadership 5 (3), 102–107.

Kshetri, Nir / Voas, Jeffrey (2017): The Economics of "Fake News". IEEE IT Professional 19 (6), 8–12.

Kühn, Kai-Uwe / Tadelis, Steven (2018): The Economics of Algorithmic Pricing: Is collusion really inevitable? Working paper. Online: https://faculty.haas.berkeley.edu/stadelis/Algo_Pricing.pdf (last acccess: 11.3.2023).

Lacuesta, Aitor / Roldan, Pau / Serrano-Puente, Darío (2020): Effects of E-Commerce on prices and Business Competition. Banco de España, Economics Bulletin 4.

Lange, Oskar (1967): The Computer and the Market, reprinted in: Nove, Alec / and Nuti D.M. (eds): Socialist Economics. Middlessex: Penguin Books, 401–402.

Laudon, Kenneth C. (2009): E-commerce: business, technology, society. Upper Saddle River, NJ: Pearson, Prentice Hall.

Malik, Ashish / Budhwar, Pawan S. / Patel, Charmi / Srikanth, N. R. (2022): May the bots be with you! Delivering HR cost-effectiveness and individualised employee experiences in an MNE. International journal of human resource management 33 (6), 1148–1178.
Marburger, Daniel (2015): Innovative pricing strategies to increase profits. New York: Business Expert Press.
Mayer-Schönberger, Viktor / Ramge, Thomas (2018): Reinventing Capitalism in the Age of Big Data. London: Basic Books.
Morris, Richard / de Vincent-Humphreys, Rupert (2019): Price-setting behaviour: Insights from a survey of large firms. European Central Bank, Economic Bulletin 7.
Norberg, Patricia A., / Horne, Daniel R. / Horne, David A. (2007): The Privacy Paradox: Personal Information Disclosure Intentions versus Behaviors. The Journal of Consumer Affairs 41(1), 100–126
OECD (2020a): Measuring the economic value of data and cross-border data flows. A business perspective. OECD Digital Economy papers 297, August.
OECD (2020b): Consumer Data Rights and Competition—Background Note by the Secretariat. 10–12 June.
Palinski, Michael (2022): Paying with your data: privacy tradeoffs in ride-hailing services. Applied economics letters 29 (18), 1719–1725.
Robbins, Lionel (1932): An Essay on the Nature & Significance of Economic Science. London: Macmillan.
Rockenbach, Bettina / Sadrieh, Abdolkarim / Schielke, Anne (2021): Paying with your personal data: The insensitivity of private information provision to asymmetric benefits. Journal of the Economic Science Association 7 (1), 64–73.
Sadeddin, Khaled W. / Serenko, Alexander / Hayes, James (2007): Online shopping bots for electronic commerce: the comparison of functionality and performance. International journal of electronic business 5 (6), 576–589.
Schechner, Bam (2017): Why Do Gas Station Prices Constantly Change? Blame the Algorithm. The Wall Street Journal. Updated May 8, 2017 6:41 pm ET. Online: https://www.wsj.com/articles/why-do-gas-station-prices-constantly-change-blame-the-algorithm-1494262674 (last access: 10.06.2023).
Schreiner, Michael / Hess, Thomas. (2015): Why Are Consumers Willing to Pay for Privacy? An Application of the Privacy-freemium Model to Media Companies, in: Proceedings of the 23rd European Conference on Information System, http://aisel.aisnet.org/ecis2015_cr/164/ (last access: 10.06.2023).
Serenko, Alexander / Hayes, James (2010): Investigating the functionality and performance of online shopping bots for electronic commerce: a follow-up study. International journal of electronic business 8 (1), 1–15.
Schwalbe, Ulrich (2018): Algorithms, Machine Learning, and Collusion. Journal of Competition Law & Economics 14 (4), 568–607.
Solove, Daniel J. (2021): The Myth of the Privacy Paradox. 89 George Washington Law Review 1, GWU Legal Studies Research Paper No. 2020–10, Available at SSRN: https://papers.ssrn.com/sol3/papers.cfm?abstract_id=3536265 (last access: 10.06.2023).
Stigler, George J. (1961): The Economics of Information. Journal of Political Economy 69 (3), 213–225.
Suntum, Ulrich van / Böhm, Tobias / Oelgemöller, Jens / Ilgmann, Cordelius (2011): Walter Eucken's Principles of Economic Policy Today. CAWM Discussion Paper No. 49. Preliminary version. August.
The Economist (2017): The world's most valuable resource is no longer oil, but data, print edition, 6 May.
Yue, Xiong (2017): Will "Big Data" Make a Centrally Planned Economy Possible? Mises Wire: Mises Institute. Online: https://mises.org/wire/will-big-data-make-centrally-planned-economy-possible (last access: 14.3.2023).

Chapter 5
Primacy of Monetary Policy

To destroy the bourgeois order, one must devastate its monetary system. (quote attributed to V.I. Lenin)[1]

All efforts to realise a competitive order are in vain as long as a certain stability of the value of money is not assured. (Eucken 204, 256, own translation)

5.1 Basic Considerations

While the previous chapter dealt with the price system as the "centrepiece" of the market economy, the following chapter is devoted to the medium in which prices are formed and expressed, money. Of course, this topic is very closely related to that of the formation of prices in the narrower sense. And, as we will see, beyond that, monetary policy naturally has a whole range of crucial cross-cutting effects.

This complexity requires a somewhat more detailed approach than in the previous chapter, which is why the considerations on monetary functions, monetary systems and the challenges of digitalisation will be preceded by some basic considerations. On the one hand, these should serve for a better orientation, but on the other hand, their presentation is necessary because the effects of digitalisation actually also come in at the fundamental level, as will be shown.

The chapter proceeds as follows. The first Sect. 5.1.1 takes as its starting point the importance of the claim for *stable money*. If stable money is not guaranteed, "(…) all efforts to realise a competitive order are in vain" (Eucken 2004, 256, own translation).

---

[1] This is, nota bene, what he is said to have said. I owe Dietmar Meyer the hint of another reference, J.M. Keynes: "Lenin is said to have declared that the best way to destroy the Capitalist System was to debauch the currency. By a continuing process of inflation, governments can confiscate, secretly and unobserved, an important part of the wealth of their citizens. (…) Lenin was certainly right. There is no subtler, no surer means of overturning the existing basis of society than to debauch the currency. The process engages all the hidden forces of economic law on the side of destruction, and does it in a manner which not one man in a million is able to diagnose". from: The Economic Consequences of the Peace, Chap. 6, "Europe after the Treaty".

© The Author(s), under exclusive license to Springer Nature Switzerland AG 2024
J. J. Dötsch, *Economic Policy in the Digital Age*, Contributions to Economics,
https://doi.org/10.1007/978-3-031-53047-0_5

The second Sect. 5.1.2 shortly introduces the basic elements of monetary systems and the perspective of the Freiburg School.

5.1.1 The Claim for Stable Money

This chapter explains why the demand for a stable value of money is central to the economic system.

At present, it seems that issues of monetary stability have become more relevant than at any time since the Second World War. The Euro crisis and, most recently, inflation have become pressing questions. The concrete causes of the current problems cannot be discussed here. But the fact of the current crisis underlines that the focus and the demands of the Freiburg School are as relevant as ever.[2]

Prices and the medium in which they are expressed, money, are one of the central themes of the Freiburg School. What is more, it is no coincidence that Eucken's constituent principle, which relates to money, is also explicitly underlined by an attribute chosen by Eucken: It is the "primacy" of monetary policy. What first and foremost mattered to him was the stability of the value of money and the ways in which this could be secured. Prices must be able to make goods and services comparable with each other, but comparability is only possible through a *stable* measure. It is certain that Eucken strongly emphasised the aspect of stability against the background of the severe monetary and economic crises at the beginning of the twentieth century. They clearly demonstrated that the devaluation of money not only causes a decrease in wealth but can lead to severe problems of economic coordination in general and in the end to severe social and, as the first half of the twentieth century showed, dangerous political problems.

The stability of the value of money has been discussed for as long as money has been used as a means of payment. This is a complex relationship on which there are controversial views that cannot be discussed separately here (see for an overview, e.g., Glasner 2021). However, there is no doubt that if money is to fulfil its functions, the stability of its value is indispensable. In this context, digitalisation brings new challenges, which will be focused on in the following. To put it succinctly, these are, on the one hand, changes with regard to the prerequisites for existing currencies and, on the other hand, the phenomenon of new, digital currencies. The fact that

---

[2] Different schools of economic thought have different answers to economic crises, just as they look at fundamental questions from different angles. We do not want to give the impression that Eucken and the Freiburg School offer the only or the best answer. Nor, of course, is the Freiburg School by any means the only one to have dealt with the problem of stable money. In the present considerations, it is much more a matter of demonstrating, as also stated in the introduction, that digitalisation is not a superficial phenomenon, but a form of technical change that—far more than all other technological revolutions before it—really also affects the fundamental principles of the market economy. Therefore, the *question* chosen here because of the perspective—to what extent does digitalisation affect the stability and functionality of money?—is important, and it is not the intention to weigh the perspective of the Freiburg School in detail against the perspective of other schools, be they classical, (post-) Keynesian, monetarist, liquidity theory or whatever.

digitalisation poses completely new challenges from both perspectives will become clear in the following, even if we maintain a relatively high degree of generality in our analysis.

In order to understand the extent to which digitalisation poses a special challenge to monetary policy, we must first explain what exactly is at stake here. In doing so, we must first make some distinctions between certain problems of monetary policy.

5.1.2 Monetary Systems

In order to understand the special transformational effect of digital technology on money, we first need to understand the institutional framework and the techniques used to create money. Accordingly, this section focusses on the monetary system.

With regard to the problem at hand, Fiedler et al. (2019, 11) distinguish between the aspects of technology and the architecture of a monetary system. In simplified terms, the term *architecture* refers to which institutions can issue which money under which conditions and in what form it comes into circulation. The Freiburg School term for this would be *monetary order*, which summarises the legal foundations that clearly define which institutions are involved in the circulation of money and provide institutional arrangements or rules so that money can fulfil its functions (see below). Another common term for this is "monetary constitution" (see, e.g., Köhler 2015), emphasising the legal aspect. "Monetary system" would be the customary term today. The term *technology* then refers to the concrete realisation of what is used as money, e.g. shells, gold coins, paper money or electronic money.

Laidler (2017, 13) provided an instructive setting of four elements that form such a monetary order: (1) a set of goals for the monetary authorities; (2) institutional arrangements that permit those goals to be attained; (3) private sector expectations consistent with them; and (4) political arrangements that permit goals to be changed, institutions to be modified and through which the monetary authorities can be held accountable for their performance. These points are taken up again at the end of this chapter to examine the extent to which digitalisation requires changes here.

That a new technology would require changes with regard to the monetary order is not obvious at first. In developed economies, a two-tier system based on central bank money and deposits in commercial banks is commonly established. Electronic payments or electronically processed transfers have been commonplace for quite a long time—and without changing anything in the familiar architecture. But this, as we will see in the following sections, could now be changing.

The primary aim is to illustrate that every form of monetary order, the design of which has been the subject of heated debate for some time now, is faced with fundamentally new challenges. Accordingly, the aim is not to offer a comprehensive review of the current discourse on the possibilities of reforming the current monetary system.[3] The point is to show what these specific challenges due to digitalisation are and in what way they are fundamental.

It is precisely for this reason that the position of the Freiburg School seems accurate in this context, as it addresses the *basic* problems of a monetary order. It will be their guiding questions that we will use here to make the scope of the current change visible. Köhler (2019) has pointed out that a summary account of the monetary policy position of the Freiburg School—i.e. of all its representatives, not just those of Eucken—has so far been lacking. Thankfully, he has also provided this account with a view to the history of economic thought and has reduced the monetary policy goal of the Freiburg School to a catchy formula: Its goal is to create a monetary constitution "(…) which is to be oriented towards monetary stability, to be institutionally designed in such a way that citizens can find a stable monetary system" (ibid., 23, own translation).

If we want to understand what challenges digital technology poses to such a constitution of money, a number of questions arise, from which the sequence of the following sub-chapters results. Accordingly, the following chapters progress from the general to the specific. It seems appropriate, given the dimension of the change, to really start with the very basics.

5.2 The Role of Money in the Economy

This chapter is devoted to the role of money in the economy. These are very fundamental considerations that have to be made because the circumstances to which they refer have come under new conditions as a result of digitalisation.

The chapter is structured as follows. The first Sect. 5.2.1 explains the crucial questions of the functions of money and their prerequisites in a market economy as well as the possible threats to these functions. The chapter deals with two sides of the same coin in different sections, namely first the functions of money before moving on to the next level, namely monetary systems in Sect. 5.2.2. The chapter thus paves the way for answering the question of how digitalisation poses a new challenge here, which is addressed in Sect. 5.3.

5.2.1 Money Functions and Their Prerequisites

This chapter introduces basic questions of monetary theory in order to be able to adequately show where change through digitalisation comes in.

[3] The current inflationary developments have considerably fuelled the debate on problems of the monetary system and monetary policy. Of course, this cannot be addressed here. Likewise, the attempt to only halfway depict the debate on the claims of Modern Monetary Theory and the corresponding opposition would go far beyond the objective of this contribution. Rather, the aim is to illustrate the extent to which fundamental relationships have been placed under new conditions by digitalisation. Where appropriate, reference is of course made to the corresponding discussion.

In order to explain what role money plays in a market economy, it is again worth starting from the question of what function this market economy is supposed to fulfil in the first place. Let us first simply assume the existence of a market economy.

A market economy is a coordination system for reducing the phenomenon of scarcity. In this system, what is scarce is not determined and proclaimed by some individuals or any groups, but this evaluation is left to the individual actors. The phenomenon of scarcity is, of course, already familiar to cultures that use the barter economy. However, there are a couple of "(...) problems that plague bartering (...)" (Naghshpour 2013, xvi). The barter economy sets systematic limits to the reduction of scarcity, because, as we have seen in the previous chapter, it does not allow for an efficient division of labour and is therefore accompanied by considerable losses in productivity. Only the use of money makes an effective division of labour possible.[4] Market economy, division of labour and money obviously belong inseparably together. So, what is the specific role of money here?

This role is commonly described in terms of three, sometimes five or even six (e.g. Flynn 2018) different money functions. In the following, we will focus on three money functions. Money is:

(1) a *means of exchange*. Instead of e.g. a dog or liquor for a new hairstyle, one exchanges a good or service for an agreed amount of money. At the moment of this kind of use, the exchange accordingly becomes a payment, and therefore to speak of a "means of payment" is functionally equivalent. Accordingly, money is also
(2) a *measure of value*. The respective current (market) values of dogs, liquor and hairstyles can be offset against each other without having to exchange them in real terms, especially since with three goods three different exchange ratios are already possible. Money eliminates "(...) the need for double coincidence of wants under barter" (Gerba and Rubiuo 2019, 37; see also Brunnermeier et al. 2019, 8).[5] Money hence serves, in other words, as a *unit of account*, as numéraire, and allows "(...) to mitigate the problem of tracking the relative prices of multiple different goods in an economy" (Brunnermeier et al. 2019,

[4] For the purposes of this study, it is not expedient to present the complex history of the theory of what money actually is. This is an exhaustively discussed topic in economics and philosophy alone. However, due to the remark in the text that the—moneyless—barter economy sets limits to the possibilities of the economy, it should be pointed out that intermediate forms do exist and in this respect the question of what can serve as money in which form also forms a subject of investigation for cultural anthropology, among others. The relevant discourse on forms of money that do not correspond to the modern concept of money relevant to these considerations can be summarised under the collective term "primitive money". Einzig (1966) has presented an extremely broad and instructive study on the topic. It is remarkable that his definition of "primitive money", which must satisfy a sufficient degree of generality, does not seem to deviate that far from a modern concept of money: "It may be defined as a unit or an object conforming to a reasonable degree to some standard of uniformity, which is employed for reckoning or for making a large proportion of the payments customary in the community concerned, and which is accepted in payment largely with the intention of employing it for making payments" (Einzig 1966, 317).

[5] The problem of double coincidence was thus problematised for the first time in by Jevons (1876), to whom, along with Menger (1892), the conception of the money functions, as they are also used here, can be traced back.

7). Since dogs age, and the hairstyle may be more important next month than today, money is also

(3) a *store of value*. Regardless of the form money takes, whether it ultimately represents a claim in the form of paper money or has an intrinsic value in the form of gold[6] (which is nevertheless tied to certain conditions and subject to fluctuations in valuation), money can therefore also be seen as an asset. Fiedler et al. (2019, 37) even emphasise that "(…) money becomes an 'asset' because it is a claim".

In addition, further functions can be differentiated, some of which can be derived from the previous ones. Sometimes the function as a medium of exchange is differentiated as two functions, namely medium of exchange and (4) means of settlement. Since money is also a store of value (more on this below) and there is no money to which no one would claim property rights,[7] the function of (5) means of transferring value is also found, since money can be given away, bequeathed, etc. Fiedler et al. (2019) point out that "(…) money constitutes a category of its own as it is neither an object of consumption (it does not directly satisfy human need) nor a means of production (the usefulness of money to allow for increasingly complex production process does not depend on its quantity)".

The functions mentioned are, of course, interrelated or inseparable, so that it would be futile to draw up a sequence with regard to importance. Insofar as we are dealing with a medium of interaction, *general acceptance* would of course be a central prerequisite. But of course, acceptance necessarily breaks down when other functions are not fulfilled.[8]

In this way, the use of money enables a functional reduction in complexity, which can also be interpreted as a reduction in transaction costs. Money, in this sense, facilitates a division of labour with regard to any goods and services, which can be differentiated as far as it is worthwhile—expressed in units of money—for the respective participants. Money thus makes it possible to coordinate the conduct of any number of individuals who neither know each other nor need to know anything about each other.

---

[6] For the sake of completeness, it should be noted that this formulation is also problematic depending on one's point of view, because depending on the situation one is in at the time, "intrinsic values" are of course quite different. If in doubt, remember, you can't eat gold. Gold, however, has the *functional* advantages of being scarce and also of having no debtor.

[7] This applies under the condition that it is not central bank money that has been completely devalued for the time being. Müller and Kerényi (2022, 125) seemingly try to stress the importance of the central banks, stating that they "(…) have been providing societies and economies with reliable, valuestoring money, for hundreds of years". One would like to exchange Reichsmark with them or make bets on the Hungarian Forint. The assertion in the text above does not apply, of course, if the money referred to here has disappeared and been forgotten; however, even found money is only due to the lucky finder if the origin of this money precludes the claims of others; heir investigators are not accidentally a profitable business.

[8] The complementarity of money functions means that the disruption of even one function can trigger a self-reinforcing process, which is partly due to the fact that the use of a currency is based on network effects. Thus, fleeing a currency because one assumes the disruption of even just one function becomes a good reason to flee that very currency.

The specific social coordination enabled by money is such a fundamental fact that sociological systems theory uses the binary code of "payment" or "relevant non-payment" (see Baraldi et al. 2021, 89) to distinguish the social system, "economic system", from other social systems and, accordingly, economics use the term of "externalities" in case of effects which are not factored in monetary terms. The social act of paying can certainly be understood as the basal medium or the basal act of "the economy",[9] and it is money that makes the modern form of the economy based on the division of labour possible. A thorough investigation is thus called for when either the relevant *medium* or the relevant *act* in which this medium fulfils its function is subjected to change. The previous chapter had focused on the act of paying in the sense of the concrete emergence of the price. Now we will focus on the medium.

Where can such changes in the medium occur in principle? The functions mentioned seem self-evident at first. In practice, however, problems arise in connection with the fact that a medium can only function as money under certain conditions. In order to exchange it for any goods and services and to be able to relate them to each other—i.e. to pay for them—the medium must be *divisible*. It must be safely *transportable*, in whatever form. It must be *durable*. It must be *free of manipulation* so that the partners in a transaction are not exposed to risks for the benefit of third parties. The means of payment must be *generally accepted*—a quality that is already apparent from the foregoing. These requirements are already obvious in the context of very less complex transactions. Accordingly, many of these conditions have been discussed almost as long as money has existed[10]and this discussion "(…) is part of a long historical interaction between technology and society" (Söderberg 2018, 2). These preconditions are—such a high degree of generality must be allowed here—always and everywhere important. They are important even when we are not talking about a medium in the narrower sense, a medium with a physical quality such as commodity money.

In addition, there is another important aspect. Money must be scarce per se so that it can function at all as a measure and as an indication of scarcity.[11] What is relatively

[9] This is not the place to discuss the borderline between economics and sociology. Some anthropologists would then have a different view of the same object area. Let us—without lapsing into economic imperialism!—simply assume here, with good reason, that the economy is also a part of the social, which we can certainly differentiate from other parts of the social on the basis of the above-mentioned code.

[10] Accordingly, we cannot engage in a detailed discussion of monetary theory here either, but we will start with the fundamentals in order to be able to show where the change that goes hand in hand with digitalisation starts in this context. Instead of a detailed discussion that would not be very useful, we will refer to the telling disclaimer by Crespo (2021, 459): "The topic of the nature or essence of money has produced an abundant literature without reaching a uniform conclusion. It has drawn the attention of famous philosophers, sociologists, and economists such as Aristotle, Nicholas Oresme, David Hume, Adam Smith, Ferdinando Galiani, Georg Simmel, Max Weber, Carl Menger, Georg F. Knapp, John Maynard Keynes, Karl Polanyi, Ludwig von Mises, Friedrich von Hayek, and Joseph Schumpeter, among others".

[11] This is a fundamental assumption that also underlies the approach of Jevons and Menger. See, for example, Hull and Sattath (2021), 6; 17. Things that are not scarce cannot have any stable value

scarce must be paid for with as relatively much money. Only this makes it possible in a market economy to combine competition for performance with maximum productivity through a maximum degree of division of labour with anonymous accounting of individual needs.

Since all these preconditions are always important for the functioning of the medium of money, namely, to express the prices formed by the conduct of market players, they can be summarised under the postulate of a *stable money value*. How these preconditions can be guaranteed without a regulator being constantly forced to intervene, how money can be kept scarce in concrete terms and how the value of money can be kept stable under present circumstances, is the subject of monetary orders or the monetary constitution.

5.2.2 *Monetary Systems: What Questions Arise in the Digital Age*

This chapter deals with the effects of digitalisation on monetary systems.

The goal of the theoretical considerations on an appropriate monetary system derives from the function that money has in the market economy. A corresponding "monetary constitution", i.e. a legally secured system of conditions and institutions that ensures the existence of money and thus the function of prices, should provide rules that keep the value of money as stable as possible while preserving the greatest possible freedom of individuals. In addition to the postulate of freedom, it also follows from the function of prices outlined in Chap. 4 that money must function "automatically" and cannot be entrusted to the higher reason of special chosen ones. This cannot function at all because of the very function that prices have.

As mentioned above, the question of a "monetary constitution" that meets these demands is an important subject of the deliberations of the Freiburg School.[12] In 1970, Folz presented a detailed account of Walter Eucken's reflections on monetary

---

at all in a system of relative values. Walras (2014) already points to this: "only scarce things and all scarce things are (…) appropriable, (…) valuable and exchangeable" (ibid., 20); "(…) a thing is scarce, in economics, the moment that it is useful and limited in quantity "(ibid., 21); "(…) things that are useful but that exist in unlimited quantities are also not appropriable". As noted above, this cannot be the place of a comprehensive discussion of money theory. In any case, the central idea in Walras's theory of money, namely "(…) to stabilize price variations by regulating the supply of money" (Walras, cited by Cirillo 1986, 215), refers to the function of the numéraire, according to which money is not "(…) purely a 'veil' in the sense that an exchange system could work without" (ibid.), but rather "(…) a third commodity of invariable value" (ibid.). Walras' theory has not spoken the last word either (accordingly, we cannot go into questions of neutrality of money and the "classical dichotomy" here) but here we accept the scarcity of money as its fundamental prerequisite for it to function (as a numéraire) at all. That *scarcity itself* is the central basis for the functionality of money in the first place is also elucidated by Halaburda et al. (2022, 21): "Scarcity matters for both medium of exchange and store of value".

[12] Similar to the above reference to the broad discussion on monetary theory, it should be noted here that there is of course also a discussion of proposals for monetary constitutions, and this was

theory and policy in German. Köhler (2019) has provided an instructive overview of the position of the Freiburg School, which unfortunately is not available in English. The distinctions he makes are extremely helpful for the purposes pursued here and should serve here as a concise overview of the position of the Freiburg School.

First of all, a monetary system no longer has to be fundamentally invented, but can be presupposed in developed economies. In order to systematise the relevant interrelationships of a monetary order appropriately, Walter Eucken distinguished three different monetary systems in his "Foundations of economics". These monetary systems initially focus on the question *of how money is created* in the first place. Strictly speaking, one could therefore speak of money creation systems, not, more generally, of monetary systems.

The distinction into three types is similar to that of the two ideal–typical economic systems of the centrally planned economy on the one hand and the market economy controlled by prices on the other, because they do not occur in a pure form in reality as designed from the drawing board.

In the first system, media also have an intrinsic value function as "commodity money". Obviously, this used to be precious metal, but depending on the economic situation, it could also be liquor (see Eucken 1940, 117ff; on this, classically, Folz 1970, 40). The individual actors in the economy can thus decide concretely whether they derive utility from the function of a medium as money or from its material value (Köhler 2019, 24).[13]

In the second system, money arises as a means of exchange for a good or service. If such a bill is returned by the debtor, the money disappears from circulation (ibid., 24). Accordingly, money can also be created by a central bank, for example, which ties the money to an underlying good with a stable market value, e.g. the bank buys precious metals. If it sells the corresponding precious metal, the money is accordingly withdrawn from the economic cycle again. Since the value of money was here usually linked to the value of precious metals in this way of money creation, it is also referred to as *metallism* (see, e.g., Cesarano 2014).

In the third system, money is created by granting credit, commonly known as *fiat money*. Here, the creation of money is not preceded by a barter transaction as in the second system. Such a paper currency, in which the medium in the narrower sense has no relevant material value anymore, is accordingly the antithesis of the first system, while the second system occupies an intermediate position.

Ultimately, money only functions on the basis of the actors' trust that they will also receive a real countervalue or service for their money. The medium of money—the other functions notwithstanding—means here nothing else than a documented claim on the one hand and a promise on the other. Claims and promises represent

particularly the case at the time of Eucken. See, for example, the still instructive contribution by Bernholz (1986).

[13] Of course, the situation is more complex. For example, if a precious metal is an intrinsic value of the medium used as money, this does not mean that the officially given form of this money is allowed to be destroyed at all, nor that this, to stay with the example of coins, would even be a technologically simple undertaking for the average user of money. For our purposes, it must suffice to make clear the differences between the general-typical systems.

the different sides of the market in all transactions; in the end, however, they fall back to the central banks, following the path of money creation.[14] Since the issuance of money is almost always a privilege of the rulers, this form of money creation, when carried out by the state by declaring any medium (even one that is worthless in and of itself) to be legal tender, is also called "chartalism" (see, e.g., Rossi 2012). In this context, further differentiations can be made in order to describe the special characteristics of digital forms of money. This will be the subject of Sect. 5.4.

Whichever way money is created, and whichever medium is used for it, as written above, an important precondition for the medium to function as money is the confidence of the users that it will function as money. The metallistic solution of money creation means a technological assurance of scarcity, all others are ultimately a contractual solution. However, in developed economies, it is above all the third system that is decisive. On the one hand, it is the most elastic with regard to the dynamics of the economy.[15] On the other hand, many people in charge are interested in increasing the money supply for political purposes, and this is easiest with fiat money. Of course, the expansion of the money supply carries the risk of inflation.

So, while on the one hand the flexibility of the fiat money system is advantageous, on the other hand the risk that the value of money will destabilise—that is, the function of prices will be disrupted—is relatively high. In this context, therefore, very important balancing problems arise that cannot be discussed in this framework. However, it is important to keep this in mind if one wants to understand how digital technology poses a new challenge in this context, as will be discussed below.

Accordingly, this gives rise to guiding questions with regard to possible regulatory concepts. One is, to what extent is there a need to reform the existing order in order to provide users with relatively better money (Köhler 2019, 46). We will not pose this question here in principle but focus on the extent to which digitalisation brings new challenges. In other words, the question which must concern us here is to what extent the *preconditions* of good money or the *functioning* of good money can be *threatened by digital technology*. To this end, the following chapters take up two fundamental complexes that capture the problems of function and technology from different perspectives. First, the central topic of *inflation* in Sect. 5.3 and then the highly topical problem area of digital currencies in Sects. 5.4. Section 5.5 then brings the insights gained together to form conclusions.

---

[14] This context is the starting point of both a much extended academic discourse and, increasingly, the public debate, in that since the Federal Reserve's temporary abandonment of the gold standard in 1971, an exponentially growing set of claims has been matched by ever more—questionable—promises.

[15] Without being able to give an adequate account of the discussion in this regard, it should be noted that, strictly speaking, it is of course a matter of greater flexibility for politics, which in a fiat money system is able to cushion short-term problems of the economy with monetary means. We will not discuss here in which case this makes sense or not over which time horizon. What is indisputable, however, is the fact that this possibility alone creates an "inflationary bias" among those in power, which, *ever since* fiat currencies have existed, has *always* led to inflation, i.e. in the long run to destabilisation and thus to the destruction of the money functions. See Bernholz (2015), 18f.

5.3 Inflation

The following chapter is dedicated to one of the most central questions that arise in connection with money, namely the phenomenon of *inflation* and especially the extent to which it can be linked to digitalisation.

The inflationary developments in the early 2020s made the problem of inflation topical.[16] Within the framework of these considerations, it is of course not possible to discuss the numerous problems associated with the problem of inflation or the different inflation theories (overview, for example, Frisch 2010). Inflation itself is already one of the most discussed phenomena in economics.[17]

However, if stable money is a central requirement that results, among other things, from the function of prices discussed in the Chap. 4, then the extent to which digitalisation can be a factor that can contribute to the destabilisation of the value of money, i.e. a reduction in the purchasing power of a currency, must also be taken into account. This is the subject of this chapter. It proceeds in two steps.

Section 5.3.1 endeavours to untangle the problem of monetary stability. Since the extent of monetary depreciation is usually approached by empirically tracking certain aggregate values, Sect. 5.3.2 deals with the concrete efforts made in this regard.

5.3.1 Disentangling Stability Targets

This section endeavours to differentiate the factors and processes that lead to inflation.

Stability of money is of utmost importance for the stability of the whole economy and society. The *economic* argument is that otherwise economic entities would not be able to calculate and to plan and accordingly; if one of the money functions does not work out, the division of labour could no longer unfold. And the *normative* argument that is inextricably linked to the economic argument is that only those who are able to plan individually are free.

Inflation is an extremely complex problem area in which different causes can have an effect, the weight of which is assessed differently in each case, depending on the situation on the one hand and the theoretical conviction of the observer on the other. Before his discussion of various inflation theories, Frisch (2010) starts with a rather general definition by Laidler and Parkin (1975, 741), because "(…) although it lacks precision (…) (it) has an advantage in that it corresponds to common usage:

---

[16] It is possibly one of the most pressing problems the global economy faces today. There is no doubt that the political measures taken in the wake of the Corona pandemic have damaged the highly differentiated value chains, and the current conflict over the Ukraine and the uncertainties that accompany it have certainly played a role. But one should not underestimate that the current inflationary developments are an obstacle of their own kind to the recovery of the international division of labour.

[17] See, e.g., Gillman (2023), Holanda Barbosa (2017), O'Neill et al. (2017).

'Inflation is a process of continuously rising prices, or equivalently, of continuously falling value of money'".

From this definition, a basic problem can already be derived for the purposes of our considerations. For prices are demanded for goods and services, but these are always relative prices of the goods and services to the monetary value or to a nominally expressed amount of money, but the reverse is also true: that the value of the respective item is a relative price that can be expressed in units of goods or services. What used to be officially communicated as the inflation rate is also a bundle of goods selected from statistical points of view.

What the measured variable is and what is the measure, however, cannot be clearly decided in the end, since none of the observed variables is really constant. The question arises as to whether a methodical distinction should be made between monetary stability on the one hand and price stability on the other. Now, logically, this is in our perspective hardly separable, since rising prices lead to a relative decline in the value of money[18]; accordingly, this is an old chicken-and-egg problem, the problem of which we do not want to go into any further theoretical detail. In a way, this situation is reminiscent of Heisenberg's uncertainty relation. Ultimately, a relative increase or decrease in the purchasing power of a given currency can only be determined on the basis of representative variables, e.g. goods and services.

The causes that are used to explain the loss of purchasing power of a currency are correspondingly diverse. This can include an increase in money supply, a surplus in demand or an increase in public spending (which implies, of course, an increase in demand); finally, inflationary spirals can also occur if, for example, employees react to the increased price level with wage demands. However, these are only a few important drivers for inflation, and though one may assess such a bundle of causes, it is never an easy task to be able to clearly isolate the role of individual factors. In essence, it is always about *two facets of one and the same connection*, monetary stability on the one hand and the question of how prices are formed on the other.

This perspective is unavoidable for several reasons. The provision of money in today's developed economies is a public task that has been taken over by the central banks (see Singleton 2011). If states are interested in a prosperous functioning of their economy, they must also be interested in a sustainably functioning money and payment system, i.e. in stable money and stable prices (see European Central Bank 2023a).[19] This is the reason why central banks use to set inflation targets. Central banks, *cum grano salis*, try to manage the inflation expectations of economic agents

[18] See—as one possible example among many—the statement of the European Central Bank: "Our job is to maintain price stability. (…) We keep prices stable by making sure that inflation—the rate at which the overall prices for goods and services change over time—remains low, stable and predictable" (European Central Bank 2023a).

[19] These explanations are, of course, extremely condensed and with regard to the institutional conditions of money creation too short. It should therefore at least be mentioned that the creation of money is a task that certain groups have usurped and secured for themselves through state power, today in the form of central banks. But whether this serves the cause is an entirely different question. The fact that those responsible have *never* acted sustainably in this regard is as obvious as it is extensively documented. This is why Friedrich August Hayek wanted to wrest the creation of money from the public purse. Since an appropriate discussion of a monetary constitution would be

and thus provide an element of economic policy-relevant building of confidence and trust in the respective currency.

Nevertheless, the question of a special and separable *effect of digitalisation* at this aggregation level seems to be virulent and this is also shown by the discussion in the academic world as well as the efforts of the central banks themselves.

5.3.2 Channels of Impact

The following section outlines the ways in which digitalisation can have an impact on inflationary developments.

There is a rich literature on the role of digitalisation in the context of inflation phenomena (see, e.g., Csonto et al. 2019, especially the literature on p. 8f.) as in other areas, the effects are assessed differently (ibid., 5). The European Central Bank aptly summarises the current situation as follows: "The impact of indirect effects (of digitalisation, J.D.) on inflation is manifold and ambiguous" (European Central Bank 2021, 86).

The main reasons for the quite different assessment of the influence of digitalisation on the value of money lie in four fundamental methodological problems.

Firstly, there is the problem of adequately capturing the phenomenon of inflation in the first place, as discussed in the previous section. It is extremely difficult to isolate and weight individual factors in a web of complex interdependencies that also develops dynamically. This leads to the following problem.

Secondly, there is the problem of adequately capturing what digitalisation actually is. There is simply no uniform measure of the extent of digitalisation. Some approaches distinguish between a digital sector in the narrower sense—i.e. e-commerce, platforms, etc.—the digital sector in the broader sense (see, for example, Goolsbee and Klenow 2018)—and the digital economy, those economic activities that are more or less based on the use of data (Csonto et al. 2019), i.e. a much broader approach. The range of representations that state statistical offices, central banks and research institutes put together is very broad.[20]

Thirdly, there is the problem of being able to state whether and which price changes were directly caused by digitalisation and which were not.

Fourthly, even if one has helped oneself heuristically with the definition of certain proxies, the question arises as to how inflationary effects come about at all.

Charbonneau et al. already proposed a segmentation of three "channels" in 2017, which provides a good orientation for our purposes. The first is a "direct channel",

---

a volume in itself, we must focus here on the concrete effects of digitalisation. In this respect, these considerations can contribute an element to a discussion on an appropriate monetary constitution in the digital age. Hayek again: "I don't believe we shall ever have a good money again before we take the thing out of the hands of government, that is, we can't take it violently out of the hands of government, all we can do is by some sly roundabout way introduce something that they can't stop" (Hayek 1984). If digitalisation holds new ways to do so?

[20] An instructive, tabular overview of these approaches is provided by Csonto et al. (2019), 15.

in which technological progress reduces prices for ICT-related goods and services. The second channel describes changes in market structure and behaviour due to the new technology and also the new transparency discussed in the previous chapter. The third channel deals with the effect of technological progress on productivity.[21]

Two years before the studies by Charbonneau et al. (2017), the Swedish Riksbank (2015) presented an instructive and still frequently cited study on the question of inflation that concerns us here. It unfolds a somewhat more complex picture than that of the French colleagues, but the argumentation of specific directions of effects mediated by many participants and elements is basically the same. Firstly, the new technology enables ICT production to be made cheaper, and it leads to cost reductions in production via the possibilities for automation and, via the new transparency, to greater competitive pressure due to better informed customers and thus to lower market-ups and correspondingly lower prices again.

The study was quite trendsetting, because the factors stressed are still decisive for the discussion today. The academic discourse either delves into the consideration of individual elements—this then accordingly also in different disciplines—, while studies concerning monetary policy rather take the overall effects into account.[22] This assumption is not unfounded and empirical studies (as e.g. Csonto et al. 2019) also seem to confirm this tendency. But it should be noted that these assumptions are made at a relatively high level of aggregation. They remain tied to bundles of implicit preconditions and it is no exaggeration to say they are formulated with some optimism. Accordingly, the conclusions also remain relatively abstract. On closer inspection, be it with regard to the composition of the corresponding basket of goods used to measure inflation, the inflation concepts used, the assessment of the scope of the impact or the time period used as a basis, the studies do show uncertainties.

It is fair to say that studies of price stability at such a high level of aggregation—i.e. explicitly with a view to the phenomenon of inflation—come to similar conclusions as those that deal with a smaller segment of the economy. Coffinet and Perillaud (2017) formulate quite aptly that "(…) the increasing use of the internet is likely to have a disinflationary effect in the short-term, the long-term effects remain

---

[21] This is again an extremely controversial connection, which will be discussed in more detail in the chapter on labour and income.

[22] *Nota bene*: this chapter focuses on the problem of monetary stability. Now, as already noted elsewhere, it is not always easy to distinguish whether the value of money is decreasing or whether certain goods are simply getting more expensive. Of course, they may become more expensive, i.e. scarcer, because they become better from the customer's point of view, more technically complex, etc. (so-called hedonistic regression). They may also become more expensive because there is a change of constellations on the market, e.g. processes of monopolisation. However, it seems helpful to keep in mind that "(…) money constitutes a category of its own as it is neither an object of consumption (it does not directly satisfy human need) nor a means of production (the usefulness of money to allow for increasingly complex production process does not depend on its quantity)" (Fiedler et al. 2019). Accordingly, this chapter focuses on the "category of its own" and other chapters illuminate this topic from other perspectives, namely the extent to which digitalisation can lead to different behaviour in markets—and in this respect, of course, also influences prices. These are two sides of the same coin.

difficult to identify" (Coffinet and Perillaud 2017, 19). Csonto et al. (2019) also observe minor short-term effects, while the long-term effects are difficult to assess. And Charbonneau et al. (2017, 11) express themselves very cautiously that digitalisation "(...) can have a small dampening effect on inflation", with which, if one still includes the limitations of the empirical basis, they actually say close to nothing. Even for the early short study by the Swedish Riksbank (2015, 59), the effects are, overall, "uncertain". Remarkably, a possible connection between the use of digital technology and the velocity of money is almost nowhere explicitly considered and is not mentioned at all, for example, in the corresponding, quite prudent report by the European Central Bank (2021).

Without being able to go into inflationary theories at this point, inflation, in the most succinct formulation, i.e. a reduced value of money over a representatively broad group of goods and services, means that the stability of money is impaired.[23] All forms of destabilisation accordingly mean that the function of prices as the central coordination mechanism of the market economy is disturbed. This entails corresponding welfare losses, since the functions of money described briefly at the beginning of the chapter are impaired.

In summary, one can say that at this level of aggregation, the effect of digitalisation on monetary stability tends not to be inflationary, but rather the effects with regard to transparency, competition and productivity tend to point in the direction of a weakening of inflation.

5.4 Digital Currencies

The following chapter deals with a new medium of exchange, so-called digital currencies. It is structured as follows:

Section 5.4.1 briefly introduces the background and establishes a connection with the other considerations made in this book.

Section 5.4.2 discusses the general characteristics and technical aspects of the new phenomenon.

---

[23] Admittedly, there is also a debate about what inflation actually is. Gaffard (2018, 2), who then traces the positions of Friedman, Wicksell and Keynes, etc., in his contribution, summarises the topic provocatively and succinctly: "The question remains whether we are dealing with a monetary phenomenon in the sense that it is attributable to mistakes in discretionary monetary (and fiscal) policy, or whether it is a phenomenon anchored in disequilibrium adjustments on gods and labour markets". Against this background, it is easy to formulate the view put forward in this contribution: namely that inflation is of course and always a "monetary phenomenon", which has different, primarily monetary and/or fiscal policy causes, but to whose different manifestations the "disequilibrium adjustments" mentioned above can either contribute causally—and secondarily—or are consequences of the process caused primarily by monetary policy. In short: do one thing without omitting something else. A structural separation is simply not realistic.

Section 5.4.3 raises the question of whether this new phenomenon, even if it is commonly called "digital currency" or "digital money", is really money in the true sense. Section 5.4.4 focuses on one special variant that is indeed money in the true sense of the word, namely central bank digital currencies (CBDCs).

This account is limited to the effects of this phenomenon on the stability of money. What cannot be dealt with in this framework are the numerous concrete regulatory issues that touch on this topic. Instead, the concluding Sect. 5.5 brings together the problems that have arisen and presents them as concrete, interrelated economic policy challenges.

5.4.1 Background

This chapter briefly outlines the background to the emergence of the phenomenon known in everyday language as "digital currencies".

The previous sections have mainly dealt with the question of how digitalisation influences the *processes* of price formation on the micro-level on the one hand and of price stability at the aggregate level at the other hand. What we had assumed so far was, of course, that it is all about goods and services on the one hand and money—first and foremost denominated in a central bank currency—on the other.

What has not been taken into account is the fact that so-called *digital currencies* or *digital money* have also been experimented with for some time on the basis of new technologies and what this could mean for the market economy. The emergence of this phenomenon raises a whole series of questions and is nowadays one of the most hotly debated topics.[24] Of course, central banks are also concerned with this phenomenon. Their interests will be discussed in more detail below. Why "digital money" at all? Aren't the existing currencies or possibilities given by the recent monetary systems sufficient?

Numerous aspects play a role here. One is the demonstrably gradually diminishing role of cash in transactions in modern economies (see, e.g., Khiaonarong and Humphrey 2019, 23). Apparently, more and more payments are being made electronically, i.e. also digitally. In this context, publications like to mention a transition to a "cashless society" as background (e.g. Fiedler et al. 2019, 9). This trend is indeed understandable, in some countries more, in some countries less. This trend is, of course, again only an expression for a rather wide range of very different phenomena that digitalisation produces in this context. In the narrower sense, i.e. the discourse of monetary theory, one also speaks of "trends of dematerialisation and informatization of money" (Nishibe 2020, 314).

Nevertheless, it should be pointed out at this point that there are very different causes for this trend. For example, the successively lower significance of cash has

[24] This discussion cannot be reproduced here in its breadth. This chapter focuses on the extent to which this new phenomenon poses new challenges to the stability of money.

cultural causes such as the willingness to gladly (and unquestioningly) accept innovations, which is likely to be more pronounced, e.g. in China than in Europe as can be seen from, e.g. the spread of Alipay wallets (Aveni and Roest 2017); there are economic causes, such as transaction cost savings; however, there are also self-reinforcing effects in the digital world, for example, when transactions with cryptocurrencies spread on certain social platforms. Some of these aspects will be discussed later when we look more closely at the relationship of cryptocurrencies to traditional central bank currencies. Is this a development that corresponds to desirable public goals? Does it affect the monetary system?

It seems, again, expedient to refer to the distinction used by Fiedler et al. (2019, 11) between the *architecture* and the *technology* of the monetary system. They pointed out that the long-standing practice of electronic payments, transfers, etc., has hardly affected the respective architecture so far. Remarkably, however, they also come to the conclusion that this could possibly change with the emergence of cryptocurrencies (ibid.). This seems to be a good indication of the scope of the digital transformation, namely that it is reshaping what has remained unchanged for a long time, or at least can potentially do so.

The following chapter focuses on the phenomenon that the medium of money itself can be replaced by "digital money" or "digital currencies" under certain circumstances and that this phenomenon indeed challenges for the architecture of current monetary systems. That there *is* already an influence on the economy and the international monetary system seems undisputed (see IMF 2021a, 2021b, 6). However, this chapter aims to describe more precisely where the—perhaps only potential—change in the architecture through the digital transformation comes in and what this means for the principle of the "primacy of monetary policy", i.e. the safeguarding of monetary stability.

5.4.2 Some General Characteristics and Technical Aspects

This chapter deals with the basic characteristics of digital currencies and how their technological basis differs from traditional money.

Section 5.2.2, with reference Eucken, distinguished monetary systems with regard to the ways in which *money is created*. Apart from the fact that this money must be countable and durable, there are actually no requirements for its physical properties. How is this relevant in this context? To the extent that, to put it succinctly, contemporary forms of money, which have to fulfil the functions discussed in Sect. 5.1.1, have no intrinsic value, but are merely a claim (Fiedler et al. 2019, 37). It is ultimately irrelevant what concrete medium (paper, plastics, brass, etc.) is used for exchange and calculation. It is therefore obvious that with cash first and foremost the aspect of counterfeit protection plays a role, but all other technical specifications are actually irrelevant for the functionality. Of course, in view of its function as a store of value, durability would also be an important aspect. Money should not go bad like a cocoa bean (see Rivero 1990). In the age of negative interest rates, this aspect nevertheless seems less trivial than it initially appears.

Accordingly, it is irrelevant whether the money is called Dollar or Euro, or in whose units it is settled and exchanged by shifting it from one digital account to the other. What is decisive in this respect is that the respective issuing central bank is responsible for the stability of its currency, i.e. the value of the claim expressed with the nominal value does not become smaller over time. This is easily understandable if the respective transaction takes place in one and the same currency area.[25]

One can probably assume with good reason that currencies of developed—or, better, "healthy"—economies fluctuate less than a stock market price and that this is also an expression of the relative stability of the payment medium used. So, you cannot pay with just anything, but participants in market activity will naturally resort to something that fulfils the money functions as well as possible. Either way, everyone is free to hold cash in different currencies, for example, if one currency is considered a relatively better means of storing values,[26] to hold demand deposits in the national currency or to keep a foreign exchange account. What can be actually paid with depends on the respective currency area; the exchange of currencies in order to participate in transactions in different currency areas can lead to exchange rate-related profits or losses according to the fluctuations.

So why "cryptocurrencies" now? What have we been missing this medium for? How is it different from other deposit money? What exactly is this phenomenon? It should be noted that there is no uniform definition at all (Söderberg 2018, 1). The somewhat loose term of "digital money" encompasses various forms and it is to be expected that further forms will appear (IMF 2021b, 5). The European Central Bank defines the term "cryptocurrency" as "a type of unregulated, digital money, which is issued and usually controlled by is developers, and used and accepted among the members of a specific virtual community" (European Central Bank 2012). This is also followed by Söderberg (2018, 1), who speaks of "(…) digital units that are created and transferred between the users through the use of cryptography".[27] The European Commission (2020b, 34) prefers the term "crypto-asset": "'crypto-asset' means a digital representation of value or rights which may be transferred and stored electronically, using distributed ledger technology or similar technology".

[25] This is, of course, a simplification. Currency areas do not have to be identical with national economies. The dollar area, for example, is of course much larger than the USA, a fact that has its advantages for some participants and is sometimes defended fiercely. This can have different reasons, which cannot be discussed here. Nor can the aspect of money markets, including currency speculation, be dealt with here. However, we will see that operations with "cryptocurrencies" must be assigned to another market.

[26] The differentiated use of currencies depending on their function naturally also has a corresponding influence on the value depending on the volume of demand, a phenomenon known as "Gresham's Law". This will be discussed in more detail in the next sub-chapter.

[27] The technical side of the cryptographic process in the narrower sense cannot be dealt with further here. Most crypto-assets are based on the blockchain, but not all (such as IOTA). The technology itself, the distributed ledger technology, is almost irrelevant in the context considered here, since in principle all media that meet certain functional requirements can be declared money. We only consider the special possibilities that arise on the basis of the new technology.

This term is quite an apt description. Nevertheless, variations in the terms "currency" and "money" are also commonly used in the relevant literature, depending on the focus. We will use these terms synonymously in the following. This does not imply any analytical limitations for our focus on the extent to which these phenomena represent a challenge for traditional money and the corresponding monetary systems. In addition, the corresponding citations to the conceptually heterogeneous discourse are less misleading. However, the extent to which this phenomenon can actually be understood as "money" is the subject of the next sub-chapter.

There are now more than 10,000 of these unregulated phenomena on the markets.[28] Whereas with a traditional currency there is a public issuer, the central banks, which influence the existing money supply, cryptocurrencies are privately emitted. This entails another crucial difference. For in currency areas, real central bank money is only available to citizens as cash; both companies and citizens have their accounts with the commercial banks, which are supplied with central bank money by the central bank. Only within the network of these private intermediaries are payment transactions possible for citizens and businesses. This is correspondingly different with cryptocurrencies, where the level of commercial banks can be completely eliminated and transfers among the participants of such a "community", each of whom accepts a particular cryptocurrency, are possible directly as a peer-to-peer procedure. This is generally faster and also cheaper (IMF 2021b, 5).

Moreover, they also move outside of the usually nationally determined currency areas and are in principle global. Instead of a local community, they are bound to a "virtual community of interest" (Nishibe 2020, 315). Cryptocurrencies "(...) can be distributed much more widely, including across devices and borders" (IMF 2021b, 6). They can be monetised, e.g. transferred into units on a bank account denominated in a central bank currency when sold, but they only exist digitally and are not realised physically.

Whereas central bank currencies are issued by a public institution which, as an entity of the state, provides the medium that is solely permitted as a public means of payment for paying taxes, cryptocurrencies are based on decentralised, private networks. The founder of bitcoin, known under the pseudonym Satshi Nakamoto, is often quoted as saying that this is "(...) a new electronic cash system that uses a peer-to-peer network to prevent double-spending (...)" that is "(...) completely decentralized with no server or central authority" (quoted after Luther and Smith 2020, 433).[29]

---

[28] It is important to bear in mind that this number has grown with astonishing dynamism so far. Söderberg (2018) still mentioned about 1500.

[29] Luther and Smith (2020) also refer very clearly to the title of the "popular" book by Ammous (2018): The Decentralised Alternative to Central Banking. Luther and Smith's (2020) contribution is noteworthy in that they further differentiate the commonly used pair of opposites of centralised vs. decentralised and distinguish between a "centralised payment mechanism process", a "decentralised payment mechanism process" and "distributed payment mechanisms". Accordingly, they also classify bitcoin as neither "centralised" nor "decentralised payment mechanism", but as a "distributed payment mechanism". For our purpose, namely to make clear the influence on monetary stability and the contrast to the principle of the conventional architecture of the banking system, we

Apart from the central bank and the commercial banks, no one actually owns central bank money, only in the token form of cash, and citizens as well as companies need a third party—commercial banks—as a "central node" of their trust in order to be able to settle transactions among themselves (see Luther and Smith 2020, 343). According to the mechanics of the transaction, it is also a centralised principle, even in the case when the clearing process takes place over several layers.

While in a modern central bank system fiat money can potentially be created in unlimited quantities,[30] the possible quantity of cryptocurrencies produced through so-called mining can be technically limited due to a mathematical procedure that is fixed at the beginning (and the same mechanism excludes attempts at counterfeiting through the corresponding encryption technology). This is a remarkable and perhaps not unintentional parallel to metallism in money creation (see Sanderson 2015; Cesaranao 2014), where money creation is limited by the physical scarcity of the underlying resource of the currency. Söderberg (2018, 2) therefore speaks of "digital metallism" with reference to Maurer et al. (2013), an aspect that will be taken up again in the final considerations of this chapter.

While the security promise in the central banking system refers on the one hand to the counterfeit-proofing of cash and the stability of the currency due to the state claiming it as legal tender, a cryptocurrency offers greater security against access by third parties, i.e. the state. Private "wallets", in which the quantities of units of the respective cryptocurrency, each with defined property rights, are stored instead of accounts in commercial banks, are safe from account blocking, safe from transaction fees, transfer limits and the like; they completely elude the access of third parties and are anonymous.

Even a quick look around reveals a remarkable variety of variants of this phenomenon. There is also talk of eMoney, stablecoins—crypto-assets whose value is linked to the value of a regular currency—such as Tether to the US dollar—or to a bundle of regular currencies—as in the case of Facebook's attempt at "Libra" or "Diem"—tokenised bank deposits, tokenised financial assets and others. This is not the place to go into the details of the concrete *technological* possibilities. Let's focus on the question of the relationship between crypto-assets and central bank money—in other words, whether cryptocurrencies are *money* at all. This is the focus of the next paragraph.

can stick to the commonly used pair of opposites. Ultimately, following the logic, "decentralised" and "distributed" have one thing in common: they are not central.

[30] Unlimited quantity is a technical possibility of fiat money systems that is actually subject to only two restrictions: One is some form of agreement or confession, economic policy commitments, self-binding of governments and all other forms of treaties and promises which are altogether, in all experience, not worth the ink. The other restriction is a corresponding successive devaluation of the value of money when the money supply grows faster than economic output, i.e. the argument of the quantity theory: If the money tap is left open, at a certain point the currency collapses on its own.

5.4.3 Are Cryptocurrencies Money at All?

This section addresses the question of how cryptocurrencies are actually money and what the relationship is between the two.

In everyday language, one generally speaks of "digital currencies" or "digital money" when talking about bitcoin, for example, and usually also when differentiating between various forms of digital money. This is also, only to mention a prominent example of relevant literature, the title of IMF (2021b)—"Rise of Public and Private Digital Money"—here both types of "money" obviously fit under one hat (see Adrian and Griffoli 2019).

This section takes a closer look at the extent to which we can really speak of *money* in the true sense of the word in this context (see Sect. 5.2.1) and what this means in terms of the stability of ordinary central bank money. In a first step, one must ask to what extent these phenomena can fulfil the functional requirements of money or not. In a next step, due to the technological novelty and the new possibilities associated with it, the question must be asked again as to what these phenomena can do better, if anything, than conventional central bank money. And thirdly, it must be discussed to what extent these phenomena endanger the stability of existing central bank money or pose new challenges to certain functions of central bank money and the price system accordingly.

Let us start from the current situation and look first at the functional requirements for money. In doing so, we can follow on from the basic considerations in Sect. 5.2.1 and focus on three functions in particular. So, are crypto-assets a "means of payment"? Yes, but only to a very limited extent. This already makes the *motivation* to acquire crypto-assets clear: Very few owners of crypto-assets will hold them because they intend to actually pay with them, unless, for example, they are involved in criminal activities, which is also the case to a considerable extent (on this, e.g. Foley et al. 2019; Paquet-Clouston et al. 2019), or want to avoid tax obligations; this would be a motive why the anonymity guaranteed by cryptographic technology would be of quite outstanding importance and would accordingly become a reason to *avoid* legal means of payment. In this context, it proves its worth that crypto-assets are token-based, not account-based—and then also faster and more flexible than the usual giro money. As a means of payment, crypto-assets are in any case—at present—not accepted to the same extent as central bank money. No ice cream, no car for digital money—still; however, a trend seems already emerging (see, e.g., Coinmap 2023; Deloite 2022; Businesswire 2020).

It is quite true that crypto-assets can function because there is an unspoken agreement *among the users* to use the respective medium as a means of payment. So, like central bank money, crypto-assets function based on the common assumption of acceptance. However, with the big difference that in the case of crypto-assets, a contract has been concluded between the users on the use of the asset, whereas in the case of the use of central bank money, a rule is imposed on the exchange partners. But the communities using crypto-assets are—still (!)—relatively narrow communities, even if their networks are principally global *ab ovo*, i.e. geographically potentially larger than national areas.[31] Furthermore, this function may be tied to the fact that a certain community, a corresponding virtual network, already exists beforehand and ties its own currency to the existing community, as the IMF (2021b, 15) has also pointed out. The corresponding network externalities play a role here, which the platform already brings along as a basis.[32] One could think of Facebook's "Libra" or "Diem", or of communities that do not want to be seen at all. In this context, one speaks of so-called digital community currencies (see, e.g., Nishibe 2020). The connection of social platforms with a digital currency, of course, potentially leads to a whole new dimension of the accumulation of user data (see Fiedler et al. 2019, 16), a point that will have to be addressed from a different perspective below. This function as a means of payment is therefore severely limited overall.

The above motivation also seems significant with regard to the function of the *store of value*. One remembers that one of the reasons for Bitcoin, which was launched in 2009, was the dissatisfaction with the existing system that arose in the course of the global financial crisis (see Davis 2011). If crypto-assets could neither then nor now fulfil the usual function as a means of payment, do they then offer themselves as a store of value in competition with central bank money? This is certainly more likely. Holders of crypto-assets who are not primarily interested in anonymous payment will consider it worthwhile *not* to invest their money in a central bank currency but hope for an increasing value of their investment. Accordingly, unlike the majority of those who hold central bank currencies in accounts, they act as speculators or investors (Söderberg 2018, 5; Auer et al. 2021, 6) or give a crypto-asset better chances as a long-term store of value (see, for example, Félez-Viñas et al. 2021). Current inflation expectations in the major currency areas will reinforce this trend (see, for example, Feyen et al. 2022 or Smales 2021).[33]

Thus, although crypto-assets fulfil this monetary function, they have a much more pronounced character as speculative instruments than central bank money. This characteristic is partly a consequence of the fact described above that they are not a regular means of payment. For the less they can be used as a means of payment, the more

[31] This is a potential, but it does not have to be the case. Such communities can also be regionally limited. See, for example, the interesting study by Pédussel Wu et al. (2023).

[32] Admittedly, the connection addressed here is even more complex, as it is ultimately the platforms that are both the product and the medium of the transformational effect of digitalisation; the connection will be taken up again in later chapters.

[33] This is an assumption that is all the more obvious the more crisis-ridden the situation is for traditional currencies, or rather, how crisis-ridden it is assessed to be. This can already be empirically verified, see, for example, Conlon et al. (2021). However, the situation is not clear-cut; that bitcoin plays a role as an inflation hedge remains to be seen; in any case, Choi and Shin (2021) show that its price development against the backdrop of crises is different from that of gold, and bitcoin is therefore "not a safe haven". In their empirical study, Kikuchi et al. (2021) attest at least bitcoin, Ethereum and Ripple a strikingly good stability. However, the development can also be interpreted in such a way that cryptocurrencies are not being bought as inflation hedges, but simply because central bank money has been available very cheaply for a long time and has accordingly formed speculative bubbles; against the background that the balance sheet of all cryptocurrencies which are not backed is ultimately completely empty, the growth in the volume of crypto-assets would be the result of a whole crowd following the greater fool theory.

their value is exposed to the fluctuations of supply and demand against central bank money, without there being any interconnection with complex real economic coordination processes. For this reason, cypto-assets are also much more volatile than central bank currencies (Auer et al. 2021, 6; Bains et al. 2022); they have a "(…) dynamic instability problem. It may suddenly lose its transaction value if people believe that in the future, others will not accept it in exchange" (Brunnermeier et al. 2019, 24). And for precisely this reason, its potential to serve as a measure of value or a means of settlement, i.e. a unit of account for any transactions, is also limited. There is thus, so to speak, a problem of its own at the level of convertibility, or rather, regardless of whether one "monetises" one's crypto-assets into any regular central bank money or puts its value into another, more promising crypto-asset, the exchange costs are potentially greater. Certainly, the last point does not fully apply to such crypto-assets whose value is linked to a central bank currency or a bundle of central bank currencies, i.e. backed crypto-assets or so-called stablecoins (see Auer et al. 2021, 7). But the decisive limitation of the first aspect, namely acceptance as a general means of payment, also applies to these.

If something is money, insofar as it fulfils the above-mentioned monetary functions, then the question of whether cryptocurrencies are money must currently be answered in the negative (see Ammous 2016). On closer inspection, one should not be deceived by the use of the term, even if its name and use in niches make it seem so. Jackrabbits are not rabbits—and cryptocurrencies are therefore not currencies, and they are not money. At the same time, however, it is undeniable that *with regard to certain functions*, i.e. not simultaneously, there is definitely a competitive relationship. In this respect, the question must be asked under which conditions the one species is contesting the place of the other.

Brunnermeier et al. (2019) have pointed out that digitalisation leads to a differentiation of monetary competition with regard to different monetary functions, where differentiation and thus also—to stay with the image—a crowding-out effect unfolds can be well explained with reference to Gresham's Law, which is relevant in this context. If two different types of money are in circulation, in the classic case silver coins and gold coins, which have the same denomination and can be exchanged one to one, the currency that is considered to be a poorer store of value displaces the other, which is then hoarded accordingly. This relationship naturally also applies to convertible cryptocurrencies (Brunnermeier et al. 2019, 10). And of course, this also means that digital money or public money may be preferred *for certain functions* and, hence digital currencies "(…) could threaten individual countries' monetary sovereignty by displacing domestic currencies" (Auer et al. 2021, 9).

It was already indicated above that cryptocurrencies appear in connection with existing communities. Brunnermeier et al. (2019, 19) accordingly mention "digital currency areas", which, as mentioned above, can only be used within the corresponding network. They thus gain their stability from the quality of this network and thus differently from traditional currency areas in the sense of Mundell (1961). Although they are global per se, they are fragmented by different spaces of public regulation. In this respect, a complex regulatory problem arises with regard to the important question of convertibility, which sets corresponding limits to the success of cryptocurrencies in one or the other functional area.

Other barriers that were relevant for the "pre-digital era of money", such as the aforementioned network externalities or exchange costs, are also eroded in this context by the possibilities of digital technology, at least as long as we are talking about use in the digital realm, i.e. non-cash. Exchange costs would in principle be lower, because the exchange of digital currencies not only takes place without time expenditure, but also lacks a third party to whom fees might have to be paid (see Brunnermeier et al. 2019, 11). And network externalities, which also represent an obstacle to competition between currencies, now play a different role, namely in that a digital currency does not have to, but can be linked to a platform and in this respect disproportionately greater network externalities can unfold in the digital space.

5.4.4 Impact on the Monetary System

The following section deals with the extent to which crypto-assets now pose a threat to the stability of central bank money.

Asked in general terms, is the functioning of the monetary system now at risk? Or, more restrictively, are its functions in any way disrupted, inhibited or confirmed? At the moment, probably less so, at least only under certain conditions. If one looks at the role that prices have in a market economy and the extent to which alternative, digital means of payment could play a role here, there is actually no detrimental correlation of effects. So far, it does not seem comprehensible in which way the stability of existing currencies would be endangered by crypto-assets. It is therefore not surprising that research interested in the phenomenon of inflation hardly focuses on this question. For this, such a volume of existing currencies would have to be converted into crypto-assets that a comprehensible loss of value would set in. But this is by no means traceable at the moment.

The issuance of money that can be used for everyday payment is still a sovereign task. In developed economies, therefore, legal tender is generally used. In the sense of a means of payment, one cannot easily switch to alternatives. Neither on the basis of the current infrastructure, nor on the basis of the currently (still) existing trust, nor on the basis of the existing network externalities in favour of the currencies used, is it likely that an alternative, non-state means of payment will take over this basic function.[34]

[34] Given the global expansion of the money supply, government debt, problems in the banking system and inflation expectations, it may come as no surprise that crypto-assets are increasingly in demand following the rise in share prices. But ultimately, however, the thought experiment that a critical mass *could* prefer a cryptocurrency to a central bank currency is unrealistic. For state power would ban its use easily, e.g. just as "liberal" Prime Minister Justin Trudeau imposed a "bank freeze" on protesters.

However, the likelihood of using alternative means of payment or an alternative store of value increases the less trust there is in legal tender. In this sense, it is quite possible that the potential of digital alternatives is growing because the given currencies are not being used carefully. However, the central banks of the developed economies, especially in the Eurozone, seem to be working on this in a lemming-like haste. If an appropriate international division of labour can no longer be maintained with the help of legal tender, for example, because it is no longer possible to plan with legal tender, then the relevant actors will have to come to an agreement on alternatives. It remains to be seen to what extent crypto-assets will be assessed as an appropriate alternative.[35]

Last but not least, this is not only a question of monetary policy, but also a question of the extent to which large platforms can develop their possibilities and succeed in outstripping the possibilities of public actors (see Auer et al. 2021, 6). It is hardly possible to predict what the results of this tension will be; for, due to the possibilities of digitalisation, the complexity is infinitely greater than ever before.

5.4.5 About the Idea of Central Bank Digital Currencies

The following section now turns to the question of what significance a digital central bank currency (CBDC) can have.

There has been quite an intense debate on this for almost half a decade (see Auer et al. 2021; Agur et al. 2022; Panetta 2021a, b, c) and according to Boar and Wehrli (2021) until 2020 already 86% of central banks conducted research in CBDCs and until 2021 more than 50 central banks had already published their results. Let us review some basic aspects for an explanation.

As mentioned above, the legal tender used today is fiat money, which is only accessible in two forms, either in the form of cash, i.e. token-based, or in the form of reserves. As far as access to money is concerned, the architecture of our monetary system is two-tiered. The reserves are only accessible to the commercial banks. The commercial banks therefore play, in a sense, a role as an intermediary that can provide accounts to non-banks, i.e. citizens and businesses, and create money denominated according to the respective central bank's unit of account by issuing credits.[36] Non-banks accordingly have claims on commercial banks in the form of these accounts denominated in a currency. Here, the money is correspondingly account-based, i.e.

[35] Of course, this will ultimately be a question of power alone and not a question of economic sense or convictions, see the comment and the example in the previous footnote. However, the opportunities offered by digitalisation were already surprising. They will not be the last.

[36] For the sake of completeness, it should be noted that commercial banks are of course not the only intermediaries, but also savings banks, money market funds and so on. This is not further differentiated in the following because it would not provide any further clarification for the focussed problem area.

the money can be clearly assigned to an owner by a third party—the intermediary, a commercial bank (see Brunnermeier et al. 2019, 5).

This is the common architecture in developed economies, at least as far as the role of the respective players is concerned. In this framework, in a cashless economy, citizens would not have access to central bank money in the narrower sense. The extent to which money in circulation is or is not linked to a particular asset, such as gold, is another question, which will be touched on again in another context below. Digital technology now makes changes possible also with regard to this characteristic architecture of the monetary system. And remarkably, the possibility of introducing digital central bank money is being considered openly by many central banks. What is this all about?

Without going into the technical aspects in a narrower sense, the basic idea of a CBDC is that private households or businesses now have direct access to a central bank account—similar to what was previously the exclusive case for commercial banks. "CBDCs can be defined as a form of digital money, denominated in the national unit of account, which is a direct liability of the central bank" (Auer et al. 2021, 3, referring to Group of central banks 2020; see also Bank for International Settlements 2020, 5). It would be "(...) an electronic form of central bank money that can be exchanged in a decentralised manner known as *peer-to-peer*, meaning that transactions occur directly between the payer and the payee without the need for a central intermediary" (Bech and Garatt 2017, 56).[37] This basic idea certainly allows for several variations. CBDCs could be token-based or account-based, used for wholesale or for retail and based on either distributed ledger technology or on the traditional technological infrastructure (see Auer et al. 2021, 3). Basically, the role of commercial banks could then only be optional for citizens and businesses, not unavoidable as it is now. This constellation would force commercial banks "(...) to make their deposits more attractive and increases the costs of funds for commercial banks" (ibid., 15).[38]

CBDCs would allow central banks to add a new form to the existing forms of central bank money, i.e. cash *and* their settlement accounts. The central bank's reserves would then be merged with CBDC, so to speak "(b)ase money is extended beyond cash and reserves to a third aggregate state—unless reserves are simply merged with CBDC units by granting unrestricted access to reserve accounts" (Fiedler et al. 2019, 17). The European Central Bank describes its thought experiment of a digital euro as "(...) an electronic equivalent to cash. And it would complement banknotes and coins, giving people an additional choice about how to pay" (European Central bank 2023b).[39]

---

[37] Bech and Garratt use the term "central bank cryptocurrencies" because of the underlying technology, but this makes no difference.

[38] This summarised with reference to Andolfatto (2021), Keister and Sanches (2019) and Chiu and Koeppel (2019).

[39] In principle, this idea is actually not new; Auer et al. (2021, 4) also refer to the proposal by Tobin (1987).

What would be the essential difference to other crypto-assets and what advantages would a CBDC offer? The possibilities pose fundamental questions. The publicly accessible motives seem to be stressed differently in different jurisdictions (Auer et al. 2021, 7). The main difference would of course be the issuer itself. A unit of a CBDC would be a claim against a central bank, "backed" by the state. A CBDC would accordingly be denominated in the respective national currency and could serve as a numéraire just like the latter. This would be a legal tender that, unlike private cryptocurrencies, could be used everywhere for payment.

However, the central banks never tire of putting the advantages of CBDCs in the shop window. It does not seem unreasonable to treat the example of the European Central Bank as typical. Let us take a closer look at each of the arguments and then comment on how they fit with the role of central banks of keeping prices stable.

On the operational side, there would be faster payment processes than before. And with a view to social goals, one also foresees financial inclusion. The European Central Bank hopes "(...) (i)t could foster financial innovation and improve the overall efficiency of the payments system" (European Central Bank 2022). But the question arises as to whether a public institution is needed to increase innovation and efficiency. It does not seem at all clear to what extent the infrastructural advantage of a CBDC would be decisive compared to the possibilities of the conventional money system and make new things possible.

In a two-page document, the European Central Bank also assembles further arguments, such as the need to keep pace with changes in the modes of payment because "(...) retail payments are also undergoing a disruptive transformation" (European Central Bank 2023b, 1; see also idem 2020, 9f.; Bindseil et al. 2021, 5). However, the question remains as to what extent this would result in a specific task for a central bank.

The European Central Bank openly fears that "(...) in a digital world (cash) could become marginalised as a means of payment" (European Central Bank 2023b, 1). But why should a central bank care if users prefer non-cash payments?

Accordingly, it claims to have to keep up with this and pretends to respond "(...) to the increasing demand for safe and trusted electronic payments" (European Central Bank 2022). Did anyone need the central bank for that?

It envisages the digital Euro as an "(...) anchor of stability for the payment and monetary systems" (ibid.), which at the same time "(...) would also strengthen the monetary sovereignty of the Euro area (...)" (ibid.). But it is another question how well the very same central bank has performed in making its currency an anchor of stability. The institution of the central bank itself would gain sovereignty through such an instrument, not the corresponding currency area. It is not comprehensible on the basis of economic arguments to what extent the possibility of additional liquidity "(...) would preserve the role of central bank money as a stabilising force of the payments system" (European Central Bank 2022, 2).

One gets the impression that the responsible at the European Central Bank, just as other central banks, either does not believe any of these words, or that these official pronouncements have been left to the pen of an anonymous undergraduate marketing student intern. Nevertheless, this explanation is hardly credible. Given that the European Central Bank was unable to preserve the stability of its currency, perhaps only the phrase "to preserve the role of (the) central bank", regardless of money—"whatever it takes"—corresponds to the real motives.

In their instructive paper, Fiedler et al. (2019, 9) have assembled the essential arguments on a more abstract level, namely "(…) higher revenue, efficiency of the payment system, traceability of illegal transactions, surveillance, upholding the public monopoly of money, countering competition" (Fiedler et al. 2019, 9). These "advantages" may be possible motives for central banks. Instead of all the far-fetched benefits mentioned above, it seems more like central banks want to limit or avoid the dangers of a new type of currency competition with digital alternatives. As long as money is issued by public institutions, it makes sense in principle for the respective currency to be exposed to competition,[40] namely to prevent the respective actors from adapting monetary policy options to the political weather or certain interests. Moreover, the "surveillance" motive mentioned in the quote must not be underestimated. A CBDC would give central banks an unprecedented amount of potential power *beyond monetary policy.* A possibility that is of course not even mentioned in the official announcements. The "bank freeze" in Canada was a foretaste of this.

While digital currencies can be a way to differentiate risks in private portfolios, for example to cushion the effects of shocks or to hedge against expansionary, inflationary monetary policy of central banks, *the more alternative currencies can be used, the more limited the central banks' room for manoeuvre in monetary policy.* With the introduction of a digital currency, central banks could expand their possibilities to set the interest rate, in a cashless society, indeed, at any positive or any negative level (Bordo and Levin 2017, 12f.). Of course, this would only be possible if there were no alternative to cash or an account at a commercial bank. But it would be naïve to think that central bankers have not thought about this yet.[41] The question would be whether such an intervention would be appropriate, i.e. in the context of the role of prices and money in a market economy as described above. This can hardly be affirmed.

From this perspective, the introduction of a CBDC seems a bit like a delayed reaction to a process in which many actors are switching to digital, private money and at this moment the previous intermediaries, the commercial banks, are also potentially losing importance. On the other hand, this limits the monetary policy competence of central banks, and one may assume that they want to have as much competence as possible. To return here to the money functions that can be unbundled in the digital space (see Fiedler et al. 2019): On the one hand, it seems understandable

[40] The debate on currency competition, especially with regard to competition between public money and private money, has of course been going on for a long time, see, classical, Hayek (1976), Brunnermeier and Niepelt (2019), Bech and Garrat (2017), but the possibilities of digitalisation are adding a new dimension.

[41] The European Central Bank still officially emphasises the advantages of physical cash. But the potential of digital central bank money for surveillance and control alone should give the citizens of a free society pause for thought. "Nobody has any intention of building a wall" as Walter Ulbricht said 1961.

at this point that digital money is increasingly used as a store of value, while central bank money has a competitive advantage as a unit of account because it is a legal tender.

But in this respect, two developments seem to be emerging. On the one hand, people are paying less and less in cash and more and more electronically. In the given architecture of the financial system, however, this means that the users of money do not actually pay with central bank money, but with liabilities of the commercial banks, which are tied to the "anchor" of central bank money and are interchangeable with each other, since they are denominated accordingly in one currency. On the other hand, there are the new digital currencies. The larger the digital networks or platforms are, the larger the network externalities generated on them become, which with increasing size simply makes it seem less necessary that digital units of account used on such platforms are somehow "backed". This could potentially lead to a crowding out of central bank money and thus restrict the central banks' room for manoeuvre in monetary policy. These are, indeed, revolutionary prospects.

However, the possibilities of CBDCs would go beyond this. By being used in a cashless society, the central bank would have considerably more information about the actual use of the currency and allow for much more specific interventions instead of the usual interventions (Auer et al. 2021, 19 with reference to the meanwhile published study by Davoodalhosseini 2022). If one sees this possibility together with the increased scope to set positive or negative interest rates for all, then these technical possibilities blur the boundary between monetary policy and fiscal policy (see Basetto and Sargent 2020). And even more so than is already the case.

The issuance of CBDC would hence on the one hand cushion the competition of private issuers with regard to certain monetary functions,[42] and this would save the monetary policy options of the central bank system over another period. The possibility of convertibility to other forms of digital money would again establish a kind of uniformity of money in the first place (see Brunnermeier et al. 2019, 26). On the other hand, the commercial banks will also be interested in prolonging as long as possible an architecture with which they have been able to do excellent business for a long time period. For this, however, they first need a central bank currency. What lies ahead is more a question of practical realities and, ultimately, contingent wrangling among regulators and interest groups.

[42] Brunnermeier et al. (2019), whose lucid and instructive contribution has been cited here several times for good reasons, believe that in a cashless society "(...) private issuers would lose the discipline of public money, and their issuance would instead be shaped by other market forces" (26); but this is an irritating statement against the background that one can associate many terms with "public money", but probably very little with "discipline". It is precisely the lack of it that erodes its function as a store of value.

5.5 Conclusions

This chapter brings together the aspects of money discussed in the previous sections for further consideration.

One could probably still subscribe to Eucken's statement that "(…) all efforts to realise a competitive order are in vain as long as a certain stability of money is not assured" (Eucken 2004, 256, own translation). It pragmatically bridges the sometimes rather abstract discussion about the desirable range of inflation targets. It is about a *certain*, but principle stability of money, not about more or less one or two per cent inflation. Does digitalisation now pose new challenges to this fundamental monetary policy goal of a certain stability? What are the *special transformational effects* of digital technology? The following sections present some conclusions. To discuss this appropriately, four complementary perspectives need to be considered.

In order to give an adequate account on the effects of digitalisation on money, firstly, the concrete formation of prices discussed in the previous chapter must also be taken into account. Secondly, digitalisation creates a new form of currency competition that has not existed before and that must also be interpreted in the context of the previously mentioned aspect. Thirdly, at this point and as in the previous chapter, reference must again be made to the instrumental character of the economy and thus correspondingly also the instrumental character of money, namely in order to be able to answer the normative question, whether a humane social order is served by these instruments or not. And then, fourthly, the question must also be raised—we do not presume to be able to fully answer it here—which economic policy cornerstones, or more precisely: the above-mentioned elements of a "monetary order", are now facing new challenges.

It can be stated that the new way of forming prices described in the previous chapter does not seem to have a significant impact on the stability of money itself. Higher degrees of product complexity due to digitalisation can lead to a justified, selective price increases, but this does not seem to lead to a *certain stability* of money being affected by the effects of digitalisation. However, money is apparently not worth more either, for example because digitalisation would make productivity gains possible.

The following three sub-chapters examine the phenomena that are characteristic of the age of digitalisation and that go beyond the causal relationships that are relevant even without digitalisation.

Section 5.5.1 treats once again the topic of price formation and the phenomenon that digital technology can partially absorb the role of prices.

Section 5.5.2 focuses on the money functions and the extent to which digitalisation has an impact on aspects of currency competition.

Section 5.5.3 deals with the corresponding economic policy problem, namely the question of an appropriate monetary order in the age of digitalisation.

5.5.1 *Crowding-Out Opportunities*

The following section illustrates the connection between the role of stable money in a market economy and the digital revolution in price formation.

Let us first make a fundamental observation and consider an aspect of the instrumental character of the economy. In this context, a closer look reveals that acquiring, possessing, holding and finally spending money under the condition of a stable monetary value enables citizens to participate appropriately in economic activities. This is the core aspect of monetary stability in the context of price formation. However, the phenomenon described in the previous chapter, namely that the use of the price system is now partly relatively more expensive due to the possibilities of processing big data, means in this context that this participation-enabling role of stable money is pushed back in favour of the role of processing big data. This aspect of participation is not usually counted among the functions of money at all[43]—possibly because until the digital age it could simply be assumed that money was the exclusive medium of encoding scarcity and thus a kind of "language" of the economy (see Brunnermeier et al. 2019, 7; Issing 1999). However, as the previous chapter has shown, this is partly a thing of the past.

This means that no matter how stable money is in and of itself, participation in the economic process, which is based on the normative claim and prerequisite of the freedom of all individuals, is pushed back by the processing of big data because this form of coordination is cheaper than coordination with the help of money. Whereas in the pre-digital age the destabilisation of the value of money was equated with a threat to freedom and thus at the same time with a threat to participation in the economic process (see the quote attributed to Lenin at the beginning of this chapter), digitalisation poses a new threat in this respect that is initially independent of the value of money itself. In this respect, it is fair to say that digitalisation *endangers a role of money that could previously be protected by monetary stability.*

This has created a new problem that does not concern money itself in a narrower sense; but it is rather a very important reason why a currency should always be handled with care, as will be shown below. With regard to the actors, digitalisation thus takes away a significant piece of manoeuvring mass from the public regulator, whose task it would be to allow individuals to pursue their individual plans freely by guaranteeing monetary stability. In this context, it is important to note that state competence is indeed needed, i.e. it is desired in order to secure the event of the market as an event of free interaction.

However, whether the absorption of this new, digital sphere of reality through instruments such as a central bank digital currency is a desirable idea in the sense of a free, humane society, seems rather doubtful.

---

[43] However, this aspect appears among the arguments for a central bank digital currencies under the label "social inclusion". We cannot go into the problem of what exactly is meant by this inclusion, but it seems worth pointing out that in its own context this argument seems rather flimsy.

5.5.2 Unbundled Competition

This section deals with the new phenomenon of how digital technology enables a kind of unbundling of monetary functions.

A new kind of currency competition occurs, or more precisely a kind of competition between different, digital offers for the relatively better fulfilment of functions previously bundled in the medium of money. Two functions in particular come into consideration here.

On the one hand, the function as a means of exchange or means of payment with regard to the concrete handling of the payment process. With crypto-assets, it is possible to pay as anonymously as with cash, only easier (you don't have to take a suitcase with you for large sums, so it is also safer), faster and independent of the distance between the transaction partners. It may be that this payment process is also cheaper than carrying out a digital transaction in a central bank currency via an intermediary such as a commercial bank. The use of cryptocurrencies can therefore save transaction costs under certain conditions (see IMF 2021b, 5). Expressed somewhat laxly, one could also say with reference to the basic requirements for money that cryptocurrencies are simply better "transportable". Depending on which aspects are predominantly important for the transaction partners, this could lead to a respective displacement of central bank money. The question would be *at what scale would this then lead to a loss of value of central bank money.*

A similar effect can be assumed for the second function, namely the store of value function. Instead of storing value in a central bank currency—whether in cash or as a claim in the account of a commercial bank—one can finally also store in form of crypto-assets. Admittedly, as described above, such investments are still primarily speculative today; cryptocurrencies are in this respect, to refer again to the basic requirements of a medium serving as money, less "durable" than large central bank currencies. Accordingly, the expectations associated with such investments will also be characterised by uncertainty. However, one must also take into account that using central bank currencies as a store of value is currently punished by the market: hence the flight into other assets.

This can change, however, the more such communities that accept a cryptocurrency reach a critical size on the one hand, and on the other hand, the more central bank currencies of a corresponding size are not dealt with in a prudent manner. That is supposed to happen. But whatever the case, there is a differentiation process behind both processes that does not seem to be conducive to the requirement of money to have an instrumental character. In the case of careless handling of a central bank currency, the case is obvious. But in the second case, the question must be asked whether the non-pecuniary costs of belonging to a certain community (see European Central Bank 2012) are in the sense of an instrumental character for the realisation of a decent order. The costs on the side of the individual participants consist of a loss of freedom due to a developing information asymmetry, which tends to be misjudged by the individuals, expressed in monetary units. This situation is discussed under the term "privacy paradox" (see, e.g., Solove 2021; Norberg et al. 2007). On the other hand, the term "virtual community of interest" used by Nishibe (2020, 315) expresses a social differentiation that probably also runs counter to the basic idea of the function of money as a guarantee for equal participation opportunities. It is correct that both issues mentioned here do not directly concern the store of value function, but are problems arising from a prerequisite for the full functionality of non-central bank currencies, namely the critical size. Last but not least, these tendencies are inherent. They result from the aforementioned possibility of unbundling the money functions (see Fiedler et al. 2019).

With this new form of unbundling of monetary functions and the fact that new competitive relationships are unfolding in the digital space with this possibility, is the monetary stability of central bank currencies at risk? This will depend, as said, first of all on the magnitude of the evasion of national bank currencies. For the time being, with a view to the efficiency of the economy, there is nothing at all wrong with actors using different means of payment. Who would want to ban barter in a community if it could solve its scarcity problem better that way? At best the state and its politicians, which would like to participate in every exchange with a tax.

With regard to the connection between the three poles of the state, society and the economy envisaged here, two fundamental problems arise. Firstly, similar to what was described in the previous paragraph, central banks as an actor are deprived of room for manoeuvre by new crypto-assets. However, one could also be happy about this from a monetary policy point of view. After all, crypto-assets can be kept scarce per se, they are—and this is the Achilles' heel of central bank currencies at this moment in time from the perspective that unbundles the monetary functions—"free of manipulation". Apart from the fluctuation of the value of a crypto-asset, neither the freedom of the citizens nor their anonymity is affected when they use crypto-assets to substitute central bank money with respect to certain money functions. This, in turn, is a phenomenon of crowding-out public competence, which does *not* seem detrimental in terms of freedom and the coordinative challenges of the economy, i.e. different from the above-mentioned processes of crowding out.

Therefore, the project pursued by so many central banks to introduce central bank digital currencies seems to be more of a political move to at least compete for a while in the context of the function of money as a means of exchange in order to maintain the existing power. It also opens up an opportunity for the central banks to expand their power if necessary. It costs the European Central Bank nothing to announce today that "(p)rivacy protection must be of the highest standard, and users should be able to choose how much information they want to disclose—but always in compliance with the applicable law" (European Central Bank 2022, 2). But even if we assume that central bankers today are all angels, there is no guarantee that their successors will be. And data protection is an object of policy. The introduction of CBDCs would be an (initially potential) attractive gain in control for politicians and thus a loss of freedom for citizens, quite similar to what we observed with regard to the processing of data on platforms in the previous chapter. It is understandable that the activity of platforms under the big techs is viewed critically; it is less understandable how citizens are served when public authorities would use the same means. Or would this be an effective antidote to the problems listed above?

In other words, would a competition between the public central bank and the digital ecosystems for knowledge advantages concerning the medium of payment be expedient, i.e. would this competition be *instrumental* in the sense of a free, humane order? Hardly. CBDCs would indeed limit the security of citizens from the fantasies of those in power. The fact that a central bank uses normative imperatives in the form of arguments as "inclusion" to expand its possibilities beyond the monetary sphere—albeit only potentially at first—seems to be a worrying development.

With an expansion of the sphere of state observation and surveillance, the CBDCs threaten to be a public counterpart of the crowding-out effects described with regard to the price system. And with this, the other monetary policy danger beyond the impact of digitalisation, namely a new possibility of creating even more liquidity with CBDCs, has not even been addressed. However, this is not the subject of this study.

5.5.3 Who Will Guard the Guards Themselves?

This chapter focuses on the question of the influence of digitalisation on the institutional framework of a monetary system, its *architecture.*

What is remarkable about the current processes is, quite fundamentally, that a technological change is also gaining influence on the architecture of the monetary system. How can this be differentiated?

The legal safeguard of this architecture can be described as the financial constitution, which, if one follows Köhler (2019), "(…) is to be oriented towards monetary stability, to be designed institutionally in such a way that citizens can find a stable monetary system" (own translation). The institutional design meant by this, which can be described as "monetary order" using a term from the Freiburg School, is thus affected accordingly by these processes. To get one's bearings on the four components of a monetary order proposed by Laidler (2010, 2017), then new challenges can be derived for all four. Since this is not a comparative monetary policy study in detail, but rather a study on the specific, new impact of digitalisation on monetary policy, we are content with the publicly available goals of the European Central Bank, whose challenges, we believe, are fundamentally transferable to other monetary authorities.

If we look at the first component, "a set of goals for the monetary authorities", then, with reference to the European Central Bank, in accordance with TFE Article 127 (1) the "(…) main objective (…) to maintain price stability" should be mentioned first. This objective has already been discussed above. The addition formulated in the same legal basis that the central bank "(…) shall act in accordance with the principle of an open market economy with free competition, favouring an efficient allocation of resources" (ibid.) seems *prima facie* unproblematic. Behind this demand stands the economic argument for stable money derived from the role of a functioning price system. The wording of the legal basis, however, does not cover the new type of competition between new, digital media for the fulfilment of separate, unbundled money functions that have become possible due to technological development. It is indeed possible that "(...) an efficient allocation of resources" can be achieved relatively better through this competitive relationship than through the medium of traditional central bank money.

In any case, this is a complex discussion on the borderline between law and economics. It is of great importance, however, that in the search for solutions, the decisive instrumental character must remain in focus, namely that the solution must always also—insofar as one wishes to normatively commit oneself to this—serve the overriding goal of a humane social order. According to the above, this also applies to the considerations of the extent to which the central bank itself enters the terrain of the "open market economy with free competition" or whether it should rather not do so. In the case of the European Central Bank—and in accordance with the economic arguments for a functioning monetary system also for other central banks—a clear answer must be found for the problem area that arises here, insofar as the TFE Article 127, Paragraph 2 also names "(...) to promote the smooth operation of payment systems" among three other "basic tasks".[44] The question is particularly complex because monetary policy objectives can be viewed less than ever in isolation. And when Laidler (2017, 4) points out that "(...) each element of any monetary order needs to be compatible with the others if the whole is to function coherently, and they can be incompatible in an endless variety of ways", then the second sub-sentence is extremely explosive with regard to the instrumental relationship between economy and society in the digital age.

In this respect, the fundamental problems that have been mentioned must first be addressed before the concrete monetary order can be shaped, the second component of which, according to Laidler, is "institutional arrangements that permit those goals to be attained". In line with the above, there can be no economic recipe for this, either now or in the future. For first of all, the responsible actors must be aware of the normative problem area and follow normative decisions in their pragmatic approach. That this is credibly achieved is ultimately the prerequisite for the third component in Laidler's scheme, namely "private sector expectations consistent with them".

From a pragmatic point of view, this third component is complementary to the fourth, "political arrangements that permit goals to be changed, institutions to be modified, and through which the monetary authorities can be held accountable for their performance". However, this is, first of all, a challenge for political practice, the core problem of which was already formulated two millennia ago by Juvenal, *Quis custodiet ipsos custodes*?[45] Remarkably, the possibilities of digitalisation provide new opportunities to address this question. At present, central banks tend to interpret the possibilities of digitalisation as a way of expanding their (monetary) policy

[44] The other three are: "to define and implement the monetary policy of the Union", "to conduct foreign-exchange operations consistent with the provisions of Article 219" and "to hold and manage the official foreign reserves of the Member States". They will not be dealt with in more detail here, as none of these three is affected in the narrower sense by the effects of digitalisation which is focussed on.

[45] The quotation is taken from the sixth of his satires, lines 347–348. The question is an expression of moral indignation, since the wives of the Romans would seduce even the guards assigned to guard their marital fidelity. Money is always seductive.

competences. However, digitalisation also offers the possibility to achieve exactly the opposite. In principle, scarcity of central bank money could be decreed by algorithm on the basis of blockchain technology, just as the quantities of bitcoin and other crypto-assets are in principle limited. This would therefore be a kind of digital gold standard for central bank money.

In principle, this would mean that the discussion about the pros and cons of the gold standard would have to be reopened. Whether scarce money is on the wish list of political leaders and powerful interest groups is a pragmatic question that cannot be resolved here either. Ultimately, the question of maintaining a financial constitution is crucial and thus as old as Western culture itself—*Quis custodiet ipsos custodes*? The answer is that the guardianship should not be entrusted to men in the first place. All experience and theory supports that "(…) (l)ong-term monetary stability—an inflation-free monetary system—can be maintained only if politicians and central bankers have no discretionary authority to influence the stock of money" (Bernholz 1986, 496).

In this context, it is a question of both a monetary policy creed and a clear normative positioning of those in charge as to what instrumental character they ascribe to the economy and for what. It will not be possible to take this off the shoulders of those responsible with any theory. But it is possible that it is digital technology which can contribute to a solution that neither monitors the people nor the money, but politicians to make sure they do not take any advantage of it.

References

Adrian, Tobias / Griffoli, Tommaso M. (2019): The Rise of Digital Money. International Monetary Fund FinTech Notes no. 2019/001.

Agur, Itai / Ari, Anil / Dell'Ariccia, Giovanni (2022): Designing central bank digital currencies. Journal of Monetary Economics 125, January, 62–79.

Ammous, Saifedean (2016): Can cryptocurrencies fulfil the functions of money? Columbia University. Center on Capitalism and Society. Working Paper No. 92, August.

Ammous, Saifedean (2018): The bitcoin standard: the decentralized alternative to central banking. Hoboken, New Jersey: John Wiley & Sons.

Andolfatto, David (2021): Some Thoughts on Central Bank Digital Currency. Cato Journal 41 (2), 343–351.

Auer, Raphael / Frost, Jon / Gambacorta, Leonardo / Monnet Cyril / Rice, Tara / Shin, Hyon Song (2021): Central bank digital currencies: motives, economic implications and the research frontier. BIS Working Papers No 976.

Aveni, Tyler / Roest, Joep (2017): China's Alipay and WeChat Pay: Reaching Rural Users. CGAP Brief. Washington, DC: World Bank.

Bains, Parma / Ismail, Arif / Melo, Fabiana (2022): Regulating the Crypto Ecosystem. The Case of Unbacked Crypto Assets. International Monetary Fund FinTech Notes Notes no. 2022/007.

Bank for International Settlements (2020): Central bank digital currencies: foundational principles and core features. Report No. 1, October.

Baraldi, Claudio / Corsi, Giancarlo / Esposito, Elena / Walker, Katherine (2021): Unlocking Luhmann. A keyword introduction to systems theory. Bielefeld: Bielefeld University Press.

Basetto, Marco / Sargent, Thomas J. (2020): Shotgun wedding: Fiscal and monetary policy. NBER Working Paper 27004.

Bech, Morten L. / Garratt, Rodney (2017): Central bank cryptocurrencies. BIS Quarterly Review, September, 55–70.

Bernholz, Peter (1986): The implementation and maintenance of a monetary constitution. Cato Journal 6 (2), 477–517.

Bernholz, Peter (2015): Monetary regimes and inflation: history, economic and political relationships. Cheltenham: Edward Elgar.

Bindseil, Ulrich / Panetta, Fabio / Terol, Ignacio (2021): Central Bank Digital Currency: functional scope, pricing and controls. European Central Bank Occasional Paper No. 286/2021.

Boar, Codruta / Wehrli, Andreas (2021): Ready, steady, go?—Results of the third BIS survey on central bank digital currency. BIS Papers No. 114.

Bordo, Michael D. / Levin, Andrew T. (2017): Central Bank digital currency and the future of monetary stability. NBER Working paper 23711.

Brunnermeier, Markus / Niepelt, Dirk (2019): On the equivalence of private and public money. Journal of Monetary Economics 106, 27–41.

Brunnermeier, Markus K. / James, Harold / Landau, Jean-Pierre (2019): The Digitalization of Money. National Bureau of Economic Research Working Paper 26300, September.

Businesswire (2020): HSB Survey Finds One-Third of Small Businesses Accept Cryptocurrency, 15.01.2020. Online: https://www.businesswire.com/news/home/20200115005482/en/HSB-Survey-Finds-One-Third-Small-Businesses-Accept (last access 23.02.2023).

Cesarano, Filippo (2014): The Puzzle of Metallism: Searching for the Nature of Money. History of Political Economy 46 (2), 177–210.

Charbonneau, Karyne / Evans, Alexa / Sarker, Subrata / Suchanek, Lena (2017): Digitalization and Inflation: A Review of the Literature. Bank of Canada Staff Analytical Note. Ottawa, Ontario, Canada: Bank of Canada.

Chiu, Jonathan / Koeppel, Thorsten (2019): The Economics of Cryptocurrencies – Bitcoin and Beyond. Bank of Canada Staff Working Paper 2019–40. Ottawa, Ontario, Canada: Bank of Canada.

Choi, Sangyup / Shin, Junhyeok (2021): Bitcoin: An Inflation Hedge but Not a Safe Haven. Finance Research Letters 46, Part B, May.

Cirillo, Renato (1986): Leon Walras' Theory of Money. The American Journal of Economics and Sociology 45 (2), 215–221.

Coffinet, Jérôme / Perillaud, Simon (2017): Effects on the internet on inflation: an overview of the literature and empirical analyses. Fifth IMF Statistical Forum, 17-17 November, Washington D.C.

Coinmap (2023): Crypto ATMs and Merchants of the World. Coinmap. Online: https://coinmap.org/view/#/world/14.43468022/-17.22656250/2 (last access: 23.02.2023).

Conlon, Thomas / Corbet, Shaen / McGee, Richard (2021): Inflation and cryptocurrencies revisited: A time-scale analysis. Economics Letters 206.

Crespo, Ricardo F. (2021): On Money as a conventional sign: Revisiting Aristotle's conception of money. Journal of Institutional Economics 17 (3), 459–471.

Csonto, Balazs / Huang, Yuxuan / Tovar, Camilo.E. (2019): Is Digitalization Driving Domestic Inflation? IMF Working Paper 19/271.

Davis, Jashua (2011): The Crypto-Currency: Bitcoin and its mysterious inventor, in: The New Yorker, 10. October.

Davoodalhosseini, Seyed Mohammadreza (2022): Central bank digital currency and monetary policy. Journal of Economic Dynamics and Control 142, September.

Deloitte (2022): Merchants getting ready for crypto. Merchant Adoption of Digital Currency Payments Survey. Online: https://www2.deloitte.com/content/dam/Deloitte/us/Documents/technology/us-cons-merchant-getting-ready-for-crypto.pdf (last access: 23.02.2023).

Einzig, Paul (1966): Primitive Money: In Its Ethnological, Historical and Economic Aspects. Oxford i.a.: Pergamon Press.

Eucken, Walter (2004): Grundsätze der Wirtschaftspolitik. Herausgegeben von Edith Eucken und K. Paul Hensel. Tübingen: Mohr Siebeck.
European Central Bank (2012): Virtual Currency Schemes. Frankfurt a.M.: European Central Bank.
European Central Bank (2020): Report on a digital euro. European Central Bank. Online: https://www.ecb.europa.eu/pub/pdf/other/Report_on_a_digital_euro~4d7268b458.en.pdf(last access: 5.3.2024).
European Central Bank (2021): Digitalisation: Channels, impacts and implications for monetary policy in the euro area. ECB Occasional Paper, No. 266, 1, Frankfurt a. M.: European Central Bank.
European Central Bank (2022): The case for a digital euro: key objectives and design considerations. July. Online: https://www.ecb.europa.eu/pub/pdf/other/key_objectives_digital_euro~f11592d6fb.en.pdf (last access: 31.01.2023).
European Central Bank (2023a): Monetary Policy. Online: https://www.ecb.europa.eu/ecb/tasks/monpol/html/index.en.html (last access: 5.3.2024).
European Central Bank (2023b): Digital Euro. Online: https://www.ecb.europa.eu/paym/digital_euro/html/index.en.html (last access: 30.01.2023).
European Commission (2020): Proposal for a Regulation of the European Parliament and of the council on Markets in Crypto-assets, and amending Directive (EU) 2019/1937. Brussels, 24.9.2020 COM (2020) 593 final.
Félez-Viñas, Ester / Foley, Sean / Karlsen, Jonathan R. / Svec, Jiri (2021): Better than Bitcoin? Can Cryptocurrencies Beat Inflation? Available at SSRN: https://deliverypdf.ssrn.com/delivery.php?ID=752123112086066120109068004095078023006042023048070022113019026098095071101120087089054030034103008038096119018082101114085097126071075054031100121077004025027029090085079018085001007004104064087120109081029018065103102091024022022101103121000007111065&EXT=pdf&INDEX=TRUE (last access: 10.06.2023).
Feyen, Erik H.B. / Kawashima, Yusaku / Mittal, Raunak (2022): Crypto-Assets Activity around the World: Evolution and Macro-Financial Drivers. Washington, D.C.: The World Bank.
Fiedler, Salomon / Gern, Klaus-Jürgen / Stolzenburg, Ulrich (2019): The impact of digitalisation on the monetary system, in: European Parliament: The Future of Money. Compilation of papers. Study requested by the ECON committee. Monetary dialogue, December, 5–29.
Flynn, Dennis (2018): Six monetary functions over five millennia: A price theory of monies, in: van der Spek, R. J. / van Leeuwen, Bas (eds): Money, Currency and Crisis. In Search of Trust, 2000 BC to 2000 AD. New York: Routledge, 13–36.
Foley, Sean / Karlsen, Jonathan / Putnins, Talis J. (2019): Sex, drugs, and bitcoin: How much illegal activity is financed through cryptocurrencies? The Review of Financial Studies 32 (5), 1798–1853.
Folz, Willibald (1970): Das geldtheoretische und geldpolitische Werk Walter Euckens. Berlin: Duncker und Humblot.
Frisch, Helmut (2010): Theories of Inflation. Cambridge: Cambridge University Press.
Gaffard, Jean Luc (2018): Monetary theorey and policy: the debate revisited. LEM Working paper Series 37. Pisa: Laboratory of Economics and management. Institute of Economics Scualo Superiore Sant'Anna.
Gerba, Eddie / Rubio, Margita (2019): Virtual Money: How Much do Cryptocurrencies Alter the Fundamental Functions of Money? In: European Parliament. Study, requested by the ECON committee. Monetary Dialogue, December 2019. The Future of Money. Compilation on papers. Policy Department for Economic, Scientific and Quality of Life Policies. Directorate-General for Internal Policies, November, 30–60.
Gillman, Max. (2023): The spectre of price inflation. Newcastle: Agenda Publishing.
Glasner, Davis (Ed.) (2021): Studies in the history of monetary theory: controversies and clarifications. Cham: Springer.
Goolsbee, Austan / Klenow, Peter (2018): Internet Rising, Prices Falling: Measuring Inflation in a World of E-Commerce, in: AEA Papers and Proceedings 108, 488–492.

Group of Central Banks (2020): Central bank digital currencies: foundational principles and core features. Joint Report 1, October.

Halaburda, Hanna / Sarvary, Miklos / Haeringer, Guillaume (2022): Beyond Bitcoin. Economics of Digital Currencies and Blockchain Technologies. Second Edition. Cham: Palgrave Macmillan.

Hayek, Friedrich August von (1976): Choice in Currency. A way to stop inflation. London: The Institute of Economic Affairs.

Hayek, Friedrich August von (1984): Interview. Online: https://www.youtube.com/watch?v=CBIidtaUCzs (last access: 4.11.2023).

Holanda Barbosa, Fernando de (2017): Exploring the Mechanics of Chronic Inflation and Hyperinflation. Cham: Springer.

Hull, Isaiah / Sattath, Or (2021): Revisiting the properties of money. Sveriges Riksbank Working Paper Series, No. 406, Stockholm: Sveriges Riksbank.

IMF (2021a): IMF Policy Paper. 2021 Compehensive Surveillance Review - Overview Paper. Washington. D.C.: International Monetary Fund.

IMF (2021b): The Rise of Public and Private Digital Money: A Strategy to Continue Delivering on The IMF's Mandate. Policy Paper No. 2021/055, International Monetary Fund.

Issing, Ottmar (1999): Hayek – Currency Competition and European Monetary Union. BIS Review.

Jevons, W. Stanley (1876): Money and the Mechanism of Exchange. New York: D. Appleton and Co.

Keister, Todd / Sanches, Daniel R. (2019): Should central banks issue digital currency? Federal Reserve Bank of Philadelphia Working Papers no. 19-26.

Khiaonarong, Tanai / Humphrey, David (2019): Cash Use Across Countries and the Demand for Central Bank Digital Currency. International Monetary Fund Working Papers 2019/046.

Kikuchi, Tatsuru / Toranosuke, Onishi / Ueda, Kenichi (2021): Price Stability of Cryptocurrencies as a Medium of Exchange. (November 11, 2021). JPS Conf. Proc. 36, 011001. Available at SSRN: https://ssrn.com/abstract=3961305 or https://doi.org/10.2139/ssrn.3961305

Köhler, Eckehardt A. (2015): Renewing the search for a monetary constitution: reforming government's role in the monetary system. Washington, D.C.: Cato Institute.

Köhler, Eckehardt A. (2019): Die Geldordnungstheorie der Freiburger Schule, in: Ordo: Jahrbuch für die Ordnung von Wirtschaft und Gesellschaft 70 (1), 21–49.

Laidler, David (2010): EMU as a monetary order. Commetary, in: M. Bordo and L. Jonung: Lessons for EMU from the History of Monetary Unions. London: Institute of Economic Affairs, 59–61.

Laidler, David (2017): Economic ideas, the monetary order and the uneasy case for policy rules. Journal of Macroeconomics 54 (A), 12–23.

Luther, William J. / Smith, Sean Stein (2020): Is Bitcoin a decentralized payment mechanism? Journal of Institutional Economics 16, 433–444.

Maurer, Bill / Nelms, Taylor / Schwarts, Lena (2013): When perhaps the real problem is money itself!: the practical materiality of Bitcoin. Social Semiotics 2 (5), 1–17.

Menger, Karl (1892): On the Origin of Money. The Economic Journal 2 (6), 239–255.

Mundell, Robert A. (1961): A Theory of Optimum Currency Areas. The American Economic Review 51 (4), 657–665.

Müller, János / Kerényi, Ádám (2022): The Rise of Central Bank Digital Currencies. Financial and Economic Review 21 (3), 122–148.

Naghshpour, Shahdad (2013): The fundamentals of money and financial systems. New York: Business Expert Press.

Nishibe, Makoto (2020): The present and future of digital-community currencies: RAMICS 2019 in Hida–Takayama keynote speech. Evolutionary and Institutional Economics Review 17, 327–343.

Norberg, Patricia A., / Horne, Daniel R. / Horne, David A. (2007): The Privacy Paradox: Personal Information Disclosure Intentions versus Behaviors. The Journal of Consumer Affairs 41 (1), 100–126.

O'Neill, Robert / Ralph, Jeff / Smith, Paul A. (2017): Inflation. History and Measurement. Cham: Palgrave McMillan.

Panetta, Fabio (2021a): Hic sunt leones – open research questions on the international dimension of central bank digital currencies. Speech at the ECB- Central Bank Research Association (CEBRA) conference on international aspects of digital currencies and fintech, Frankfurt am Main, 19 October 2021. Online: https://www.bis.org/review/r211118c.pdf (last access: 10.06.2023).

Panetta, Fabio (2021b): Central bank digital currencies: a monetary anchor for digital innovation. Speech by Fabio Panetta, Member of the Executive Board of the ECB, at the Elcano Royal Institute, Madrid, 5 November 2021. Online: https://www.ecb.europa.eu/press/key/date/2021/html/ecb.sp211105~08781cb638.en.html (last access: 10.06.2023).

Panetta, Fabio (2021c): Designing a digital euro for the retail payments landscape of tomorrow. European Central Bank. Online: https://www.ecb.europa.eu/press/key/date/2021/html/ecb.sp211118~b36013b7c5.en.html (last access: 10.06.2023).

Paquet-Clouston, Masarah / Haslhofer, Bernhard /Dupont, Benoît (2019): Ransomware payments in the Bitcoinecosystem. Journal of Cybersecurity 5 (1), 1–11.

Pédussel Wu, Jennifer / Metzger, Martina / Neira, Ignacio Silva / Farroukh, Arafet (2023): What determines demand for digital community currencies? Our Village in Cameroon, Working Paper, No. 209/2023. Hochschule für Wirtschaft und Recht Berlin, Institute for International Political Economy (IPE), Berlin.

Rivero, Piedad P. (1990): When cocoa was used as currency. The Unesco Courier 1990 (1), 16–20.

Rossi, Sergio (2012): Chartalism, in: The Elgar Companion to Post Keynesian Economics, Second Edition. Edited by J. E. King. Cheltenham: Elgar, 79–82.

Sanderson, Henry (2015): Digital currencies: A gold standard for bitcoin, in: Financial Times, 15th May.

Singleton, John (2011): Central banking in the twentieth century. Cambridge: Cambridge University Press.

Smales, Lee A. (2021): Cryptocurrency as an Alternative Inflation Hedge? Online: https://papers.ssrn.com/sol3/papers.cfm?abstract_id=3883123 (last access: 30.01.2023).

Söderberg, Gabriel (2018): Are Bitcoin another crypto-assets money? Sveriges Riksbank. Economic Commentaries No. 5, 14th March.

Solove, Daniel J. (2021): The Myth of the Privacy Paradox. 89 George Washington Law Review 1, GWU Legal Studies Research Paper No. 2020–10. Available at SSRN: https://papers.ssrn.com/sol3/papers.cfm?abstract_id=3536265 (last access: 10.06.2023).

Sveriges Riksbank (2015): Digitisation and Inflation. Monetary Policy Report, February.

Tobin, James (1987): The case for preserving regulatory distinctions. Proceedings of the Economic Policy Symposium. Jackson Hole: Federal Reserve Bank of Kansas City, 167–83.

Walras, Léon (2014): Elements of Theoretical Economics Or the Theory of Social Wealth. Edited and translated by Donald A. Walker and Jan van Daal. Cambridge: Cambridge University Press.

Chapter 6
Open Markets Under Pressure

Competition is one click away. (Larry Page)

6.1 About Openness of Economies in the Digital Age

This chapter addresses the question of the extent to which the principle of open markets in the digital age needs to consider new dimensions. To make it clear that this is a complex interplay of several factors that goes beyond questions of the effect of trade barriers, this chapter briefly introduces the meaning of this claim, the implications of which will then be explored in greater depth in the following chapters against the background of the digital transformation.

The first Sect. 6.1.1 shortly explains the economic arguments of the claim for open markets and which areas it can be concretely addressed. Section 6.1.2 deals with the special role of the state in this context.

6.1.1 Openness as a Multidimensional Demand

The following chapter discusses the extent to which the demand for open markets fundamentally goes beyond a mere postulate of free trade.

Economics has always been committed to the demand for open borders for trade in goods and services. Among other things, to fully exploit the potential of the division of labour at the international level. However, this openness should not only be interpreted as a principle of free *trade*, but also, quite necessarily, has an implication for competition policy, that is to say no company should be protected from competition merely because it is a domestic one. For companies to be under the pressure of competitors, markets must be contestable. Domestic companies will not offer better goods and services if they are protected from competition from abroad. And the same applies to companies that are guaranteed a monopoly position by the state for certain

© The Author(s), under exclusive license to Springer Nature Switzerland AG 2024

J. J. Dötsch, *Economic Policy in the Digital Age*, Contributions to Economics,
https://doi.org/10.1007/978-3-031-53047-0_6

goods or services. Whatever the case may be, the always relevant question in this context is *what the barriers of a market are* in the first place. Basically, there are three ways to answer this question.

Firstly, the borders can be defined administratively, i.e. on the basis of *national borders*. The market then corresponds to a national economy and the concept of the market accordingly coincides with that of the economy. From this perspective, issues concerning international trade come into focus accordingly.

Secondly, this is the more complex approach; one can try to clarify the question in terms of *competition* by defining which market is relevant, i.e. where competition as a coordinative mechanism begins or should begin (see Sullivan 2021). In this sense, barriers to market entry can also have to do with the administrative barriers of a national border, but can also arise independently from national borders, among other things, for technological reasons, economies of scale, cost advantages or anti-competitive practices.

Thirdly, it is essential to consider the role of the *state*. For, on the one hand, markets can be threatened by the state if it acts in the interests of certain groups. Then, too, the market is correspondingly less open because competition is impeded. On the other hand, the state must provide the appropriate institutional setting so that coordination processes run as far as possible according to the market principle. The state must allow and encourage an economy that is as efficient and humane as possible.

In this sense, we understand here open borders for trade and the maintenance of the principle of competition as two aspects of one and the same claim. Since, as the previous paragraph suggested, the state has a special role to play, the following sub-chapter deals briefly with this problem.

6.1.2 The Special Role of the State

This section briefly points out how far state regulation can run counter to the principle of market openness.

The state has a special role insofar as it is the public regulator. From the first perspective mentioned in the previous section, the state plays an important role in shaping trade policy. In the second, the perspective of ensuring competition and free entry to markets, it seems useful to introduce a further distinction, namely between the protection of competition from monopolies and cartels on the one hand and the protection from distortions by state intervention, on the other. From a pragmatic perspective, this corresponds to the state's commitment to *enforce* the principle of open markets, on the one hand, and to *commit* itself to this principle, on the other.

At this point, it should be noted once again that the present account deviates from Eucken's original conception. This difference between the *constitutive principle* of keeping markets open, on the one hand, and the *regulatory principle* of competition policy, on the other. Both aimed at ensuring that the coordination of economic activity should proceed according to the principle of the market, i.e. competition. In our perspective, it makes sense to deal with these aspects together and to shed light on *what challenges the digital transformation poses* for economic policy.

6.2 Borders in a Digitalised World

The following chapter discusses the question in which way digitalisation plays a role with regard to the degree of the openness of economies and focuses on problems of cross-border exchange. On the one hand, this can be understood as an effect on already existing contexts, such as the phenomenon of servicification in international value chains. On the other hand, however, digitalisation in the narrower sense also poses a new challenge in international business, as data transcends borders and offers new opportunities for companies and users.

The remainder of this chapter is structured as follows. Section 6.2.1 focuses on the concrete trade policy dimension of this issue. Section 6.2.2 draws attention to the fact that the public regulator, with a view to securing freedom and security—a humane order—for its citizens, is also faced with new balancing problems in this context. Section 6.2.3 focuses on the interaction between the regulator and the regulated. This already seems to be a controversial topic in this problem area insofar as "tech giants" (see Kerber 2022) are emerging as new dominant and widely influential players on the stage of the global economy. Section 6.2.4 draws the attention to the demand for public regulation by interest groups.

6.2.1 National Economies, National Borders

The following section is devoted to the question of the openness of markets at the level of national economies.

The basic conviction of free trade policy, which has dominated for years, is that open markets lead to relatively greater prosperity for all participants in the long term (Panagariya 2019).[1] And in this respect, the most measures to protect or close markets in some form can also be linked to international trade issues. Common issues are import restrictions such as tariffs, quotas, subsidies, as well as the broad arsenal of non-tariff barriers to trade. What they all have in common is, on the one hand, that they relate to the phenomenon of cross-border trade and regulations. They therefore always become relevant in the context of clear-cut borders. What they have in common too is that existing national economies are to be more or less exposed to the output in goods and services of other national economies, according to the

[1] Of course, the dominance of this paradigm seems to be crumbling at present for a variety of reasons. Neither the theoretical discussion of free trade nor the causes of the current change can be addressed here in a detailed manner. The phenomena and processes discussed below also run independently of this. They are possibly accelerated by the current developments of de-globalisation (see, e.g., Goldberg and Reed 2023; Irwin 2020; Kim et al. 2020) in the traditional sense.

will of the politically relevant actors. In this perspective, the market is defined by national borders and thus corresponds to a national economy; the degree and type of its openness are the subject of the respective policy.

Do national borders still play a role for the phenomena of digitalisation that are relevant in this context? At first glance, the opposite seems to be the case. Digital technology is both the driver and the backbone of the international division of labour and hence lowers barriers to international trade (Casalini et al. 2019, 4). Global value chains, or better, global value networks, in which different organisational units in many countries take on sub-tasks, are able to work because large amounts of data cross borders (Burri 2021, 7). Data transcends borders and time zones and can in principle be monetised at any location. Worldwide availability of data, for example via cloud services, is now a widespread basis of business processes and the basis of entire new business models (Pasadilla et al. 2020, 2).

Global value chains can no longer be managed without digital technology at all. Behind the international flows of goods and services that have long been well captured under the buzzword "globalisation", parallel worlds of data flows and digital infrastructure have developed accordingly. They are the basis for maximising the potential of the international division of labour. The Covid-19 pandemic has made it clear how thin the ice is now; the same pandemic has also become a driver of digital solutions. This is comprehensible, e.g. as far as the markets for end consumers are concerned, because a considerable share of the international trade is now conducted via e-commerce (see International Trade Administration 2023; Wang 2022). Digital goods are available worldwide at one click.

The so-called *servicification* that accompanies the differentiation of international value creation (see, e.g., Rickards 2019, 7f.) leads, among other things, to the fact that "(…) 50% of the world's traded services are already digitised" (Burri 2021, 7; see also Miroudot 2017). Digitalisation has made it possible for numerous services themselves to be traded worldwide today. In this way, digitalisation has led to a further push of this servicification phenomenon (see, e.g., Lanz and Maurer 2015). Today, the volume of trade in services exceeds the volume of trade in goods (Pasadilla et al. 2020, 1; see Ratna and Kim 2016, 426).

All this has two important implications. Firstly, with respect to the international division of labour and international markets, national borders become ultimately less significant. This is certainly not an immediate consequence of digitalisation only, but a development in which digital possibilities form an organic component that promotes a further *erosion* of national borders.

Secondly, this erosion, not the sudden disappearance of borders, also means that borders also get more indistinct in the age of digitalisation. They get more indistinct because capturing and regulating the digital side of these global processes is not a trivial task. Digitalisation blurs the distinction between the creation of goods and services in general (see Casalini et al. 2019, 9). For example, it is not easy to decide whether a 3D-printed item is a traditional commodity or a service. A similar problem is encountered in the clarification of all possible "smart" devices that were simply not smart before (see ibid., 11). Even the question of what is to be understood by a "delivery" at all is no longer self-evident. In any case, the relationship between goods and services has become considerably more complex. Additionally, there is the problem of digital dependency relationships across the entire value creation networks, because "(…) a simple digital trade transaction rests on a series of trade-related factors that enable or support the transaction" (ibid.). It is, therefore, no exaggeration to say that digitalisation has had a fundamental impact on *what* is traded and *how* it is traded.

Fundamentally, the question of a greater or lesser degree of openness is an important subject of national economic and *trade policy*. For in this context, it is of course also a question of what conditions should be created for the companies of a national economy so that they also benefit from the global interdependence enhanced by digitalisation. In the digital age, this question of the openness of an economy becomes correspondingly more complex, because the degree of openness can no longer be easily controlled by the customs at the border; the question becomes one of digital infrastructure, control and access to data. This has accordingly both complex technical and regulatory aspects.

The next chapter focuses on the question of how digitalisation affects international trade regulations.

6.2.2 Trade Barriers in the Digital Age

The following section discusses how to regulate border crossings in the digital age in concrete terms.

In terms of international trade, the openness of markets means that it is permitted to "(…) foreign suppliers to compete in national markets without encountering discriminatory, excessively burdensome or restrictive conditions" (Casalini et al. 2019, 5). In the relevant WTO agreements, the principles of non-discrimination against non-domestic goods and services apply accordingly.[2] What does digitalisation mean in this respect?

In principle, national borders seem to be all too easy to cross digitally, "(…) global digital trade is hard to stop at the border" (Burri 2021, 8). This becomes clear if one compares the above-mentioned growth in the volume of international trade in services from the liberalisation push in the 1980s, to its peak before the global financial crisis in 2008, with the growth in international data flows in just one decade. While the former grew approximately by a factor of 10, the latter grew by multiple times over (see, e.g., OECD 2020, 25). However, data is not only an element of international value chains but is also traded in its own right (see, e.g., Pasadilla et al. 2020, 1).

---

[2] The principle of equal treatment upon market entry, irrespective of the origin of a good or service, is laid down in the international trade agreements under the umbrella of today's WTO as the principle of the "Most Favoured Nation"; if the goods and services are already offered on a national market, the principle of "National treatment" applies, i.e. in this case, too, there must be no discrimination.

Accordingly, trade barriers relating to data traffic in particular have received increased attention in recent years. As early as 1998, the WTO had set up a "Work Programme on Electronic Commerce" in this context (WTO 1998).[3] The United States International Trade Commission (2013, 2014) developed a corresponding framework relatively early on, which Burri (2021), among others, also refers to and which is used here too.

Companies can be obliged to carry out certain activities within the country's borders, such as stationing servers there or giving preference to national IT service providers. This is known as "localisation measures". These measures can, by causing higher costs, be a barrier to market entry or a competitive disadvantage for foreign firms (see Burri 2021, 10 with reference to OECD 2015). Thus, the regulation of data use potentially also becomes part of industrial policy (Pasadilla et al. 2020, 3).

So-called data privacy and protection measures are to be assessed as a non-tariff trade barrier. Regulations on the handling of data apply within certain national borders, and if they differ, they can constitute a non-tariff trade barrier. This is the prominent problem area of *interoperability*, which means the "(…) ability of a system, product or service to communicate and function with other (technically different) systems, products or services" (Kerber and Schweitzer 2017, 40). This problem area has a technological aspect, but also a legal aspect. The latter, in particular, is effective in the sense of a border, as it falls within the sphere of competence of national policies or jurisdictions. However, interoperability is an important prerequisite for fully exploiting the potential of digitalisation. The next sub-chapter will go into this in more detail. However, companies will also engage in more or less risky activities in different countries with a view to possible penalties for violating data protection regulations; this also applies to the aspect mentioned in the previous paragraph (Pasadelli et al. 2020, 5).

Another problem is posed by "intellectual property-related measures", an area that has been prominently discussed since the TRIPS Agreement but which has become more explosive today in the age of digitalisation. This is because intellectual property rights are of course not only of central importance for all types of content providers, but also quite generally crucial in connection with the processing and monetisation of data. Burri (2023, 560) provides a detailed account of the respective issues such as "(…) foreign websites that facilitate IPR infringement; software piracy; circumvention of technological protection measures; cybertheft of trade secrets; trademark infringement related to domain names". In addition, there is censorship[4] of content and cybersecurity. "Border measures" in the narrower sense are more of a side issue,

---

[3] A precursor would be the OECD's Guidelines on the Protection of Privacy and Transborder Flows of Personal Data, as early as 1980.

[4] In this context, the term "censorship" refers to the state's intervention in certain content, either when the political position expressed there is not allowed to be heard or even expressed, but also, of course, when any standards are violated, such as ethical ones in advertising. Both the fact that the internet is the best-monitored space on the planet and the experience that in liberal nations platforms are more likely to eradicate unpopular opinions than the state are among the apparent paradoxes of the new age.

but they play a role insofar as the end result of e-commerce can actually be a physical package at the customer's premises. Are we able to say in which direction the openness of the markets has developed in recent years?

Trends can be traced quite well by looking at the development of international trade in services, which is, as said above, closely interconnected with cross-border digital traffic. A good approach to understanding current developments is the "Digital Services Trade Restrictiveness Index" (Digital STRI), which "(...) identifies, catalogues, and quantifies cross-cutting barriers that affect trade in digitally enabled services" (OECD 2022a, 15) and documents different degrees of openness with regard to the corresponding regulation. In total, about one hundred categories of policy measures are recorded. These can be assigned to four overarching groups, namely (1) infrastructure and connectivity, (2) electronic transactions, (3) payment systems, (4) intellectual property rights and a corresponding fifth residual category for other barriers, whereby the first category is the most important with 64% (OECD 2022a, 16).

Which industry is particularly affected by which factors is another question, because this is the starting point of the corresponding industrial policy considerations. The relevance of barriers in the digital age is accordingly a burning issue. A broad approach is offered by the "Digital Trades Estimates Project" (DTE 2023) of the European Centre for International Political Economy, which has 64 economies on its screen and focuses on four different areas, namely (1) fiscal restrictions, (2) establishment restrictions, (3) restrictions on data and finally, in a narrower sense, (4) trading restrictions.

Not surprisingly, such taxonomies can then be used to trace the greater or lesser degrees of openness of national economies or regions. Behind the disparities that then become visible, i.e. a more or less pronounced openness, a self-reinforcing process can possibly be assumed. The more highly digitalised companies or companies with digital business models are located in a country, the higher the capacity for infrastructural expansion, which rapidly increases the gap to countries where no such players are located. From this perspective, the situation is actually not dissimilar to that of development gaps in the pre-digital age, because successful industries not only induce agglomeration effects, but also, depending on their complexity, coupling effects on the entire national economy and, accordingly, accumulate more capital in the long run. In any case, the corresponding indices show that this is a strongly dynamic development.

Beyond the question of infrastructure, the coordination of the legal framework and the corresponding policy across borders are also relevant (Mitchel and Neha 2020, 1; Ahmad 2019, Kerber and Schweitzer 2017). Based on this background, one can also speak of "digital markets" where the regulations are uniform. A clear example of the high pressure to move in this area is the fact that the "EU Digital Single Market" is one of the six priorities of the European Commission. By "(...) eliminating barriers to pan-European online services for citizens, public administrations and businesses". The European Commission hopes to achieve economic growth and generate more jobs (EU4Digital 2023).

Looking at all these advantages that digitalisation is supposed to promise the economy, can a distinction be made between national or regional integration, i.e.

openness of a digital market from its international embedding? Or, to put it another way: What are the reasons for wanting to protect a digital market? This question is addressed in the following section.

6.2.3 Balancing Restrictions

This chapter examines the extent to which digitalisation gives rise to new trade-off problems with regard to the degree of openness of national economies.

International trade—with or without the free trade paradigm—is regulated for a variety of motives. The protection of domestic industries (for whatever reason) was already mentioned at the beginning of the chapter. Other economic motives can be the growth of the economy through an intended increase in exports. In addition, the protection of citizens also plays a role, for example with regard to the public good of security, which restricts the trade in weapons, or consumer protection, which can be used to justify qualitative barriers. The success of domestic industries, on the one hand, and the protection of citizens, on the other, are the two determining poles of regulation in the digital age as well. However, they have entered into a new relationship with each other. This section is dedicated to this.

With regard to consumer protection, privacy concerns should be mentioned first. The relationship between privacy and competition or the competitiveness of companies and the economies that are home to them is the subject of a bountiful amount of literature.[5] For, as already mentioned in connection with the role of prices, competition is about the discovery of knowledge, and accordingly the possibilities of encoding any facts in the form of data, which are available today through digitalisation, are of decisive importance. Accordingly, there is a complex relationship between data protection and competitiveness. If some companies have access to more data than others, they have a correspondingly greater potential to turn this data into competitive advantages. The impact of the European Data Protection Regulation in Europe on the innovative capacity of companies is also being discussed (see, e.g., Blind et al. 2022).

This extremely complex area is discussed in detail in the following chapter on the problem of property and freedom of contract. In this chapter here, the focus is only on the fact that the different regulatory treatment of this issue in different jurisdictions is tantamount to a form of boundary demarcation in the digital space and hence a reduction of openness. If such reductions are asymmetrical, they potentially unfold effects on the potential economic activity and thus influence the relative competitiveness of the jurisdictions. This can, but does not have to be, a reason for the regulations to become less strict systemically.

From this perspective, consumer protection also unfolds an important dimension in the age of digitalisation with regard to the "openness" of the market and specifically

[5] See, for example, early on Stigler (1980), Posner (1981), Hermalin and Katz (2006), Calzolari and Pavan (2006), Acquisti et al. (2016).

with regard to the competitiveness of the companies located in an economy. Stricter data protection regulations and requirements in an economy can accordingly be a burden for the companies located there, not only because they restrict the use of customer data or data on third parties, but also because they may have to invest in expensive data protection measures. Moreover, such regulations place a burden on the regulator, who is responsible for enforcing the law accordingly (detailed in Chander et al. 2021; Lukings and Lashkari 2022, 165f, also Voss and Bouthinon-Sumas 2021). This means correspondingly higher public costs and is therefore a critical balancing problem.

Overall, the relationship between data protection and competitiveness depends on the respective industry as well as on the type of data collected and the legal environment (see, for instance, Blind et al. 2022). Of course, robust data protection can also be an element of competition for better service quality, for example in the area of consumer communication or professional social networks (see Esayas 2018). The role of data is probably the most central aspect of business in the digital age and is therefore discussed in detail in the following Chap. 7.

One option that falls into this area is data residency regulations, a type of localisation measure. Such data residency rules require that certain types of data be stored in the country or region where they were collected or originated and not transferred or stored in other countries. Regulations of this kind can also play a role in the international competitiveness of companies by affecting their ability to operate in different countries. First of all, naturally, such regulations can also have the effect of protecting domestic companies from international competitors (see Castro and McQuinn 2015). They can have both positive and negative effects on international competitiveness. On the one hand, data residency rules can help protect the privacy and security of personal data by keeping it under the jurisdiction of the country where it was collected. This can increase consumer trust in companies and improve their reputation, which can lead to a competitive advantage. On the other hand, data residency rules can also create additional costs and complexity for companies, especially those that operate in multiple countries and may need to set up redundant structures (Pasadilla et al. 2020, 6). Compliance with these regulations may require companies to invest in new data storage and processing infrastructure, which can be expensive and time-consuming. This can put them at a disadvantage compared to companies that are not subject to these regulations. Overall, the impact of data retention regulations on international competitiveness depends on a variety of factors, including the specific regulations, the industry and the market environment.

Just as with arms trade, aspects of national security also play an important role in this context. For this reason, there are de facto interventions in international data flows that have economic relevance but are not primarily economically motivated. Aspects of national security therefore also form an important area for exceptions within the WTO (Lukings and Lashkari 2022, 148). Either way, digitalisation has also considerably increased the complexity of this area, as trade interests must now be weighed against security interests in an environment that is not only politically and economically, but also technologically highly insecure (Mishra 2020).

Such balancing problems are very characteristic for considerations in this context. For example, it is sometimes not easy to decide whether cross-border data flows are goods or services, a "classification dilemma" that has been discussed by lawyers dealing with international trade issues since the WTO programme of 1998 (Burri 2021, 12). This is one of the reasons why individual states have tended to agree on the basis of preferential trade agreements in this area (ibid., 13; see also Mitchell and Neha 2020). Thus, digitalisation fundamentally changes the basis on which cross-border trade has been discussed so far. This is because the new problems can no longer be easily captured by the previous schemes of liberalisation of international trade in goods and services (see already Cho and Kelly 2013), but require "(…) regulatory cooperation and interfacing domestic regimes, so as to provide interoperability and legal certainty" (Burri 2021, 20).

The fact that the situation is not straightforward can also be seen in the nature of data itself. Just as the distinction between goods and services has become more complex, it is not always possible to distinguish clearly between personal and non-personal data. However, the question of how the data is classified and legally recorded accordingly is relevant for the degree of the openness of markets. On the one hand, companies are dependent on personal information in order to be able to offer their goods and services in a customised way. On the other hand, personal and non-personal data are generated and processed throughout the entire value chain (Pasadilla et al. 2020, 4). Clearly separating this not only means a theoretical or legal challenge, but in practice also additional technical effort and thus additional costs (Casalini and Gonzálzes 2019, 33). This connection may be problematic especially for small and medium-sized enterprises, insofar as they cannot shoulder the costs of high data protection requirements (Pasadilla et al. 2020, 6). In this context, the extent of the restrictions on generating data may also become an important factor for competitiveness.

Some of the problems addressed here fall within the scope of the discussion on "interoperability" (see Kerber and Schweitzer 2017). There is no universally valid definition for this term. It is generally used to refer to the possibilities that a product, service or system has to network with other products, services or systems, which is a very important characteristic in the digital age. Basically, this is not an either-or question, but there are different horizontal as well as vertical manifestations based on technological as well as legal decisions. From a legal perspective, interoperability can be established by common standards or the reciprocal recognition of equivalence.

The phenomenon affects the problem area dealt with in this section in two ways. Firstly, interoperability always goes hand in hand with data traffic. In this respect, there is the possibility of erecting barriers through legal regulations in this area. These regulations could then be justified with arguments such as those above. However, such regulations also have a direct impact on the processes operating in the respective markets. For the highest possible degree of interoperability can lead to a reduction of transaction costs and economies of scale, but, on the other hand, also restrict competition for better standards (see below). However, natural monopolies can also and especially develop through standards (Kerber and Schweitzer 2017, 43).

What has still not been considered in this section is the aspect of environmental protection mentioned at the beginning, which is, after all, an important motive for regulating trade. In the digital age and in the "digital economy", this aspect is actually not insignificant either. Although a crypto-asset has no national currency area, it is well known that not only is cryptocurrency mining energy-intensive (Bondarev 2020; Dai et al. 2022), but also the use of data centres or streaming services (Madlener et al. 2021 and the references there on p. 5). In general, social media and AI leave no small carbon footprint.

Two aspects are relevant for the problem area of this section. First, the cost of the necessary energy is an increasingly important factor. The question of whether it can be produced cheaply or whether it has to be imported to ensure that a domestic market is well supplied with it is no different here than if we were talking about steel production. Secondly, in such cases, where (a lot of) energy is used and has to be paid for anyway, AI is of course also useful in reverse (see, e.g., Liu et al. 2022). AI costs energy itself, but one can use it to better control/reduce energy consumption in a production process, for example, so that the overall net consumption is lower. The effect on the environment, or more precisely, the climate effect, is global anyway. Conversely, however, this argument will by no means be accepted in a modern liberal society. Who would want to run in the next election with the position that Facebook or TikTok should be shut down in the respective country because it is a burden on the environment?[6]

One way in which markets are less open to competitors, which is only partly related to national borders and international trade, concerns their own functioning. Section 6.3 is devoted to this problem area. Before that, the next section briefly takes a look at the state as a regulating actor.

6.2.4 Demand for Public Regulation

The following section focuses on a problem of regulation, namely the demand of interest groups working towards regulation in their own interests.

Phenomena of border demarcation, such as the examples written previously, become relevant from the point of view of market participants as a form of transaction costs, but the very fact that trade and international value creation otherwise do *not* care about borders has always been seen as socially useful.[7]

---

[6] The energy consumption for the digital infrastructure and the use of the internet therefore do not play a prominent role in the heated climate discussion, although it would certainly be due to it, even if the estimates differ: As Andrae (2020, 19) calculates, the electricity consumption of modern information technology already accounted for around 7% of global consumption even before the pandemic; almost four per cent of greenhouse gas emissions are part of the footprint of the "digital world" according to Bordage (2019, 9). If we look at the entire value chain required for digital technology, the picture is even worse, because the production of all these smart devices requires both energy and raw materials (see, e.g., Schwarzer and Peduzzi 2021).

[7] "Change through trade" has accordingly been a maxim of international politics for a long time. Friedrich August von Hayek pointed out the multiple meanings of the Greek word "katallasein",

In addition to controlling cross-border trade, the state can also intervene in the market in other ways. For example, it can nationalise certain activities or intervene in price formation through various forms of state intervention;[8] in addition, there is a wide range of forms of privileging certain companies, for whatever reason. All this leads to the corresponding markets being less open to competition. To define whether the principle of competition is impeded it is then more appropriate to use the term *relevant markets*, as it is usual in competition theory and policy (see e.g. Eben/Robertson 2021).

The reduction in openness that takes place in this context leads to less competition and thus correspondingly to relatively poorer market performance. This connection is anything but trivial, both theoretically and in concrete economic policy practice, and has accordingly raised a whole series of complex questions in the literature. With regard to the relevant actors, a distinction can be made between the perspective of the actors on markets—i.e. suppliers and consumers of goods and services—and the regulator as an actor. The regulator sets the rules of the game within which the actors on markets can act. Accordingly, it is naturally obvious that there is also a *demand for regulation.*

The new institutional economics has focused on this phenomenon with its theory of "regulatory capture" (see Stigler 1971; overview in Dal Bó 2006). It thus addresses a problem that had already preoccupied the Freiburg School half a century earlier, which, against the backdrop of a wartime economy and isolationism, addressed the damage caused by an intertwining of state and economy that served the interests of semi-public interest groups. The problem of appropriate regulation and intervention is always and everywhere problematic; firstly, of course, in that it opens up the possibility of rent-like incomes accruing to those who are no longer exposed to free-market mechanisms through regulation. Accordingly, of course, actors in the market have every incentive to steer the regulators' motivation in a favourable direction through a share of this rent in advance.

The economic problem that is independent of this grievance is that the competitive processes of selection and steering are now taken over by agents which pretend to be wiser than the market. For, in principle, there is a problem of adequate knowledge here, under which premises markets or certain actors should be protected or steered in some form. Friedrich August von Hayek has accordingly condemned such regulations that aim at redistribution towards political goals such as "social justice" as an economically absurd "pretence of knowledge" (1988). In principle, this problem always exists when the coordination guided by price signals is distorted or suspended by measures influencing competition.

---

which stands for both "exchange" *and* "to make a friend out of an enemy". Admittedly, this seems to be an overstretched interpretation of the matter in modern industrial society. Whether the expectations of forcing change by restricting trade are more promising is a different kettle of fish.

[8] At the time of writing, the most prominent example in the shadow of inflation and major geopolitical conflicts is the "price caps".

In the digital age, too, industrial policy and the market for regulation form a difficult problem area. An example of this that is probably also perceived by the wider public is the regulation of the provision of driving services, a market whose practices have been shaken most prominently by Uber (see OECD 2007). It will not be possible to make clear statements about the extent to which markets dominated by digital business models are more or less susceptible to the problem of regulatory capture or not. In any case, the complexity of what can and should be regulated has increased.

6.3 Monopolisation

This chapter examines the implication of the demand for open markets in terms of competition problems and primarily addresses the increased tendency towards greater concentration and monopolisation as a result of digitalisation.

The claim of open markets essentially means that markets are open to competitors. In this respect, this has implications for competition policy. This chapter explains the connection between digitalisation and tendencies towards monopolisation. The remainder of this chapter is structured as follows.

Section 6.3.1 focuses on the fundamental connection between competition and technological progress. This seems a particularly noteworthy aspect insofar as, from the perspective of economics, technological change always has an impact on structures and processes in markets. Gains in advantage are the central incentive for entrepreneurial behaviour. What does the new digital technology mean in this context?

Section 6.3.2 is devoted to perhaps the most prominent topic of economics in the digital age. It turns its focus to platforms and concentrates on the phenomenon of indirect network externalities underlying the platform economy. It links this aspect to the function of competition to discover, generate and distribute knowledge and considers the possibility of using knowledge differently and more cheaply on the basis of big data technologies than through the price mechanism.

Section 6.3.3 concludes this area of phenomena with a price theory perspective on the phenomenon of zero marginal cost and the importance of economies of scale.

6.3.1 Competition and Technological Change

The following section briefly discusses the importance of technological change and its significance for competition.

Even if there is a plethora of attempts to define competition, but also no conclusive common definition, it can be said that competition prevails on a market when different suppliers try to outdo each other with attractive offers of price/performance in order to convince customers, i.e. they put each other under competitive pressure. Competition therefore requires more than one player and larger concentrations or market shares may indicate a lower competitive pressure—but not necessarily—or it may indicate that customers have a narrower range of offers available to them.

Either way, concentration processes are neither bad per se nor to be avoided per se. Undisturbed markets can indeed show high degrees of concentration at certain points in time. This is naturally the case in the short term, because innovators find themselves in a monopoly situation the moment they are the sole supplier of a new product or service. Depending on the industry, economies of scale can play a special role. In this respect, the policy area of competition policy moves in a very important borderline area, namely in that it ensures through rules that the coordination processes take place competitively and thus that a market economy is a reality.

Be that as it may, the principle of keeping markets open, whether they are national markets or specific, relevant markets, means that actors in markets should be exposed to the pressure of competition at all times. Under this condition, market actors can only survive in the long run if they offer either cheaper or better quality goods or services, or both at the same time. If there is no more competition, there is no more market economy.

A monopoly situation that has been achieved through an advantage in price or quality due to pressure from competitors, or due to the fact that a supplier was the first to discover the need for a certain good or service in the first place, is of course not at all undesirable. After all, it is precisely this situation that provides the incentive for suppliers to make risky investments or to invest money, time and energy in research and development. All this is a fundamental component of the market economy and is necessary and desirable as long as this monopoly situation can be contested by other market players at any time.

This process of continuous creation and destruction of market structures by making economic use of knowledge was described by Schumpeter (2003, first published in 1942) as a process of *creative destruction*. The connection between technological and economic change denoted by this famous metaphor has accordingly left a lasting mark on competition policy (Ducci 2020, 10). Both go hand in hand under competitive conditions. Questions of technology as well as organisation (in this regard, relevant Chandler 1977) have accordingly influenced the debates of competition theory and policy. One such debate was, for example, the question of the relationship between company size and innovation activity, in which Schumpeter tended to emphasise company size, while Arrow (1962) emphasised competition.[9]

However, in recent times, it can be said *cum grano salis* that the importance of the dynamics of technological development with regard to the development of markets has dominated the discourse. Accordingly, Schumpeter's metaphor eventually did not seem expressive enough and was displaced by Christensen's more exalted use of the word, which addresses "radical" innovations and for whom it is rather less the destruction than the explosion causing it that seems to be important, hence the term

[9] This discussion has been conducted empirically and theoretically in great detail; generalisations are not unproblematic for this reason alone, as different sectors simply "function" differently. See, for example, Aghion et al. (2005) or Scherrer and Ross (1990).

"disruptive" innovation (Bower and Christensen 1995). The argument is basically the same as that of old Schumpeter's, whereby the focus is on the new dynamics or the speed of change; this also brings the completely new start-ups into view, which suddenly creates completely new markets.

However, one obviously already has some practice in correlating company size and innovative strength based on degrees of concentration, in finding arguments for a minimum level of competitive pressure, or else in thinking about the significance of potential competition. What influence does digitalisation have in this context? Do the central elements of the digital transformation, namely connectivity and arbitrariness of what can be coded, not mean a radical change not only at the level of certain sectors, but for the process of discovery in general? Do they lead to more concentration—and thus ultimately to a reduction in competitive pressure?

At first glance, some indications can leave the impression that this is the case. Increasing degrees of concentration can be detected across all sectors. Ducci (2020) states with regard to the USA that "(…) US Census Bureau data show increases in the revenue share enjoyed by the largest fifty firms in the timeframe between 1997 and 2012 in a large portion of US industries, with various industry-specific studies finding similar trends over longer periods of time" (ibid., 15, with reference to Council of Economic advisors 2016) as well as that "(…) more than 75% of US industries have experienced an increase in concentration levels over the last two decades" (ibid., with reference to Grullon et al. 2018) and also a lower number of new market entries.

It is not an easy task to empirically trace the extent to which such concentration tendencies can actually be attributed to the effects of digitalisation, and digitalisation alone is certainly not the decisive cause in every case. Nevertheless, it seems to be an important driver of concentration. The following reasons can be given for this. McMahon et al. (2021) were able to document in detail that digital technologies are particularly advantageous for large companies, since, firstly, high fixed costs with low marginal costs are typical and hence highly scalable (Haskel and Westlake 2018). Secondly, complementary human capital or other intangible assets must be available for their use, which are characteristic above all for large companies (McMahon et al. 2021, 4). Overall larger firms in both production and services show a positive correlation with both digitalisation and company size.[10] A third aspect that could be mentioned is that digitalisation enables productivity gains[11] at the company level (see Gal et al. 2019) and thus a higher degree of competitiveness. One has to take into account that the larger companies are usually the more productive ones. Overall, it can be said that a "(…) shift in market power towards larger firms" (McMahon et al. 2021, 4) can be observed and that digitalisation is an important factor in this development.

---

[10] In the context of digitalisation, however, higher markups are also explained by the fact that digital technologies are secured via property rights (see Calligaris et al. 2019). This is not a sufficient *cause* of company size; on the other hand, patents tend to be concentrated among large multinationals.

[11] What may be apparent at the level of companies is less comprehensible at the aggregate level of national economies. On this question, see also the chapter on labour and income and footnote 20 in Chap. 8. on the discussion regarding the "Solow paradox".

It may of course be the case that not in every sector are the special effects of digitalisation the cause of higher degrees of concentration. Higher degrees of concentration could also result from any other competitive strategy or from any other new technology that is very expensive for companies to acquire. Nevertheless, this finding seems striking insofar as digital technology must be understood as a general purpose technology and therefore affects all sectors. Furthermore, it must also be taken into account that AI, big data and networking also have an impact on how processes of economic coordination are carried out in the first place. This is not to say anything less than that the technological drivers of market activity are different and they also take on a completely different role. A tendency towards higher concentration or monopolisation can be understood as an expression of this development.

The next two sections outline the extent to which digitalisation is driving a tendency towards the formation of natural monopolies, focusing on the twin phenomena of indirect network externalities and capacities for using big data.

6.3.2 Indirect Network Externalities and Knowledge

This chapter examines the extent to which the combination of indirect network externalities and the capacity of digital technology to process data is leading to a new dynamic towards higher levels of concentration and monopolisation.

The changes in the economy due to digitalisation are commonly associated with the tech giants, especially the well-known large platforms, as almost all end consumers come into contact with them in their daily lives. In fact, the economy in the digital age is to a large extent a "platform economy".[12] The following section is devoted to the question of how this works and to what extent tendencies towards monopolisation come about as a result of this mode of operation.

Platforms or two-sided (multi-sided) markets are basically not a new phenomenon.[13] These are markets with two or more different user groups, where each group has indirect network effects on the other. Direct network effects occur when the utility of consumers increases with the size of the network in which they are participants. The standard example of this is the number of subscribers to a telephone network. In this case, all participants use the same thing and are therefore in the same network, the telephone network.

In the case of positive indirect network effects, the benefit increases when the size of another group or, according to the common usage of the term, another network increases. This is the case, for example—offline—when companies place advertisements in newspapers, from which, on the one hand, they benefit the more people read this newspaper, but on the other hand, the readers also benefit, provided that the

---

[12] Not surprisingly, a vast literature is devoted to the issues of the "platform economy". The phenomenon as such cannot be fully addressed here. For the purposes of this book, we will concentrate only on the aspects relevant to the focus of the respective chapters.

[13] See also the chapter on the phenomenon of the "sharing economy".

advertisements are of interest to them. In this case, there would be positive network externalities on both sides. Of course, negative network externalities are also possible, for example, continuing this example, if some advertisement is perceived as annoying or there are too many ads, similarly to a traffic jam representing a negative network externality in the use of the road network (Knieps 2015, 4). Whenever both groups are affected by effects, there are indirect network effects and thus a so-called two-sided market.

In this context, platforms function as intermediaries that mediate between minimum two groups or networks. The business model of such intermediaries now differs from suppliers in one-sided markets. When setting prices for the use of a platform, they now have to take into account the price elasticity of demand and supply—as in a one-sided market—but also, and this is relevant, the extent of the network effect that this creates. If the platform's user fee is increased, then this leads to a corresponding contraction of both user groups (see Evans and Schmalensee 2016). Platforms offer the opportunity to take into account the differences in the elasticity of demand among different networks. A well-known example from the old offline world is singles' evenings in pubs, where entry or drinks are free for the group whose demand is more price elastic, in the chosen example mostly the ladies. However, for the intermediary, the platform, it is possible to cross-subsidise one of the two groups.

Platforms can accordingly be interpreted as a way of reducing transaction costs. Instead of the forms of an organisation and bilateral contracts, one creates a form of coordination *between* these two forms. Both possibilities mentioned here are basically nothing new; they have existed for the offline world in principle as long as there have been newspapers, fairs or pubs. So what are the differences in the digital age that provides software-based platforms? Several aspects become relevant here. We will shortly present six aspects in the following.

Firstly, the potential customer base of platforms in the offline era was significantly limited by transaction costs. In the above example, pubs in a city have only limited possibilities to make a profitable business model out of singles' nights, because it will de facto only be profitable for a limited number. The intermediary, i.e. the pub, will come up against capacity limits if it is the only player on the supply side; if there are too many competitors, the business is not worthwhile. In this example, the potential demand is sooner or later limited by the transport costs incurred—no matter how attractive the participants may be, at some point the journey to the pub is not worthwhile. This is a phenomenon that is already captured and fruitfully applied in regional economics by the central place theory (see Mulligan et al. 2012).

For platforms on the internet, both factors are almost completely absent. An internet platform is "only a click away" and, in the example of partner search, there are no overcrowding effects—on the contrary. A software-based platform enables a basically unlimited coordination capacity of participants of any type (Tiwan 2014, 5) and can therefore form digital ecosystems (see further below). A type of congestion effect can occur in this example if the platform operator earns its money not through the two groups of partner seekers, e.g. through a participation fee, but through advertisers to whom it provides corresponding advertising space and time on its platform.

Advertising that is too frequent or too annoying, or simply needs too much advertising space, can be perceived as bothersome as in the offline world of paper-newspapers (see Anderson and Jullien 2016). However, the better the artificial intelligence used by the platform operator, the better this can be handled. This will be discussed in more detail below.

Secondly, the role of size and speed have changed radically (Mariniello 2022, 286). On the one hand, there is a tendency towards the winner-takes-it-all effect with platforms due to the existing indirect network externalities already in the offline world (on this, for example, Kuchinke and Vidal 2016): Because the larger the respective user group, the more attractive a platform becomes, a snowball effect occurs. Indirect network externalities grow exponentially with the number of participants, which—in principle—is unlimited on the internet. For new competitors, market entry is virtually impossible as soon as an existing platform has reached a critical size. For platform-based business models, the most important thing is to reach this critical size as quickly as possible.

Thirdly, based on modern data processing, the "knowledge" gained on internet platforms that is relevant for competing for customers goes exponentially beyond anything that was possible in the pre-digital age. This is because, based on algorithms, the platforms not only "know" certain data about the participants—for example, via personal input during registration—but they can also gain a basically unlimited amount of data about these participants based on tracking their online behaviour.[14] This, of course, allows them to decisively optimise the platform's offer by making it, in effect, tailor-made for all participants. The platform's offer is the possibility of the most suitable *matching* possible among the various participants. The possibility of offering this is now optimised in the digital age via the possibilities of data processing.

Fourthly, the possibilities of digitalisation mean that the principle of the platform no longer necessarily has to specialise in certain groups, such as singles or providers of overnight accommodation and those looking for holiday recreation, but can in principle be extended to everything.[15] By knowing, in great detail, the preferences and willingness to pay of users, platform providers can either monetise the data directly by selling it to data traders, or they can extend their core competence, namely that of successful matching based on the collected data and the intelligent processing of this data, to any other business area. Taking up the above example in an exaggerated way: the singles pub operator can thus open a successful gardening business or a bookshop

---

[14] Of course, this statement is only valid to a limited extent against the background of corresponding data protection regulations. However, the practice of making data and thus "knowledge" about users available is a complex problem area of its own. Chapter 7 is dedicated to this in detail.

[15] It must be emphasised that this is a possibility in principle. In fact, practice shows interesting specialisations. Meanwhile platforms such as Amazon or Alibaba network everything possible, the spread of specialised platforms such as Uber or Airbnb is also essential. Dating apps such as "Tinder", "Bumble", "Plenty of Fish" or "Hinge", to stay with the chosen example in the text, also focus on particular groups and behaviours. This is discussed in detail in Sect. 7.2. Regardless of the form in which brands and/or companies offer services, the potential mentioned in the text is very important; the chapter on the topic of property, i.e. in particular the role of data, will go into this in more detail.

ad hoc. Whereas competition as a discovery procedure in the pre-digital age could still be understood in such a way that certain suppliers specialised in certain customer wishes and the knowledge of this could be regarded as their "core competence", the core competence of platforms is potentially the sector-independent matching. Competition thus remains a discovery procedure, because this very business model is also a discovery.

Fifth, the business model of digital platforms fundamentally changes the process of competition as a discovery procedure and in a way that generates monopolistic tendencies. This is because the ecosystem of a platform no longer uses prices as signals alone to coordinate behaviour with the aim of discovering, generating and diffusing knowledge. After all, using the price system to discover scarcity would be more expensive! The ability to process big data is cheaper for the platform—and the "smarter" it is and better it is fed with data, the more users it has. This can certainly be seen as a concentration tendency that goes beyond monopolisation in the pre-digital age. It is therefore not surprising that the business models of the new tech giants are platform-based. And this brings us back to the connection between technological change, the implementation of a new business model and the tendency towards a monopoly situation mentioned above, which Ducci (2020, 19f.) describes:

> First, it favours a new wave of platform intermediation as the increasingly dominant model of the firm, where intermediaries rely on creating large networks of users that can match through the platform and where users generally benefit from larger networks due to network externalities. Second, and in addition to this effect, the digital nature of the current wave of platforms further enhances the tendency towards concentrated market structures compared to older examples of platforms through extensive reliance on big data for algorithmic predictions and digital matching.

Thus, the presence of indirect network externalities combined with the capacity to process data leads to a situation where, in terms of market structure, a few dominant players capture most of the market share.

Sixthly, it is precisely this situation that leads to lock-in effects for platform users. Such effects are primarily discussed in case the switching costs are too high. Such switching costs are those costs that a user incurs when switching from one platform to another. These costs can be monetary (e.g. a participation fee, the cost of buying new hardware or software) or non-monetary (e.g. the time and effort required to get familiar with a new platform). Studies have shown that high switching costs can act as a barrier to entry and, beyond the effect of indirect network externalities, make it more difficult for new platforms to poach users from established competitors. Lock-in effects can certainly be understood as a partial effect of the fact that platforms based on digital technology can exploit the possibilities of indirect network externalities almost without limit. It is precisely the availability of complementary products and services generated via the knowledge of possible "matches", the degree of customisation and personalisation as well as the quality of the user experience (see Gawer and Cusumano, 2014) that leads to lock-in situations.

Against this background, how should markets now be kept open? Or, asked from a different perspective, is this outcome of a discovery procedure not even desirable?

This question will be taken up again and discussed in Sect. 6.4. Before that, the aspects of cost structures and pricing will be additionally considered in the following section.

6.3.3 Cost Structure and Prices

The following section is devoted to the dimension of the phenomenon that can be captured in monetary terms, namely that markets in the digital age can be less open due to a tendency towards monopolisation. This aspect, the costs, is captured in terms of the traditional price-theoretical perspective.

A tendency towards a (natural) monopoly can exist due to the cost structure, for example, if high fixed costs but low marginal costs are incurred for the production of the corresponding service. If the quantity produced is increased when fixed costs are high and marginal costs are low, unit costs fall. The lowest unit costs are thus incurred by the company that can sell the most units. It can therefore also charge a lower price. Following this argument, only one supplier remains over time, the natural monopoly. Natural monopolies are particularly characteristic of network goods such as energy or water supply and are a topic traditionally treated in industrial economics (see, e.g., Vogelsang 2021). The successful business models of the digital age, the platform-based ones, are no different. Even if their technological development and/or ability to reach the threshold of a necessary minimum number of participants is initially costly, they can subsequently operate at almost zero marginal costs, worldwide. First come, first serve. And for a huge amount of users, this is—it seems, increasingly—the new normal.

In this context, let us return to the network effects that are important in the age of digitalisation and look at the demand situation. While a demand curve is normally falling, it is convex when network effects are present. This is because we can assume that participants have the highest motivation to join a network when this network has reached a critical minimum size. When all those participants have joined the network who have a high willingness to pay, only those participants will join whose willingness to pay is lower. To continue the previous example, if all the really love-hungry singles are already part of one of the networks in the singles bar, only those will additionally join a network there who are already halfway better supplied with partnerships by other means and therefore also have a relatively low willingness to pay. In terms of costs, this means for the platform operator that the market price generated from the payment of the participants must exceed the marginal costs to make the platform profitable at all. It must reach this critical size *as quickly as possible.*

If it can attract a sufficient number, the winner-takes-it-all effect already described in the previous section occurs. For accordingly, from this perspective, the critical size of the network is the decisive market entry barrier for a newcomer to the market, because the competitor does not have the necessary number of customers to cover the unit costs. In this respect, there is also a competition policy challenge from this perspective.

This central cost aspect of platforms is also relevant for other market situations in the digital age. For example, digital goods can very well be offered by platforms or traded on platforms. Digital goods have extremely low variable costs. Once a piece of music has been digitised, it can be made available in any quantity worldwide in real time at almost zero marginal cost. The costs for the corresponding digital infrastructure have to be paid once. From the perspective of industrial economics, the profit of a monopolistic supplier is maximised if it offers a quantity at which marginal revenue and marginal cost are equal. Assuming zero marginal costs, the quantity axis and supply curve are identical.

This cost-side phenomenon, together with the effects regarding knowledge described in the previous section, results in a pronounced financial power of the winners in the digital economy. This can then lead to the incumbents having the corresponding means to easily buy out (potential) competitors. One example that has become famous is the purchase of WhatsApp by Facebook. The incumbent was able to buy in the expected network effects at the right time in order to later use the data generated on the basis of the networks, as shown in the previous section. It is remarkable that the relevance of this situation in terms of competition policy was only perceived relatively late by the cartel authorities and corresponding regulations were made. Either way, digitalisation presents a new, extremely complex challenge, both in terms of the cost dimension briefly touched on here and with regard to the technological dimension. The following chapter is dedicated to this.

6.4 Conclusions: Competition is "One Click Away"?

This chapter brings the perspectives presented in the three previous chapters together and links them to the fundamental questions this book addresses and considers the corresponding economic policy options.

As already mentioned at the beginning of this chapter, the demand for open markets, Eucken's constitutive principle, originally has a trade dimension. However, the argument underlying this demand is ultimately one of competition policy. Competition policy, in Eucken's original scheme, is conducted as a regulatory principle. As already briefly explained in Sect. 3.2.3, under today's conditions it seems necessary to deal with competition policy issues together with those raised by trade problems.

This became particularly clear in connection with the monopolisation tendencies, to which digitalisation is leading in some areas. Of course, beyond the points already mentioned, the question arises as to whether or not digitalisation has brought about decisive changes and new challenges for the realisation of the principle of competition in general. In this context, the statement by Google co-founder Larry Page—"competition is one click away"—has become well-known (Wismer 2012). With this rhetoric he was obviously primarily alluding to a transparency effect, which has already been highlighted in Sect. 3.2.4. However, it cannot be denied that his metaphor seems a bit euphemistic.

The fact that digitalisation poses new challenges for competition policy has already become clear in the previous chapters wherever it could be shown that the new digital possibilities have an impact on the functioning principle of the market. For our considerations, a complexity problem arises here in that the effects recorded on the basis of the heuristic structure of the principles partly have a simultaneous and mutually reinforcing effect. In addition, the technology and the business models are developing at great speed and this internationally. This causes corresponding difficulties for the regulator, i.e. primarily the competition authorities and consumer protection, everywhere.

The question of the extent to which digitalisation represents a new challenge for competition policy can thus be answered with the fact that it is precisely the simultaneous interaction of these effects that has become central as a new problem of complexity. The OECD (2022b, 16) also points out that it is by no means clear for competition policy in the age of digitalisation what can be addressed by it at all. Can certain categories of challenges be summarised for competition policy, based on the details also considered in the other chapters?

The discourse on the problems of competition policy in the context of digitalisation is extremely broad, even though it is relatively new.[16] For the purposes of the present considerations, it would be a somewhat violent synthesis to try to separate phenomena relevant to competition policy in particular from others. It is precisely their interaction that poses new challenges to competition policy practice and theory.

This problem is best illustrated by the phenomenon of multi-sided markets and platform ecosystems. This is because the network externalities, together with the cost structures discussed above, lead to new monopoly tendencies. This is not a bad thing per se. In principle, the effects of such indirect network effects are desirable as long as they bring about an improvement for the consumer, on the one hand, and suppliers are exposed to competitive pressure, on the other. However, the aforementioned snowball effects can easily lead to the latter being impeded, especially if considerable switching costs arise for the consumer or if a switch is not even sensible due to the relevance of indirect network effects—the best-known example is probably Facebook. To stay with the image of Larry Page, the click is not worth it at all.

From the perspective of competition policy, this situation must be extended to include the dimension of economies of scale. Economies of scale are essential here insofar as if "(…) the cost of production is much less than proportional to the number of customers served (…) with increasing returns to scale, competition between two firms producing the same product will not allow them to cover their costs" (Crémer et al. 2020, 20). Consequently, no one enters the market. In the age of the internet, however, this means that the demand side—e.g. content or service providers—is virtually *forced* to offer customers monetarily free services and to earn money with

[16] OECD (2022b) provides an overview; from the author's point of view, the report of the Monopolies Commission (2015) still presents the fundamental problems in a relevant way; Crémer et al. (2020) present a well-founded, practice-oriented account. The series of publications of the German Cartel Authority, the "Bundeskartellamt" (2023), "Competition and Consumer Protection in the digital Economy" is digitally accessible and provides well-founded presentations on the fundamental problems of competition policy.

advertising. Monetarily free services and high levels of concentration are linked (see Barnett 2018). This leads to a self-reinforcing effect in that the supply side has an incentive to collect as much data as possible and to exploit the possibilities of working with big data as far as possible (see Monopolkommission 2015, 27f.).

This then leads to specific problems in connection with data and property rights, to the phenomenon of tech giants and the associated effects; the chapter on property is dedicated specifically to this phenomenon. Platforms become *gatekeepers*: "This refers to the position that platforms have when firms rely on them for access to consumers" (OECD 2022b, 17). Indirect network externalities, economies of scale and the role of data form the three-pole field of tension in which competition policy must move in the digital age (see Crémer et al. 2020, 20f).

Beyond this gatekeeper function, there is also a new challenge for competition policy in that the question of the relevant market has now also gained new complexity (see, e.g., Eben and Robertsen 2021). For a tech giant, it is relatively easy to penetrate completely new markets, not only because of its financial possibilities, but also because it knows how to use the possibilities of digital technology and especially the handling of big data. This is how, e.g., Google evolved from a search engine into a highly complex player. And it is precisely here that the advantage of size and scope becomes apparent.

In this respect, the market mechanisms underlying the observable processes are not new. However, it is their interplay, created by the possibilities of the digital age that now leads to a new dynamic, which is less about competition in the traditional sense, but rather about an all-or-nothing approach to the market. Accordingly, the interest of antitrust authorities focuses on the multi-sided platforms, which are reaching a new level of complexity. The competition authorities have to consider the effects of all relevant sides, i.e. the direct as well as the indirect network effects.

The fact that the-winner-takes-it-all effects exists does not necessarily mean in every case that competition no longer takes place; in some cases, it also takes place at the ecosystem level, as the OECD (2022b, 19) has stated, especially for the markets for mobile communication. The effects of platforms on competition policy are also ambiguous because competition among platforms will occur only rarely, but competition among suppliers on a platform can be particularly intense (see Dedola et al. 2023, 4; 23). Based on these correlations, competition policy monitoring of the markets will tend to focus on the observation of market behaviour and less on market structure features, such as critical concentration levels. It is then necessary to determine individually to what extent a company behaves anti-competitively, i.e. intentionally excludes others.

The extent to which market conduct is anti-competitive or not, however, is not only a problem of observation, but also an increasingly complex challenge for assessment, as has become clear in Sects. 4.2.2 and especially 4.3.3 on the topic of algorithmic pricing. On the one hand, it can be assumed that technology and business models develop more quickly than the monitoring ability and capacity of competition authorities, but on the other hand, any observation must still be followed by a debate that may be highly explosive in terms of competition theory, since the competitive effects must first be adequately understood. The fact that the German

Federal Cartel Office, one of the most respected competition authorities worldwide, only launched its—highly instructive—series of publications on the topic of "Competition and Consumer Protection in the Digital Economy" in 2017 may be seen as a vivid indication of the prevailing phase shift between science and authorities, on the one hand, and developments in the economy, on the other.

In addition to this problem of the concentration tendency and the effects of large platforms, which dominates the discourse, it should of course not be forgotten that digitalisation also creates new markets at the same time, as start-ups break up traditional market structures, as Dedola et al. (2023, 5) have found for example for specialised fintech services. In terms of competition policy, the challenge is to prevent such new companies from being swallowed up by the large incumbents to the detriment of consumers. In this context, of course, new issues arise, as, e.g., documented in Germany by the amendment of the Act against Restraints of Competition in 2017.

However, returning to the starting point of the chapter's overarching theme, it is precisely because national borders seem to play only a minor role with regard to the economic effects of digital technology that competition policy *enforcement* problems arise. Many of the digital markets are global per se. Anti-competitive behaviour can affect numerous jurisdictions, and it will not always be easy to find those responsible in the territory of an affected jurisdiction.

At present, however, international harmonisation of competition law seems to be just as much a purely theoretical idea as the possibility of enforcing it at all. This desideratum is hindered not least by national or regional industrial policy goals that may be legitimate from the perspective of national or regional economic policy, but in the global context have anti-competitive effects. This aspect refers back to the role of the state as discussed in Sect. 6.1.2.

The most appropriate summary of the challenges for competition policy may well be that the challenges of digitalisation, which start with the respective principles, together unfold a new complexity. In view of the dynamics of technical and economic developments, this complexity eludes a general, unambiguous "per se" interpretation in terms of competition policy. This new complexity requires an assessment that needs to be more small-scale, more case-by-case and more behaviour-oriented. And in any case more than just one click.

References

Acquisti, Alessandro / Taylor, Curtis/ Wagman, Liad (2016): The Economics of Privacy. Journal of Economic Literature 54 (2), 442–492.

Aghion, Philippe / Bloom, Nick / Blundell Richard / Griffith, Rachel / Howitt, Peter (2005): Competition and Innovation: An Inverted-U Relationship. The Quarterly Journal of Economics 120 (2), 701–728

Ahmad, Usman (2019): The Importance of Cross-Border Regulatory Cooperation in an Era of Digital Trade. World Trade Review 18 (1), 99–120.

Anderson, Simon / Jullien, Bruo (2016): The advertising-financed business model in two-sided media markets. Toulouse School of Economics Working paper 632.

Andrae, Anders (2020): New perspectives on internet electricity use in 2030. Engineering and Applied Science Letter 3 (2), 19–31.

Arrow, Kenneth (1962): Economic Welfare and the Allocation of Resources for Invention. The Rate and Direction of Inventive Activity: Economic and Social Factors. Cambridge, MA: Princeton University Press.

Barnett, Jonathan M. (2018): The costs of free: commoditization, bundling and concentration. Journal of Institutional Economics 14 (6), 1097–1120.

Blind, Knut / Niebel, Crispin Miles / Rammer, Christian (2022): The impact of the EU General Data Protection Regulation on innovation in firms. ZEW Discussion Papers No. 22-047. Mannheim: ZEW – Leibniz-Zentrum für Europäische Wirtschaftsforschung.

Bondarev, Mikhail (2020): Energy consumption of bitcoin mining. International Journal of Energy Economics and Policy 10 (4), 525–529.

Bordage, Frédéric (2019): The Environmental Footprint of the Digital World. Online: https://www.greenit.fr/wp-content/uploads/2019/11/GREENIT_EENM_etude_EN_accessible.pdf (last access: 27.07.2023).

Bower, Joseph L. / Christensen, Clayton M. (1995): Disruptive Technologies: Catching The Wave. Harvard Business Review. January–February.

Bundeskartellamt (2023): Series of papers on "Competition and Consumer Protection in the Digital Economy", online: https://www.bundeskartellamt.de/EN/AboutUs/Publications/Schriftenreihe_Digitales/Schriftenreihe_node.html;jsessionid=9A8BC4E6D1901EC77F646DE2FC13B171.2_cid381 (last access: 27.07.2023).

Burri, Mira (2021): Digital Trade. In Search of Appropriate Regulation. In: Fernando Esteban De La Rosa et al (eds): Justice Security and Individual Freedoms in the Digital Society. Cizur Menor: Thomson/Reuters, 213–247.

Burri, Mira (2023): The Impact of Digitalization on Global Trade Law. German Law Journal 24, 551–573.

Calligaris, Sara / Criscuolo, Chiara / Marcolin, Luca (2019): Mark-ups in the Digital Era. OECD Science, Technology and Industry Working Papers No. 2018/10. Paris: OECD Publishing.

Calzolari, Giacomo / Pavan (2006): Alessandro: On the optimality of privacy in sequential contracting. Journal of Economic Theory 130 (1), 168–204.

Casalini, Francesca / González, Javier López (2019): Trade and Cross-Border Data Flows. OECD Trade Policy Papers No. 220. Paris: OECD Publishing.

Casalini, Francesca / González, Javier López / Moïsé, Evdokia (2019): Approaches to market openness in the digital age. OECD trade policy paper. Paris: OECD Publishing.

Castro, Daniel / McQinn, Alan (2015): Cross-Border Data Flows Enable Growth in All Industries. Washington, DC: Information Technology and Innovation Foundation.

Chandler, Alfred D. Jr. (1977): The Visible Hand. Cambridge, MA: Harvard University Press.

Chander, Anupam / Abraham, Meaza / Chandy, Sandeep / Fang, Yuan / Park, Dayoung / Yu, Isabel (2021): Achieving Privacy: Costs of Compliance and Enforcement of Data Protection Regulation. Policy Research Working Paper 9594. World Bank's World Development Report 2021 Team in collaboration with the Macroeconomics, Trade and Investment Global Practice. Georgetown: Law Faculty Publications and Other Works 2374.

Cho, Sungjoon / Kelly, Claire R. (2013): Are World Trading Rules Passé? Vanderbilt Journal of International Law 53, 623–666.

Council of Economic Advisers (2016): Benefits of Competition and Indicators of Market Power. Issues Brief. Washington, DC: Obama White House.

Crémer, Jacques / de Montjoye, Yves-Alexandre / Schweitzer, Heike (2020): Competition Policy for the Digital Era. Brussels: European Commission, Directorate-General for Competition.

Dal Bó, Ernesto (2006): Regulatory capture: a review. Oxford Review of Economic Policy 22 (2), 203–225.

Dai, Min / Kou, Steven / Qian, Shuaijie / Qin, Ling (2022): Bitcoin Mining and Electricity Consumption. Boston University, Questrom School of Business, BU Open Access Articles.

Online: https://open.bu.edu/bitstream/handle/2144/43618/SSRN-id3994797.pdf?sequence=1&isAllowed=y (last access: 10.06.2023).
Dedola, Luca / Ehrmann, Michael / Hoffmann, Peter / Lamo, Ana / Paz Pardo, Gonzalo / Slacalek, Jirka / Strasser, Georg (2023): Digitalisation and the economy. European Central Bank Working Paper Series. Frankfurt am Main: European Central Bank.
DTE (2023): Digital Trade Estimates Project. European Centre for International Political Economy (ECIPE). Online: https://ecipe.org/dte/ (last access: 11.3.2023).
Ducci, Francesco (2020): Natural Monopolies in Digital Platform Markets. Cambridge: Cambridge University Press.
Eben, Magali / Robertson, Viktoria H.S.E. (2021): The Relevant Market Concept in Competition Law and Its Application to Digital Markets: A Comparative Analysis of the EU, US, and Brazil. Graz Law Working Paper No. 01-2021.
Esayas, Samson (2018): Privacy as a Non-Price Competition Parameter: Theories of Harm in Mergers. University of Oslo Faculty of Law Research Paper No. 2018.
Evans, David S. / Schmalensee, Richard (2016): Matchmakers: The New Economics of Multisided Platforms. Cambridge, MA: Harvard Business Review Press.
EU4Digital (2023): Funded by the European Commission. Online: https://eufordigital.eu/discover-eu/the-eu4digital-initiative/ (last access: 10.02.2023).
Gal, Peter / Nicoletti, Giuseppe / Renault, Theodore / Sorbe, Stéphane / Timiliotis, Christina (2019): Digitalisation and productivity: In search of the holy grail – Firm-level empirical evidence from EU countries. OECD Economics Department Working Papers No. 1533. Paris: OECD Publishing.
Gawer, Annabelle / Cusumano, Michael A. (2014): Industry platforms and ecosystem innovation. Journal of Product Innovation Management 31(3), 417–433.
Goldberg, Pinelopi K. / Reed, Tristan (2023): Is the Global Economy Deglobalizing? And if so, why? And what is next? National Bureau of Economic Research, Working Paper 31115. Online: https://www.nber.org/system/files/working_papers/w31115/w31115.pdf (last access: 12.09.2023).
Grullon, Gustavo / Larkin, Yelena / Michaely, Roni (2018): Are U.S. Industries Becoming More Concentrated? SSRN Scholarly Paper ID 2612047. Rochester, NY: Social Science Research Network.
Haskel, Jonathan / Westlake, Stian (2018): Capitalism without Capital. The Rise of the Intangible Economy. Princeton: Princeton University Press.
Hayek, Friedrich August von (1988): The Fatal Conceit. The Errors of Socialism. Chicago: Routledge.
Hermalin, Benjamin E. / Katz, Michael L. (2006): Privacy, property rights and efficiency: The economics of privacy as secrecy. Quantitative Marketing and Economics 4, 209–239.
International Trade Administration (2023): eCommerce Size and Sales Forecast. Online: https://www.trade.gov/ecommerce-sales-size-forecast (last access 20.03.2023).
Irwin, Douglas A. (2020): The pandemic adds momentum to the deglobalization trend. Peterson Institute for International Economics. Online: https://www.piie.com/blogs/realtime-economics/pandemic-adds-momentum-deglobalization-trend (last access: 12.09.2023).
Kerber, Wolfgang / Schweitzer, Heike (2017): Interoperability in the Digital Economy. Journal of Intellectual Property, Information Technology and E-Commerce Law (JIPITEC) 8 (1), 39–58.
Kerber, Wolfgang (2022): Taming Tech Giants: The Neglected Interplay Between Competition Law and Data Protection (Privacy) Law. The Antitrust Bulletin 67 (2), 280–300.
Kim, Hag-Min / Li, Ping / Lee, Yea. R. (2020): Observations of deglobalization against globalization and impacts on global business. International Trade, Politics and Development, 4 (2), 83–103.
Knieps, Günter (2015): Network Economics. Principles – Strategies – Competition Policy. Cham: Springer Publishing.
Kuchinke, Björn A. / Vidal, Miguel (2016): Exclusionary strategies and the rise of winner-takes-it-all markets on the Internet. Telecommunications Policy 40 (6), 582–592.
Lanz, Rainer / Maurer, Andreas (2015): Services and Global Value Chains – Some Evidence on Servicification of Manufacturing and Services Networks'. WTO Working Paper ERSD 3.

Liu, Hui / Nikitas, Nikolaos / Li, Yanfei / Yang, Rui (2022): Big Data in Energy Economics. Singapore: Springer.

Lukings, Melissa / Lashkari, Arash Habibi (2022): Understanding Cybersecurity Law and Digital Privacy: A Common Law Perspective. Cham: Springer.

Madlener, Reinhard / Sheykhha, Siamak / Briglauer, Wolfgang (2021): The electricity- and CO2-saving potentials offered by regulation of European video-streaming services. FCN Working Paper No. 5: RWTH Aachen University.

Mariniello, Mario (2022): Digital Economic Policy. The Economics of Digital Markets from a European Union Perspective. Oxford: University Press.

McMahon, Michael / Calligaris, Sara / Doyle, Eleanor / Kinsella, Stephen (2021): Scale market power and competition in a digital world: Is bigger better? OECD Science, Technology and Industry Working Papers 2021/01.

Miroudot, Sébastien (2017): Services in Global Value Chains: Trade patterns and gains from specialisation. Paris: OECD Publishing.

Mishra, Neha (2020): The Trade: (Cyber)Security Dilemma and Its Impact on Global Cybersecurity Governance. Journal of World Trade Volume 54 (4), 567–590.

Mitchell Andrew D. / Mishra, Neha (2020): Digital Trade Integration in Preferential Trade Agreements. ARTNeT Working Paper Series No. 191, May. Bangkok: ESCAP.

Monopolkommission (2015): Competition policy: The challenge of digital markets. Special Report No. 68. Special Report by the Monopolies Commission pursuant to section 44 (1) (4) of the Act Against Restraints on Competition. Bonn.

Mulligan, Gordon F. / Partridge, Mark D. / Carruthers, John I. (2012): Central place theory and its reemergence in regional science. The Annals of Regional Science 48, 405–443.

OECD (2007): Policy Roundtables. Taxi Services: Competition and Regulation. DAF/COMP 42.

OECD (2020): Measuring the economic value of data and cross-border data flows. A business perspective. OECD Digital Economy papers 297, August.

OECD (2015): Emerging Policy Issues: Localisation Barriers to Trade, TAD/TC/WP(2014)17/FINAL, 12 May.

OECD (2022a): Services Trade Restrictiveness Index: Policy trends up to 2022. February.

OECD (2022b): OECD Handbook on Competition Policy in the Digital Age.

Panagariya, Arvind (2019): Debunking Protectionist Myths. Free Trade, the Developing World, and Prosperity. Economic Development Bulletin 31.

Pasadilla, Gloria, Duval, Yann and Anukoonwattaka, Witada (2020): Next generation non-tariff measures: Emerging data policies and barriers to digital trade. ARTNeT Working Paper Series No. 187, January. Bangkok: ESCAP.

Posner, Richard A. (1981): The Economics of Privacy. The American Economic Review 71 (2), 405–409.

Ratna, Rajan Sudesh / Kim, Nayeon (2016): Potential of trade in services, in: Cho, Joong-Wan / Ratna, Rajan Sudesh (eds): The ASIA-PACIFIC TRADE AGREEMENT: Promoting South-South Regional Integration and Sustainable Development. United Nations Economic and Social Commission for Asia and the Pacific. Bangkok: United Nations Publication.

Rickards, Peter (2019): The International Trade in Services, Reserve Bank of Australia, Bulletin March 2019. Online: https://www.rba.gov.au/publications/bulletin/2019/mar/pdf/the-international-trade-in-services.pdf (last access 10.03.2023).

Scherer, Frederic M. / Ross, David (1990): Industrial Market Structure and Economic Performance. 3rd ed. Boston, MA: Houghton Mifflin.

Schumpeter, Joseph (2003): Capitalism, Socialism, and Democracy. London, New York: Routledge.

Schwarzer, Stefan / Peduzzi, Pascal (2021): United Nations Foresight Brief No. 027, November. The Growing Footprint of Digitalisation. Online: https://wedocs.unep.org/handle/20.500.11822/37439 (last access: 26.07.2023).

Stigler, George J. (1971): The Theory of Economic Regulation. The Bell Journal of Economics and Management Science 2 (1), 3–21.

Stigler, George J. (1980): An Introduction to Privacy in Economics and Politics. The Journal of Legal Studies 9 (4), Article 2.
Sullivan, Sean (2021): Market Definition. Research Handbook on Abuse of Dominance and Monopolization (Pınar Akman, Konstantinos Stylianou, & Or Brook eds, forthcoming), U Iowa Legal Studies Research Paper No. 2021-29, Available at SSRN: https://ssrn.com/abstract=3861047 or http://dx.doi.org/10.2139/ssrn.3861047 (last access: 30.4.2023).
Tiwan, Amrit (2014): Platform Ecosystems. Aligning Architecture, Governance, and Strategy. Amsterdam: Elsevier.
United States International Trade Commission (2013): Digital Trade in the US and Global Economies, Part 1, Investigation No. 332–531. Washington, DC: USITC.
United States International Trade Commission (2014): Digital Trade in the US and Global Economies, Part 2, Investigation No. 332-540. Washington, DC: USITC.
Vogelsang, Ingo (2021): The economics and regulation of network industries. Telecommunications and beyond. Cambridge: Cambridge University Press.
Voss, W. Gregory / Bouthinon-Dumas, Hugues (2021): EU General Data Protection Regulation Sanctions in Theory and in Practice. 37 Santa Clara High Technology Law Journal 1.
Wang, Alex (2022): What Is the Share of E-Commerce in Overall Retail Sales? Understanding how retailers count online and in-store purchases is key. CBRE. Online: https://www.cbre.com/insights/articles/omnichannel-what-is-the-share-of-e-commerce-in-overall-retail-sales (last access: 08.03.2023).
Wismer, David (2012): Google's Larry Page: "Competition Is One Click Away" (And Other Quotes Of The Week). Forbes, October 14. Online: https://www.forbes.com/sites/davidwismer/2012/10/14/googles-larry-page-competition-is-one-click-away-and-other-quotes-of-the-week/ (last access: 27.07.2023).
WTO (1998): Declaration on global electronic commerce. Adopted on 20 May 1998. Online: https://docs.wto.org/dol2fe/Pages/SS/directdoc.aspx?filename=Q:/WT/MIN98/DEC2.pdf&Open=True (last access 16. February 2023).

Chapter 7
Private Property

> The first and chief design of every system of government is to maintain justice; to prevent the members of a society from incroaching on one anothers property, or seizing what is not their own. The design here is to give each one the secure and peacable possession of his own property. (Adam Smith 1762, 47)

7.1 Preliminary Considerations

This section briefly explains why it makes sense to combine *private property*, which appears as a constitutive principle in Eucken, with the two regulatory principles of *freedom of contract* and *liability*.

Private property, ownership of the means of production, is one of the most important prerequisites for the emergence of a market economy. In Eucken's original conception, this was above all considered as an own principle in order to distinguish it from the idea of collective ownership, which at that time was also seen as a way of adequately containing the problems of the economy.

Nowadays, the existence of private property in developed economies is presupposed. Moreover, it must be clear that private property can only become a factor in the economy if the corresponding institutional framework conditions create incentives for it. This includes *freedom of contract* on the one hand and *liability* for one's own actions on the other. The latter two are listed as independent principles in Eucken's original concept.

This chapter has "private property" in its title, but the two other important prerequisites—freedom of contract and responsibility—will be dealt with at the same time, because only under the condition of the last two factors does private property fulfil its function in the market economy. Similarly, Suntum et al. (2011, 11) has already summarised these three principles as his claim for a "Framework for Efficient Property Rights". As will be shown, this aspect has become considerably more complex under the conditions of digitalisation. At the centre of it all is probably the most decisive element of the digital economy: data.

© The Author(s), under exclusive license to Springer Nature Switzerland AG 2024

J. J. Dötsch, *Economic Policy in the Digital Age*, Contributions to Economics,
https://doi.org/10.1007/978-3-031-53047-0_7

The aim of this chapter is twofold. First, it aims to establish a basic understanding of those problems that arise in connection with the success factor of data and the social institutions of property and freedom of contract. Secondly, to show how, in this complex situation, new and conflicting constellations have arisen between the interests of individuals, the interests of companies, the economy and society as a whole. New structures are formed in the interaction at all the levels mentioned.

Accordingly, the chosen approach is to be understood as a heuristic grid with which these problems are approached in perspective, but without claiming to be able to clarify them completely and conclusively. Accordingly, the remainder of this chapter is divided into three parts.

Section 7.2 focuses on the core element of the digital economy, data, and discusses how the concept of property has come under new conditions in this context.

Section 7.3 draws attention to one of the most visible symptoms of the economic and social change triggered by digitalisation, namely the so-called "sharing economy".

Section 7.4 strives for an appropriate overall view of the issues addressed.

7.2 Who Owns the Twenty-First Century's Oil?

This chapter examines what is possibly the most important element in the digital age, *data*, from the point of view of the extent to which property rights issues become relevant.

It was not because Joe Kaeser, then CEO of Siemens, was famous for his statement that data is the oil of the twenty-first century (The Economic Times 2018) that this comparison became particularly revolutionary. Nor was he the only one to say or write such. The Economist (2017) ran the same headline. Others compare data to gold (Shubladze 2023). Either way, it seems obvious that there is a lot of money to be made from data.

But while the business models of "oil barons" and "sugar barons", to stay with the metaphor, were still halfway similar, the business models in the data-based digital economy, most prominently those of the big techs, are novel. Of course, traditional business models can be optimised through the systematic extraction of data and the use of AI; products and services can be individualised, product decision-making processes can be made more efficient, and so on. But this much is already obvious from these few superficial remarks: data is a different kind of economic good than gold or oil. Not only can data itself be highly diverse, but so can its collection, processing and use; and above all, unlike oil, gold or sugar, data is anything but scarce.[1] The comparison with oil is therefore actually completely misleading. And yet, there are "data barons".

---

[1] This statement is only *seemingly* in contrast to Walras' definition used earlier. This will be discussed in detail later in this chapter.

Hardly anything is growing as rapidly in the digital age as the volume of data being produced. According to a forecast of the European Commission, the volume of globally produced data is going to grow to 175 zettabytes in 2025 (European Commission 2020). This corresponds to a fivefold increase compared to 2018. This enormous dynamic is firstly due to the fact that the costs for collecting, storing and analysing data have fallen considerably; secondly, users are more active than ever; and thirdly, the connectivity of possibly all devices through sensors within the framework of the "Internet of Things" (see OECD 2020a, b, 10). It is visible to all that data can be an element for economic success. But the question of who actually owns which data and under which circumstances is anything but trivial. This question makes the scope of the transformation through digitalisation particularly clear and crystallises completely new constellations among individuals, companies, economies—and also society.

The following sections seek to clarify this question in three steps. Section 7.2.1 focuses on the fundamental role of property rights for the market economy. Section 7.2.2 clarifies that an exclusive property right, such as in the case of tangible goods, is inappropriate for data and discusses the "bundles of rights" approach. Section 7.2.3 discusses the possible shifts among the interests of individuals, companies and the macro level of the economy. Section 7.2.4 draws the attention to the fact that new areas of tension arise for the regulation of property rights in the digital age. Section 7.2.5 shortly discusses the respective implications for economic policy.

7.2.1 On the Role of Property Rights in the Economy

The following section provides a brief overview of the role of property rights in the economy.

Private property, instead of collective ownership, is an essential prerequisite for both efficiency and freedom (see Suntum et al. 2011, 12). We have become accustomed to the existence of private ownership of the factors of production and of its outcomes as a prerequisite for a market economy.

For the time being, history has provided good examples for ending the discussion about the extent to which a more prosperous solution to the problem of scarcity could be brought about through the form of collective ownership instead of private ownership. Lack of private ownership of the factors of production means no or wrong incentives for efficient economic action. Those who have no rights of disposal over resources will not use them to the best of their knowledge and abilities. An appropriate division of labour cannot unfold, dispersed knowledge (see Hayek 1945) is not used nor even discovered (see Hayek 1968), the invisible hand of the market cannot take effect[2] and the overall level of wealth and prosperity becomes lower.

Property rights and the associated freedom to enter into contracts on one's own responsibility, to be liable with one's property or to be allowed to benefit from

[2] See Footnote 1 in Chap. 3.

the use of private property if a demand can be satisfied with it, are in this respect institutional foundations of the market economy.[3] They are fundamental prerequisites for competition to come into being. In this context, economic law on the one hand and normativity on the other hand, once again, meet as two sides of the same coin. Economically, property and freedom of contract are fundamental, as they regulate conflicts over the rival use of resources and create incentives so that scarcity can be reduced. At the same time, they are the prerequisite for the autonomous shaping of one's own life, for the preservation of the freedom of individual actors and their private autonomy.

This is intuitively understandable and a definition of ownership for tangible goods such as a bicycle will hardly be more difficult to establish than using the bicycle. This poses few difficulties because the use of material goods is exclusive, i.e. the owner can decide who uses his good. Material goods are rival in use. From an economic point of view, this exclusivity, which is ensured by the right of ownership, is also essential for avoiding the free-rider phenomenon and for incentivisation, namely when resources have to be invested for the production of a material good for which there is demand. This is the case with bicycles and also with oil drilling.

In the case of intangible goods—intellectual property—the starting point is different, because its use is fundamentally not rival.[4] Exclusivity cannot be ensured in the same way and without further ado. Intangible goods are not scarce per se. A legal definition of intangible goods therefore represents an artificial scarcity of resources by making the rights to their use available to exclusively assignable legal entities. This transfers a positive effect of property rights of tangible goods to intangible resources, because it can solve incentive problems that would arise from copying or imitating such resources. If companies or entrepreneurs cannot reap the fruits of their innovations, they have little incentive to strive for new solutions.

This is intuitively understandable with regard to patents—vaccines are probably the most prominent example at present—but also other examples such as music compositions.[5] Moreover, the last example vividly shows that the market's potential to maximise diversity and create wealth through the division of labour can be pragmatically extended. For certain classes of such intellectual property rights—such as pop songs, advertising jingles or stock sound effects like the "Wilhelm Scream"—can again create their own markets. Intellectual property rights are therefore also an essential component of the successful division of labour. In anticipation of this, it should only be noted that the change brought about by digital technology in the area of the example mentioned is not only illustrated by the enormous variety of songs, sounds, etc., but also economically, in that providers such as Deezer or Spotify offer millions of sound recordings to everyone at prices that are hardly worth mentioning.

---

[3] For the purposes of these considerations, we do not address the issues of corporate constitution and limitation of liability.

[4] See, in general, for example Besen and Raskind (1991).

[5] However, this is probably tending to become less so, at least in the public perception: "Access" has arguably become one of the most important keywords of the internet age. A clear expression of this problem context is a phenomenon like "Pirate Parties International", which would have been completely unthinkable just a few years ago.

With regard to intellectual property rights, these brief explanations and examples already show that there have emerged crucial balancing problems with regard to economic policy objectives. For intellectual property can be protected to a greater or lesser extent. If patent protection is too strong, i.e. if the patent is valid for a correspondingly long period of time or the fee to buy it is too high, this can be an incentive, but overall, it can lead to a loss of prosperity, for example if the potential of competition and division of labour cannot be fully exploited. Cinemagoers would then not only have to come on the same bicycle but hear all the actors die with the same scream.

Too little patent protection, on the other hand, would potentially weaken the incentives for research and development, namely if the profits resulting from the short-term monopolistic advantage could be imitated away too quickly. The latter also shows that under certain circumstances there may be no need for a patent at all, namely if the knowledge enabling competitive advantages can be kept as e.g. a company or trade secret and securely protected from access by third parties. Such balancing problems can be of a very different nature and also exist in other contexts and are the subject of legal regulations not least because of the interest of the directly involved parties as well as the public interest, for example in the case of appropriate citation. This problem of balancing interests will be encountered further below in connection with the "data economy".

Ultimately, a legal version of intellectual property is superfluous in the case where its creator—by whatever means—can ensure exclusivity. "Secret formulas" for remedies or drinks are an illustrative example. This is vivid, on the one hand, because a "secret formula" for a drink may well be kept exclusively in the hands of the owners for generations, since the process is unknown; on the other hand, because of the technical progress that has taken place in chemical laboratories time may well erode the trade secret by making it easy to analyse compositions and thus reconstruct a recipe. In other words, and in our context, we now have better methods for obtaining and interpreting data! This example also shows that the incentives for data holders (not named "owners" here) to make this data accessible to others, i.e. to *share* it, depend on what they have to offer on the basis of this data. If this can create competition, there is no incentive to do so. If complementary services can be developed that one cannot offer oneself, but that strengthen the overall market position, there are incentives (see Engels 2016, 5).

But if data can make one rich, i.e. if one can obtain benefits from it or gain a competitive advantage in certain contexts, then the question arises as to how data can and should be treated from a property rights perspective. But as has already become clear from the few "properties" and examples above, the question is far less clear than in the case of oil or even a piece of music. One must therefore first be clear about what the phenomenon of data actually is. This is what the following section tries to do.

7.2.2 Which Rights on Which Data?

This section combines the question of property rights with an examination of the peculiarities of the phenomenon of data.

What kind of phenomenon or what kinds of goods are we talking about with data? First, some basic questions.

Unlike material goods, data is not rival per se to begin with. Data is also produced on a large and growing scale; data isn't scarce at all. So there can obviously be no incentive problem here in that exclusive property rights must serve as an incentive for data to be produced on a sufficient scale. Rather, the opposite seems to be the case, and it is completely different than the example from the previous paragraph would suggest. Data is available, but their potential for innovation does not seem to have been fully exploited (see OECD 2019). Unlike secret formulas, some data remains unused in data silos (see De Gregorio and Ranchordás 2020).

Depending on the technological context, third parties can be excluded from the use of data. While the construction manual for a new gear shift can be easily reconstructed, owners of data can protect "their" data relatively easily through technological precautions.

Regardless of the form in which data becomes relevant from an economic, legal or normative perspective, data can be distinguished in very different ways and assigned to different categories. For example, according to the way in which it is generated, processed or used. It is often observable that in the rampant discussion about the role of data, a clear distinction is not always made. A fundamental problem in this regard is the clear definition of data relating to persons. "Personal data" is defined by the OECD (2013, 13) as "(…) any information relating to an identified or identifiable individual (data subject)". In their instructive background note on the topic of consumer data rights and competition, they contrast this category with the broader term "consumer data", "(…) to capture data concerning consumers, where such data have been collected, traded or used as part of a commercial relationship" (OECD 2020b, 7). There is data that is voluntarily given or subsequently generated, so-called inferred data; data that has been shared, stored data or data that has already been processed. Sometimes a distinction is also made between a syntactic and a semantic level of data. Based on this, data can also be distinguished according to its content, i.e. to which area of non-digital reality it refers.

At this point, it must suffice for our purposes to draw attention to this diversity of data. Of particular importance, however, is of course what this data provides concrete knowledge about, what relation it has to the world. This draws attention to the exceptionally important issue of *personal data*. This very widely discussed topic will be dealt with in more detail below. At any rate, it can be stated at this point that—it has already been briefly mentioned in connection with the problem of open borders—personal data and non-personal data cannot always be perfectly distinguished. And even if one could, this problem cannot be solved without further ado via anonymisation, since different standards can be applied for this. And "(…) (i)n practice, however, is may be (sic) difficult to safeguard anonymous data against re-identification" (OECD 2020b, 10, with reference to PCAST 2014). This is also to point out how limited the considerations set out here are. Even a differentiation like this is still quite blurred at present.

Against this background, so much can already be established that an overarching property law regulation encompassing all types of data would be completely inappropriate for the subject matter at all. The situation is more complex in that both the data themselves can be very different and the contexts in which they are generated, shared or processed. The digital economy has thus posed entirely new challenges to the legal system and economic considerations, which at the same time, as will be shown, represent normative challenges. However, if no overarching regulation is possible, then equally different, appropriate data governance solutions must be found for different contexts.

Can such contexts be systematised? For example, according to sectors, the type of participants, such as public, private or commercial, customer, supplier, etc.? This seems, *prima facie*, inevitable for an appropriate taxonomy for the use of data, but still seems to reduce the observable complexity only to an unsatisfactory extent. The next paragraph will cover this idea again.

At the same time, the question arises as to which appropriate legal category would be conducive to an adequate reduction in complexity. For this, however, neither the concept of property rights in material goods seems practicable (because data are not rival, do not wear out, lie unused in silos, have numerous different manifestations, and can be used in a much different and more diverse way), nor does the concept of intellectual property rights seem appropriate, because exclusivity is technically easier to achieve, there is apparently no lack of incentives to produce data at all and differences with regard to different types of data, such as that between syntactic and semantic levels, cannot be (meaningfully) captured by intellectual property rights. It is therefore obviously necessary to differentiate the concept of property right in a more fine-grained way in order to adequately represent the different forms. The approach of "bundles of rights" provides some useful hints. The following section is devoted to this.

7.2.3 The "Bundle of Rights" Approach on Data

This chapter presents the extent to which the "bundle of rights" approach can be a way to address the new complexity created by the role of data in the economy.

The special role of private property as a prerequisite for the functioning of markets was taken up and theoretically developed further by the property rights theory in the 1970s.[6] It addresses the problem at hand at the micro level and has the advantage for our purposes that it further differentiates the generic term "property". While in the case of tangible goods, as shown above, a particular entity corresponds to the exclusive ownership of an assignable legal entity, the theory further splits the

[6] See the seminal contributions of Coase (1960), Furubotn and Pejovich (1972) and Demsetz (2002).

difference between property and non-property and deals with composite, so-called "bundles of rights", which an assignable owner can dispose of in order to consider any properties of an entity as a resource from which he can derive benefit. "Bundles of rights" thus consist of several elements of rights of disposal by claimable persons over something, which can be both tangible and intangible in nature. This approach seems flexible enough to more adequately capture the complex phenomenon of data and its use.[7]

What elements of legal titles can such "bundles of rights" consist of? Usually four different kinds are distinguished: (1) the *usus*, i.e. the right to use something; (2) the *usus fructus*, the right to keep the proceeds from the use of something; (3) *abusus*, which is a right to change the thing concerned; and (4) the *usus abutendi*, i.e. the right to dispose of the thing concerned in whole or in part. In this last perspective, the sale of a thing can be interpreted as a transfer of the corresponding rights. This approach achieves a gain in differentiation by the fact that there does not have to be only one specific legal entity that holds such a bundle of rights, but the individual elements of the bundle can also be held by different legal entities. Accordingly, different owners can have different rights to a certain good.

For the present problem context, this seems to be a useful approach in several respects. First and foremost, it can be used to illustrate the variety of ways in which data—to stick with this general term—is used. It always refers to that aspect of the particular use on the basis of which benefits can be derived from data in each case. This is a helpful tool in this context with regard to the incentive problem already mentioned above, since a certain type of use of data is either very costly or particularly profitable. In both cases, as above, legal titles become significant, for example, by being able to establish exclusivity if it cannot be guaranteed technically, as in the case of trade secrets.

The perspective of "bundles of rights" can therefore help to clarify that in the extremely diverse use situations, it can be defined who can and should have rights to production, access, control or monetisation of data. However, given the countless contexts and diversity of data, it will not be possible to develop a valid taxonomy for all possible cases.

The perspective of "bundles of rights" is, however, an excellent instrument for making clear the new lines of conflict that have arisen through the data-based potential commodification of almost everything. For this is one of the core problems that digitalisation has raised with regard to the question of an economy that is meant to serve people and society. The question of economic commodification has become more complex and far-reaching. The next paragraph is devoted to this problem.

[7] Few have brought as much clarity to this problem area as Wolfgang Kerber, see for example the publications (2019, 2022a, b), who has examined and presented in detail the problems merely addressed here, also with a view to the concrete legal regulations and attempts at regulation in Europe, among other places. Lastly, in the instructive joint contribution with Martina Eckardt (2023).

7.2.4 *Areas of Conflict*

The following section illustrates the extent to which new areas of tension arise for the regulation of the application of property rights in the digital age.

Let us again take as starting point the central assumption that the economy has a technical, i.e. instrumental, character, and that the task of economic policy is therefore to ensure that it functions as efficiently as possible and serves a humane society of free individuals. Let us assume that individuals are interested in both the highest possible degree of individual freedom and an increase in prosperity for themselves, or at least in maintaining a level of prosperity that has been achieved. On the other hand, let us assume that politics has a duty to create the conditions to increase the level of overall distributable wealth.[8]

Following this, it would fundamentally serve the goal of prosperity if as much data as possible were collected and made available to as many participants as possible. This would enable companies to better individualise products and services and create greater potential for innovation (OECD 2020a, 14). However, this is in opposition with the fundamental value of privacy, which is a de facto legally protected area today.[9] The economy under the conditions of the digital age—i.e. making use of all forms of digital data—and *privacy* thus entail a source for complex trade-off situations (see Acquisti et al. 2016). This is, basically, nothing new, but this relationship is becoming more complicated in the digital age.

This explosive relationship between the potential for greater prosperity through data—through the more efficient usage of a hugely increased quantity of data—and the protection of privacy not only affects the relationship between individual customers and companies, but is also encountered in the relationship between individuals and the public sector. The collection of data can, for example, serve to improve the use of infrastructure, for example in the form of traffic guidance systems that relieve inner cities, reduce environmental pollution and, by improving the supply of public goods—for example air quality, available space, noise levels, etc.—can reduce externalities and lead to an increase in the level of prosperity. The same is true for many other crucial, mostly publicly provided infrastructure or services, such as health care (OECD 2020b, 23). It is important to note that here potential positive externalities, such as the ability to predict and direct traffic flows accordingly, are juxtaposed with potential negative externalities, such as the ability to negatively discriminate against customers (ibid., with reference to Gal and Rubinfeld 2019).

---

[8] We will simply take these normative assumptions for granted here. It is certainly the case that in the course of the discussion about environmental damage and currently especially climate change, an ethic of renunciation can be observed among parts of the population. A discussion of the sense and nonsense of the claims made in this area, political projects, etc. cannot be undertaken here. Apart from the debates and different policy goals on these issues, it is indisputable that the most efficient solution would be the best for the implementation of each idea. This should therefore be left to the market.

[9] In Europe this is enshrined in Article 7—"Everyone has the right to respect for his or her private and family life, home and communications"—and further specified with regard to "Protection of personal data" in the Charter of Fundamental Rights of the European Union.

The extent to which individuals are willing to give access to data, to share data or to guarantee the possibility of producing such data is a psychological question on the individual level, and at the same time a legal and thus ultimately also a political question, the answer to which is subject to normative change. What are these difficulties in detail? Two groups of problems can be distinguished.

First, there is a group of *technological problems*. It is not easily possible to clearly distinguish private and non-private data in every context. Even if one were to assume that this were the case, there would still be the problem that certain private data, even if released by an individual, could give rise to uncontrollable constellations. Because on the basis of this data, conclusions can be drawn under certain circumstances—unasked for and unobserved by, for example, public supervision—concerning third persons (one also speaks of "inferred data") who have not given their consent. From an economic point of view, this is an externality. It would be naïve to believe that companies would not want to use this opportunity to gain a competitive advantage.

A solution to this externality problem via technical procedures, such as the anonymisation or pseudonymisation of data, would have to meet generally binding standards, but such standards are certainly still a long way off.[10] However, whether anonymised, pseudonymised or not, data can be valuable, and the more data there is the greater its potential. One might get the impression that the digital age is generating its own kind of nuclear waste: "The more personal information is collected and stored, the more broadly it is disclosed, and the longer it is stored, the more likely it will be hacked, accidentally disclosed or used for illegal purposes" (Kemp 2020, 644f). No matter how one assesses the advantages and disadvantages of using private data, there is first of all a fundamental technical problem: "(...) the most de-identified consumer data can technically be re-identified" (OECD 2020a, b referring to PCAST 2014).

This initially technical question of solving the externality problem then becomes, in a next step, another economic question, because all such procedures are, of course, associated with costs. The starting point for such considerations, however, inevitably remains a normative position. For the question must be answered as to how expensive privacy should or may be for those involved. To put it simply, we then come back to the trade-off formulated at the outset, namely between a lesser or greater degree of protection of privacy, i.e. private autonomy, and a greater or lesser potential for creating wealth through data. Regardless of whether we are dealing with constellations between private individuals and companies or private individuals and the public sector, decisions in favour of one or the other technical solution shift the emphasis in one direction or the other.

In addition, there is the difficulty of separating data and the context of data (of course also collected in the form of data) with regard to their relevance to privacy issues. A high degree of generality of a regulation will therefore not be able to handle

---

[10] Since privacy concerns play a very special role in Europe, this question is also accompanied by a corresponding jurisprudential discourse. See, with a European perspective e.g. Stalla-Bourdillon and Knight (2017) and Esayas (2015). With reference to the interpretation of the legal basis mentioned in the previous footnote, see also Hallinan (2021).

the concrete situations appropriately, which means that a plethora of different regulations of data governance will have to be worked out. In this process, however, we are certainly still at the beginning of understanding (Kerber 2022b, 281), especially since different legal traditions have different views of the problem. In the United States, the meaning of privacy is evaluated differently and as such is not legally captured specifically at all, but through consumer law; accordingly, privacy issues are treated differently than in Europe. In Australia, the instrument of "consumer rights" is used. The discussion in the field of law and economics is therefore highly complex and, in fact, still quite open. Whichever way you look at it, the question of how property and freedom of contract can be implemented pragmatically in the digital age faces, still, unresolved challenges. With regard to the complexity of the issues on the one hand, and the necessarily greater variety of correspondingly smaller regulations on the other, indicates *a greater overall degree of monitoring seems to be necessary* (see Fernández-Macías 2018, 11).

The second group of problems can be summarised as *problems of market failure.* Such problems have been discussed in economic theory and literature for a long time, but they have become more complex in the digital age, which will be briefly addressed below in the problem area focused on here.

Information asymmetries are particularly relevant in this context. Private individuals will usually have relatively little idea about who collects which types of data about them in which context, and in what form they can be further processed. Basically, information asymmetries between buyers and sellers can potentially lead to worse market outcomes, which have been described by Akerlof (1970). One policy option to address the problem of asymmetric information is to require sellers to make certain information appropriately available so that potential buyers have an adequate basis for their decision to buy or not to buy. This is, of course, also possible for interactions in which data is created or used. Here, a contract would have to be concluded on the regulation of corresponding property rights, or more precisely, on an appropriate "bundle of rights" to the data.

Theoretically, this problem is taken up with the help of data protection declarations, e.g. when using all kinds of apps, etc., and to that extent the issue is solved contractually. Because these data protection declarations are also the ones that inform or should inform the customer/user about the use of rights of disposal. In practice, however, they are usually "clicked away" without being read. This may be due to laziness or irrational behaviour (see the next section), but there is no doubt that data protection declarations are specific legal texts that an average user may not be sufficiently trained to interpret appropriately. In addition, time must be taken by the user for an appropriate study and a correspondingly weighted decision. This results in transaction costs that can vary depending on the design of such declarations or due to different decision-making architectures—for example, an opt-in solution in contrast to an opt-out solution (see Borgesius 2015).[11]

[11] The keyword of decision architecture necessitates a reference to the influence of behavioural economics on regulatory approaches—"behavioural informed intervention" (Sibony and Alemano 2015, 1)—in a whole range of areas of life, which is very widely discussed under the keyword

Similar to what has already been mentioned above, the possibility of a shift in transaction costs on the one hand and the potential for innovation on the other can also be observed in this context depending on the design of decision architectures. This means that in this context, too, a balancing problem arises for the public regulator when it deems it necessary to specify requirements for decision architectures. This form of new everyday complexity is remarkable. Here, too, a new type of trade-off constellation arises with regard to possible policy solutions, in which three aspects play a role: Firstly, the transaction costs incurred, then the protection of privacy, but also freedom of contract. The more far-reaching the legal protection of private individuals, the greater the encroachment on freedom of contract.

Another case of market failure is when *people behave irrationally*, apart from their level of information. This problem has been widely studied in behavioural economics (see, e.g. Chadhuri 2021; Mallard 2017). For the subject of this chapter, the best-known example of such a case is the so-called privacy paradox (see e.g. Solove 2021; Norberg et al. 2007), which was already mentioned in Sects. 4.1.3 and 5.5.2 and for which there is ample empirical evidence. According to a survey by the European Commission, 92% of the participants were in favour of personal information on their electronic devices only being accessible with their permission and 82% also considered their consent necessary for their activities on the internet to be tracked (see European Commission 2016). But in practice, a very different behaviour can be observed: people most often "click away" the privacy statements unread, as in the example above; or they post all kinds of things on platforms, about which they well know, evaluate, process and pass on their data. This is not the place to go into the complex psychological or behavioural background of how such situations actually arise. In any case, it is remarkable that two trends can be observed that reinforce each other. On the one hand, there is a tendency for users to be increasingly indifferent to the fact that their data is being used by third parties.[12] And on the other hand, companies, recognising that there is business potential in data, are increasingly moving from passive to active data collectors (see OECD 2020b, 16). However, two aspects, which are already encountered at a fairly high level of generality, should nevertheless be mentioned here.

There is the fact that irrational behaviour can be understood a kind of complexity reduction. In a world that has been digitalised to this extent, people are not able to work through the complexity of the "bundles of rights" in every single living situation that they deal with using apps and smart devices equipped with sensors. This is precisely why, for reasons of complexity reduction, if they are asked at all, they simply click away. It is one of the very well-known characteristics of the digital age

"nudging", made popular by Thaler and Sunstein (2009). It is obvious that this approach is also a useful instrument for reducing complexity with regard to the behaviour of users on the internet. However, the problems associated with this cannot be discussed in detail here. It is noteworthy, however, that the relevance of the issues raised has grown considerably. For the context addressed here, see also Sunstein and Thaler (2003), Acquisti and Grossklag (2007) or Krebs (2013).

[12] Admittedly, differences can be observed in this respect, as the question of how highly users assess the value of their data or how important privacy is to them is context-dependent (see Acquisti et al. 2016). Nevertheless, a general tendency seems to be observable.

that masses of people are informationally overloaded; "(cookie) consent fatigue" is the decisive result for this extremely widespread overload phenomenon here (see e.g. Wein 2022). Can this be solved by an appropriate (economic) political framework? Again, only at the price of the trade-offs discussed above. The following section will revisit the problem from a different perspective.

Another problem related to market failures concerns *competition policy*. It has already been addressed from other perspectives in the preceding chapters. Data can be a decisive factor in gaining market power. Data can become barriers to entry for potential competitors, a phenomenon that has reached a completely new dimension in the context of the platform economy and platform ecosystems (see above): "(...) the exclusive control over data sets through firms with market power can allow the leveraging of this market power to other markets and foreclosure of competitors also outside of the platform economy" (Kerber 2022a, 160; see also Kerber 2019, 2022b; Crémer et al. 2019). Data can be an "essential facility" "(...) if a non-replicable and non-substitutable data set (...) is controlled by a dominant firm is a necessary input for providing services on another market" (Kerber 2022a, 169). This problem becomes particularly explosive when certain providers already dominate the market and it is therefore hardly possible for consumers to switch to alternatives. "Consumers regularly do not get a real say in questions of privacy as part of the quality of an online product, as they are usually not able to bypass certain prevalent digital service providers" (Robertson 2020, 165).

The dominant players thus strengthen their position by making more market-relevant knowledge available to them in the form of data (see Kemp 2020; Ezrachi and Robertson 2019) than would have been possible via the "discovery procedure" (Hayek) of the pre-digital age. Stucke (2018) has coined the remarkable expression "data-opolist" to describe this. In this respect, the question of ownership or the question of access to data—rights of disposal in the context outlined above—is also at the centre of completely new competition policy challenges.

Particularly striking is the emerging new entanglement between privacy issues, as mentioned above, and competition policy issues. After all, the advertising industry is a key sector for the internet economy, which has already been mentioned in previous chapters with reference to the indirect network effects. The business models used here are based on the handling of user data with the aim of tailor-made, targeted advertising (see OECD 2020a, 26, OECD b, 19). This activity, "consumer profiling" (see, early, Elmer 2004; Selinger 2018), is admittedly not unproblematic with regard to personal rights and data protection (see, e.g. Petkova and Böhm 2017 or Hacker 2017). However, the possibility for users to consent to or refuse the use of their data when using platforms using "tracking walls" (see Borgesius et al. 2017) has different consequences for small platforms such as e.g. online newspapers using tracking walls or over-the-top players that already dominate the platform market, such as Google or Facebook. In the latter case users have already clicked "yes" on the modules of the tracking wall at the very beginning and are continuously logged in anyway via their mobile devices, etc. The balancing task for regulation in the area of tension between competition effects, protection of privacy, potential progress and overall welfare has thus become considerably more complex (see Kerber 2022b; Graef and Berlo 2021;

Graef et al. 2017; Costa-Cabral and Lynskey 2017).[13] This can be attributed not least to the fact that the three problems mentioned, namely market power, irrational behaviour and information asymmetries, can reinforce each other (Kerber 2022b, 283). This connection, which challenges rule-making in competition policy as well as data and consumer protection in equal measure and in conjunction with each other, is new (Douglas 2021a, 651).

A not insignificant element of this new complexity is that the data relevant for business success is of course not only collected directly by a supplier offering its services on a website—so-called first-party data collection—but also collected via third parties. And third-party trackers can be found on the bulk of the most widely used websites as well as on most apps (see OECD 2020b, 17). Remarkably, Ezrachi and Robertson have pointed out that "(…) the majority of these trackers are controlled by a small number of data giants" (Ezrachi and Robertson 2019, 5).[14]

In order to attempt to draw a pragmatic interim result at this point, for the purposes of these reflections it seems extremely noteworthy, that the new dimension of data in the digital age generates a new kind of complexity in which aspects of data protection, competition policy issues and property rights or access rights are inextricably intertwined. The next section attempts to summarise what this means for economic policy.

7.2.5 Policy Implications

This chapter explains the extent to which the phenomena described in the previous sections mean a new challenge for economic policy.

What immediate conclusions can be drawn from the aspects presented above? Is there anything at all to be done—or can we or should we confidently leave further development to the forces of the market? Can these forces develop adequately at all in the area under consideration? If we go back to the original question of the new conditions under which private property of the means of production and freedom of contract came to exist in the digital age, the following problems can be identified in essence.

The central problem is the increased degree of complexity. Initially, it is not a problem if neither the concept of ownership of tangible goods nor the concept of

---

[13] The practice of the large over-the-top players attracted the attention of the competition authorities and the corresponding research at an early stage and, in accordance with the complexity of the subject matter, which is only briefly mentioned here, triggered a very broad discussion, the details of which cannot be reproduced in this framework. With regard to the remarkable google case, see for example Geradin et al. (2020).

[14] This knowledge secured via the data is then again the basis for the possibility of price discrimination, which is also relevant in terms of competition policy (see Fudenberg and Villas-Boas 2012) and which was already dealt with in Sect. 5.2. Conversely, it is also possible that different products or variants of are offered to different customers depending on the data available, and in this way certain groups are excluded from consuming certain products or services (OECD 2020b, 22).

intellectual property is practically applicable for securing the right to property in the data economy, but rather the more complex concept of bundles of rights can be used. The problem for (economic) policy lies in the fact that, firstly, the functioning of the data economy requires a multitude of individual data governance solutions, which on the one hand entails new transaction costs.

Secondly, such solutions, as briefly outlined above, may involve normative trade-offs to which there will be no easy answers and which, like technological development, are obviously subject to change.

Thirdly, as has also been widely discussed in competition policy in the context of the "more economic approach" (see Schmidtchen 2007; Miceli 2017; Zalewska-Głogowska 2017), this results in a considerable potential for legal uncertainty due to a lower degree of general rules in favour of individually regulated cases. These problems also show that the borderline between competition law and data protection is becoming blurred with regard to the requirements of concrete regulation and that the two areas can no longer be clearly separated (Kerber 2022b, 282, with reference to Douglas 2021b; OECD 2020b). Thus, externalities arise under different areas of regulation.

This fact should not be underestimated, because for an appropriate assessment, beyond the respective individual constellations, the technical, i.e. instrumental character of the economy must be taken into consideration. If, however, a superordinate solution is not possible, then the relationship between the conditions of the economy and society automatically shifts. It shifts towards more efficiency.

As should have become clear above, this problem is far more complex today than it was when Eucken formulated his principles. The change with regard to economic policy lies in the necessity of a shift from a more institutional approach of high generality of large scope to a more small-scale, case-by-case approach. However, one cannot help suspecting that the complexity of (economic) reality is growing at a completely different pace and one can only keep up in small steps and distinct areas. In any case, this means that adequate enforcement of the law faces difficulties arising, on the one hand, from technological and economic conditions and, on the other hand, from the fact that in many cases such problems span different jurisdictions.

The normative demand for a technical character of the economy can be seen as an indication of economic policy priorities insofar as its starting point is the idea of an independent individual who decides freely and autonomously. Private property is only one component of the fundamentally important private autonomy of responsible citizens. With regard to the functioning of the market economy, this is crucial insofar as *the consumer* should set the incentives for development. Therefore, in this context, consumer protection is required, which not coincidentally often works under the same roof as the competition authority.

But here again a remarkable dilemma arises. If one admits that consumers are overloaded, under-informed, irrational and solutions via individual consent in data protection declarations, for example, do not work adequately, then either the freedom of action of the consumer or the freedom of action of the respective service provider or both would have to be restricted. Choi et al. (2019) assume that if negative externalities outweigh positive ones, there will be a level of data collection above the social optimum even if the consumers are informed and have to give their consent (OECD 2020b, 24). Depending on which regulations are devised here, freedom of contract can be impaired.

All possible solutions to this new complexity, as discussed under terms such as "data sharing" or "open data", "data access" or "transportability", have, on the one hand, sometimes complex technical implications, but all lead back—albeit differently in each case—to the central question of an appropriate design of the "bundles of rights" and what exactly are individuals supposed to decide. An elegant way to bundle decision-making competence and make it delegable to an intermediary is the conception of so-called "data trustees" (see for an overview Specht-Riemenschneider and Kerber 2022).[15]

Whichever way we look at it, digitalisation has given rise to a new degree of complexity that suddenly complicates a fundamental principle like "property". In order to use this fruitfully in the future in the sense of both efficiency and a humane society at the same time, it seems that the inventiveness not only of computer scientists, but also of economists and legal experts together will be urgently needed.

7.3 Sharing or Owning

This chapter looks at a phenomenon that has received a lot of attention in the age of digitalisation and is considered an important growth industry, the so-called sharing economy.

Can digitalisation make more out of less and lead to a paradigm shift in the economy? A particularly prominent term for the digital age suggests such a fundamental change, or at least the potential to put some areas on a different footing than has been the case so far: the "sharing economy". What is it all about? Is it a new, more modern, different part of the economy? Is private property getting less important? Does this term capture a decisive, new element of the economy that is characteristic of the digital age?

The following sections discuss these questions in four steps.

Section 7.3.1 briefly outlines the background and some basic questions.

Section 7.3.2 discusses what can be concretely understood by "sharing economy" in the digital age. To this end, the new phenomena appearing under this label are confronted with forms of shared management or collaborative economy that already existed before the digital age.

Section 7.3.3 seeks to present the commonalities of the business models in question.

Section 7.3.4 looks at the economic consequences of the emergence of the sharing economy for the economy as a whole.

---

[15] This is a new concept, the possibilities of which are still under discussion and cannot be discussed in detail here.

Section 7.3.5 deals with the question of what these developments mean for citizens and for the regulator.

7.3.1 Background

This section briefly explains the background to the sharing economy.

In connection with the problem of allocating profits and losses that have arisen on the basis of data, the previous chapter discussed the need for a differentiated concept of ownership in the digital age and illustrated that there are novel problems of complexity and enforceability in this regard. But a change in the fundamental principle of the economy and doing business, i.e. maximising utility in a rival process, has not yet become visible at this level. Is this perhaps the case at another, more general and visible level, the "sharing economy"?

In any case, forms of sharing based on digital solutions are obviously penetrating more and more areas of everyday life—such as video sharing, car sharing, the increasing amount of flats "shared" via Airbnb in big cities or even meal sharing. In the examples mentioned, there are indeed owners; however, the operators of the dominant sharing-brands will no more have earned their money by *sharing* their property than by making more property out of it. However, if one takes into account the volume of turnover generated by business models that want to be understood as part of the "sharing economy"—40.2 billion US Dollars in 2022 after 18.6 billion US Dollars in 2015 (Statista 2023)—and if one looks even briefly at the accompanying upheavals in existing industries, then the phenomenon seems to be indeed significant and requires further clarification.

A few remarks beforehand. The meaning of the term "sharing" is in contrast to the meaning of the term "owning". And it is possibly because of this use of the term that the discourse on the topic is largely a "value and vision-loaded domain" (Codagnone and Martnes 2016, 18)—at least the choice of words gives cause for this. This may be partly intentional (see Newman 2018), partly not. However, instead of simply assuming a fundamental change in the form of economic activity behind the omnipresent dynamics, it is important to critically question what is going on.

Assuming the (presumed) difference expressed by the contrast between the terms "sharing" and "owning", which was provocatively put as the heading of this chapter, it must be noted that there was already a rich academic discussion on the possibilities of sharing and collaboration before the dawn of the digital age. In order to make the situation clear, in the following we will also briefly draw on elements of this discussion and explore the question of whether there is a shift in the digital age, even if only in terms of tendency, from private to more collective ownership, from owning to sharing, from shared work to a collaborative economy.

While the previous chapter dealt with the extent to which the concept of ownership and property rights in the data-based economy faces new challenges with regard to what is arguably the most important new element of the value chain—data—the following chapter looks at a more general level and focuses on the new business models that are spreading with extraordinary dynamism in all sectors and can be summarised under the very name of the "sharing economy".

7.3.2 A "Floating Signifier"

The following section seeks to clarify what is meant by the heterogeneous phenomena typical of the digital age that appear under the label "sharing economy".

Everyone is talking about the phenomenon of the "sharing economy". But many are talking about very different things. Sometimes the term is used synonymously with "collaborative economy" or "-consumption" (World Economic Forum 2013, 5). Why is this actually the case?

There is no consensus on a definition (Codagnone and Martens 2016, 6f.). The term first became known in a different context and even before the digital age through a publication by Weitzmann (1986). With the emergence of the internet and thus new business models, the term became known by a broader public and, barely three decades later, also became the focus of interest of the World Economic Forum. At that time, of course, the topic was already resolutely linked to the possibilities of digitalisation. The statement that this was a truly epoch-making phenomenon—"(t)he sharing economy represents one node of a much broader series of shifts underway dating back to the Industrial Revolution" (World Economic Forum 2013, 6)—may be seen as an element of the Forum's typical rhetoric. However, the statement was and is understandable in view of the scope of the perceptible changes. After all, digitalisation was supposed to make it possible to share much more in many more areas of life: "Today there are hundreds of ways one can share different kinds of assets: space, skills, stuff and time" (ibid.). And indeed, the phenomenon of sharing platforms now extends to all kinds of markets, from housing to driving services to factor markets and consumer durables and affects the whole economy and society (Codagnone et al. 2016, 8).

The preceding quotation from the World Economic Forum provides two important clues for our considerations. Firstly, it correctly captures the fact that digitalisation expands the possibilities for new, digital business models to use "space, skills, stuff and time". Secondly, the statement is also a good indication of how contradictory the discourse on the topic is, since it often works with very fuzzy or even inappropriate terms. The statement is also a contradiction in itself. Those who truly "share" their "asset", as the World Economic Forum very aptly put it, cannot earn any money from it. According to the Routledge Dictionary of Economics, an asset is "(1) a resource with a market value, (2) a unit of wealth capable of earning an income" or "(3) sufficient estate or effects to discharge the burden on an heir or executor" (Rutherford 1995, 17). Sharing an asset in the proper sense de facto does not make one rich. But this was probably no more the point of the World Economic Forum than it was of the shareholders of the most successful players in the "sharing economy".

If an asset is not shared in the traditional sense, this indicates that everything may remain the same, but the new phenomenon is obviously based on a new business model, and often built on digital technology.[16] These indeed very diverse possibilities for new business models in this area are also a reason for the variety of definitional approaches. Demary (2015, 4) formulates a rather general approach and understands it as all activities to share services, goods or knowledge; similarly, in Miller (2016, 150) individuals create goods, services, but also space and money in order to share them with each other.

The boundary between "sharing" and "collaborating" is sometimes blurred in the discourse. This is also the reason why "sharing economy" is often mentioned in the same breath as "collaborative economy" or "-consumption" (as in the aforementioned contribution of the World Economic Forum 2013, 5). Often "sharing economy", "collaborative consumption" or "-economy", "access-based consumption" or "circular economy" are simply used synonymously (Codagnone and Martens 2016, 5). In some places, however, the "collaborative economy" based on "collaborative consumption" is differentiated from sharing in the narrower sense (see, for example, Botsman 2013; Botsman and Roger 2010), but in other places it is not (such as World Economic Forum 2013, 5). Other, somehow related terms also appear from time to time, such as "access-based consumption" (Bardhi and Eckhardt 2012; Belk 2014) or "connected consumption" (Dubois et al. 2014; Schor, 2014).[17] As Codagnone et al. (2016, 20) aptly put it, "The 'sharing economy' (and other alternative labels) is used as a 'floating signifier' for a diverse range of activities (they are referring to Nadeem et al. 2015. 13). For our purposes, it will not be the aim to work out an exact typology.

However, the often encountered conceptual vagueness is unfortunate, if not even suspicious.[18] Codagnone and Martnes (2016, 18) have emphatically pointed out, with regard to the use of the term, that the discourse on this area of phenomena is a "(...) value and vision-loaded domain" and have identified three strands of this discourse. Firstly, the "non-economic social approach to consumption", which emphasises a shift from ownership to access; secondly, the economic view that the sharing economy would lead to new competitive pressures and innovation by capitalising on previously unused capacities; and thirdly, the corresponding literature from the field of business and management, which emphasises new business models. This segmentation is still accurate.

---

[16] For the purposes of this study, it will suffice to describe what is currently happening under the label of the "sharing economy"; for this explanation, the building blocks of the economic theory of sharing—such as Buchanan's "economic theory of clubs" (1965) or Becker's "theory on the allocation of time" (1965) are not absolutely necessary precisely because they deal with the actual phenomenon of sharing.

[17] A good overview of the confusion of terms and an instructive presentation of the problem is provided by Codagnone and Martens (2016); a literature review with a focus on business administration and sharing in the accommodation sector is provided by Hossein (2023).

[18] See, for example, Newman's (2018, 2) bilious critique of Uber: "Uber scrupulously refers to itself as facilitating 'ridesharing'—by my count, more than seventy of its digital press releases include the term. But, as any five-year-old could tell you, Uber's business model has nothing to do with sharing".

First of all, a few limitations in order to make an appropriate distinction for the purposes of the present considerations. It seems to make sense to start with digital technology, let us leave it for the time being with the internet in general. Koopman et al. (2015, 2) focus on the internet as a tool that is used to enable better capacity utilisation of goods by bringing demanders and suppliers together under lower transaction costs. These are therefore platform solutions. As a first delimitation, we can assume at this point that with regard to the current phenomenon of the sharing economy, the internet is obligatory. All such phenomena are based on internet platforms and use digital interconnectedness (Codagnone and Martens 2016, 6).

Thus, platforms in general, especially multi-sided platforms, come into the focus of studies on the topic (see e.g. Zervas et al. 2016). The economic effect that is decisive for the success of such business models is, as already described in earlier sections, indirect network effects, as they occur in two-sided or multi-sided markets.[19] However, as has already been explained, nothing is shared on such platforms in a revolutionary new sense. Are there, perhaps, kinds of collaboration in a revolutionary new sense on the basis of the platforms? Since the aspect of collaboration seems to be of particular importance in the context of the phenomenon of the sharing economy, at least according to the common usage of the term, it seems worthwhile to take a closer look at this here.

If there are indirect network effects, then it is not yet collaboration in the true sense. It is true that goods can be exchanged or mediated on the basis of a platform and, in addition to goods, labour or services can be exchanged or mediated; but work is not yet done on a common basis in the sense of ownership, beyond the mediation that is decisive for the platform. Even if the platform has mediated a collaboration, no new or lasting common ground is created, nor any new, common business of its own order. In order for this to come about, the profit that the platform itself generates—for example through advertising or fees—could be distributed proportionally to those who have cooperated and worked together on the basis of the platform. But this is not the case at all with the examples that stand for the success of the sharing economy. Digital platforms can organise the matching process that is necessary for a collaboration to take place. But they themselves do not handle the collaboration that comes about, they do not create anything that is more collaborative than forms of collaborative economic activity that already existed—even before the digital age.

Conversely, to clarify the issue, how can we distinguish the collaborative economy from the sharing economy that characterises the digital age? This requires some differentiating criteria. We can speak of a collaborative economy in the narrower sense if three conditions are met: firstly, if the economy is based on collective goods or on such goods where there is only a partial exclusion principle or where it is only partially enforceable or should be enforced. This applies to economic activity with common goods (see Ostrom 1990), club goods (seminal Buchanan 1965) or public

[19] A well-developed body of theory deals with multi-sided markets, which cannot be presented here. Reference is made to the relevant publications by Rochet and Tirole (2003), 991 f., Dewenter (2006), 2 f., Evans and Schmalensee (2007), 154.

goods (see Musgrave 1957).[20] Secondly, if the participation of actors in such a form of economy is long-term. Cooperation in this sense cannot be a short-term, selective one; it must at least be set up as a project. Thirdly, in a collaborative economy, members can influence the respective structure of such collaborative economies as long as they participate. In this respect, a collaborative economy is not unlike a household (see Yates 2016).

Perhaps the best-known example of collaborative economies are cooperatives in which the members' rights to use the common assets are defined and the members are thus also co-owners of these assets and have corresponding incentives to use them sensibly. Upon leaving the cooperative, these (ownership) rights expire accordingly. Although it is not an indispensable prerequisite for forms of collaborative economy, it is certainly conducive to them if the participants know each other personally, ideally if they are "tightly connected social groups" (Benkler 2004, 333) or at least if the participants are not completely anonymous[21]: "Clearly, cooperation is not so easy in the face of strangers" (N'Guyen 2019, 85). This not insignificant aspect will be discussed further below.

However, these parameters are hardly applicable to the dynamically developing and well-known phenomena of the sharing economy such as Uber or Airbnb. They are not collaborative in the original sense, and nothing is shared in the original sense. The European Court of Justice has therefore accurately described Uber as a "transportation services company" (Court of Justice of the European Union 2017), where drivers receive money from their passengers and Uber receives money from its drivers. It is significant that this made headlines, because it did not fit the image of a well-sounding "sharing economy" (for instructive and biting criticism of this, see Newman 2018 from a legal perspective).

7.3.3 The Smallest Common Denominator

This section looks at what the phenomena of the sharing economy of the digital age have in common, distinguishes them from forms of collaborative economy in the proper sense and highlights the crucial success factors.

---

[20] At this point, now from a different perspective, it becomes clear once again that property rights play a central role in a proper understanding of the processes in the digital economy. The three goods listed here have in common that they are not private goods. Elinor Ostrom has great merits in the issue of the commons; she was, *in nuce*, mainly concerned with the question of how scarce natural resources can be used collectively in a sustainable manner. Such commons are not purely public goods in that their use by one has an effect on others. Club goods are also a form of collective use, but in contrast to pure public goods or the commons, excludability is possible with club goods.

[21] Probably the best-known economic contribution to the problem of communal management of goods, "community governance", comes from Ostrom, who also formulated corresponding design principles. See Ostrom (1990). The commons problem as such cannot be discussed here. At the end of the chapter, the relevant aspects of Ostrom's approach will be briefly discussed.

Codagnone and Martens (2016, 6, footnote 5), in a broad scan of the relevant literature, have mentioned three characteristics shared by the authors, two of which will be taken up here: "a) the ability of facilitating exchange among strangers rather than among kin or within community; b) the strong reliance on technology that may also favour offline activities".[22] The participants are usually not owners of the respective platform; the platform is essentially used because of the aforementioned indirect network effects. Digital technology does not simply encourage sharing in the original sense of the word but has made the relationship to property more complex. What does this mean and how can it be differentiated?

Let us first return to the concept of "assets", which was also at the centre of the argumentation of the World Economic Forum and with whose examples we will remain. In this respect, there are basically two possibilities within the framework of the business models of the modern sharing economy. On the one hand, participants can commodify their assets—"space, skills, stuff and time"—via a platform for those periods when they are not using them for themselves. Specifically exemplified with reference to the quote: they can offer their living space via Airbnb, mathematics lessons on a tutoring platform, their mobile home to others when they themselves are not on holiday or spend their time with other people's dogs. This form of platform business model is called *peer-to-peer*; owners of assets, who can be private individuals or commercial suppliers, offer something via platforms. Peer-to-peer platforms organise two-sided markets, as was made clear above. In many varieties of this commodification of assets via a platform, the assets are those that the participants themselves can afford. Of course, they only use the platform itself, it does not belong to them.

This possibility is contrasted with so-called *asset hubs*; what is shared belongs to the platform. In this case, the idea is that participants can use something they cannot or do not want to afford themselves. The platform then makes such goods available to the users in the short term in order to make a profit from their investment in the asset. How can such sharing economy business models be further differentiated?

In principle, differentiations can be made according to the goals of the respective platform. For example, there may be platforms with, but also without the intention of making a profit. If profit is to be made, this can be done via fees at the level of the platform, for example via user fees or percentage participation of the platform in transactions among exchange partners who have found each other on the platform. Another possibility is to generate profit through advertising. This is probably the most striking variant in the digital age, which has already been dealt with in connection with the postulate of open markets and data in the previous chapters. This is because platforms on the internet are of course an excellent way of using the user data that can be generated there to tap market potential for all kinds of things—not just targeted marketing. The aspects of this that are relevant to competition policy have already been briefly discussed.

[22] Point c), "the participation of high cultural capital consumers rather than being limited to a survival mechanisms (sic) among the most disadvantaged", is no less relevant, we will come back to this in the next sub-chapter.

The actual entrepreneurial achievement, i.e. the key element of the sharing economy, is the successful provision of the platform itself. Not least in the business literature, business models that can be attributed to the sharing economy are differentiated even further (e.g. Munez and Cohen 2017; Codagnone et al. 2016, 22f.). For our purposes, let us leave it at the fundamental basis that a platform mediates the demand side and the suppply side and can benefit from this.

It is therefore legitimate to ask what the difference actually is to the platforms not known under the label "sharing". Codagnone and Martens (2016, 12) have proposed an instructive overview and differentiate among the actors involved between peer-to-peer and business-to-consumer solutions. In terms of business objectives, they distinguish between profit-orientated and non-profit solutions. In principle, this differentiation results in three groups of sharing solutions, "true sharing"—which is not for profit and peer-to-peer—and sharing solutions with profit-orientation, which can be "commercial peer-to-peer" or "commercial business-to-customer" (see Codagnone and Martens 2016, 12). This differentiation enables the categorisation of a wealth of different models and provides a good orientation for the purposes of our observations. What is dominant today under the label of the "sharing economy" will essentially be variants "commercial peer-to-peer" and "commercial business-to-consumer" solutions. Codagnone and Martens (2016) choose the term peer-to-peer because there can be consumers on both sides, but according to their observations, consumers and providers are more often confronted with each other. From an economic perspective, this is an exceptionally dynamic spread of the coordination form of two-sided or multi-sided markets. What factors lead to this?

First of all, at least as far as the peer-to-peer variant is concerned, the entry costs for such business models are relatively low. The decisive factor for market success, as already mentioned in an earlier section, is the economies of scale of the network effects that then unfold. Accordingly, it is crucial that a sufficient level of awareness is created so that the costs are covered. The main investment costs are therefore for advertising, less for the actual platform itself. Above a certain size, of course, there are correspondingly higher costs for operating an appropriate technical infrastructure. With reference to the distinction made between peer-to-peer and business-to-consumer, Einav et al. (2015) presented a study that Codagnone and Martens (2016) also refer to and which offers an economic explanation for the differentiation between the two. They base their argument on the marginal costs of production. If these are lower in the business-to-consumer area than in the peer-to-peer area, then only peak demand will be served in the peer-to-peer format. If the opposite is true, the peer-to-peer format displaces the other format: "This explains why P2P sharing platforms are successful in markets with highly fluctuating demand, such as taxi services and tourist accommodation or very short-term labour markets" (Codagnone and Martens (2016, 13).

An important factor for the spread of this form of coordination is the reduction in transaction costs it makes possible. Information and coordination costs for bringing together suppliers and consumers in all areas of life have been massively reduced by the internet. Platforms are the place where indirect network effects can be used cost-effectively, where matching among different participants can be organised cheaply

(Codagnone and Martens 2016, 8). They *prima facie* lead to a higher degree of transparency in certain markets and can significantly reduce search/information and matching costs among participants. This can be understood as a positive welfare effect.

How does this happen in detail? Platforms can reduce information asymmetries by using signalling techniques, for example, in which a supplier makes more detailed information about the characteristics of his offer accessible via the platform, for example, photos of the used car on offer or the potential rendezvous partner. This function can be complemented by so-called screening instruments, for example when users make their experiences with the above-mentioned car dealer or the lonely paramour public within the framework of a forum set up on the corresponding platform. Mutual assessment reduces uncertainties (Dang N'Guyen 2019, 88) and is, not least because of the anonymity, a key to the success of platforms, "(…) one of the salient characteristics of 'sharing economy' platforms (…). The trust that makes the 'sharing economy' possible is the combined results of users' attitudes and of how such attitudes are effectively leveraged by online reputational rating systems and liability insurance schemes" (Codagnone and Martens 2016, 22). The extent to which such instruments are then used rationally (see Mayya et al. 2023) or cause a bias to arise (see Spitko 2020) is another question.

In this respect, the new internet-based platforms are not only a novelty insofar as they bring together a larger number of potential partners, but also because intelligent technology can help to both minimise transaction costs and ensure optimal information for all participants. This is what ultimately makes a truly successful platform and indicates that, beyond the business idea and business model, the use of big data and artificial intelligence is crucial for success.

Depending on the market share the platforms have—we will discuss this problem later—it is also possible for them to impose their own quality requirements on the supply side and thus reduce information asymmetries. Accordingly, the credibility of the supply side is under pressure. Similar to the argumentation of Einav et al. above, where high fixed costs can be decisive for a differentiation of peer-to-peer and business-to-consumer solutions, Codagnone and Martens (2016, 14) mention the relevance of brand sensitivity in this context. Maintaining visibility in certain businesses has the same effect. These are not new techniques, but in general the costs of their application and the possibilities for the creation of two-sided markets have decreased decisively due to digital technology, i.e. in this case mainly the internet and user-friendly apps.

7.3.4 Economic Effects

This section addresses the question of what effects an increasing omnipresence of internet-based two-sided markets now has.

Let us focus the economic effects in the narrower sense first. In what way do the new business models influence the benefits on the sides of demand and supply? Can this perhaps be increased for all participants? The increase in market transparency, thereby the reduction of information asymmetries and, as a result, better-informed decisions can lead to better offers. Such business models can increase the competitive pressure among such suppliers who compete with each other on platforms. This can, for example in the case of providers of accommodation services, i.e. hotels, lead to a better offer in terms of price and quality. However, this is not necessarily the case and therefore cannot be generalised without restrictions. What restrictions have to be taken into account?

For example, in the case of a service such as passenger transport—the well-known example of Uber—the price can be lower than that of the previous offer—in this case that of a traditional taxi service. However, this can also be accompanied by a loss of quality. To stay with the example, the driver may not be as good as a professional taxi driver; the car might not meet the requirements for safety, space and cleanliness that would be required for a licence to provide taxi services (admittedly, platforms try to counter this with appropriate mechanisms, as briefly mentioned above). The list could be continued and is also easily transferable to other areas. After all, many "sharing" offers are based precisely on the fact that they are provided by non-professional providers. This state of affairs has been discussed in the context of minimum standards in many areas—such as the possibility of registering a trade, the German purity law for proper beer, etc.

In our context, two processes are noteworthy in this respect. First that this discussion will probably have to be conducted in ever wider areas of economic exchange. The need for regulation for the production of certain goods and services, which until now could be addressed to certain commercial structures and insofar as forms of organisation kept the costs of publicising, monitoring and enforcing rules low, will now have to be addressed to an undefined group of potential semi-professionals. This means that new transaction costs will arise at the level of the regulator, which will have to be financed through taxpayers' money.

Second, it is striking and seems novel that a remarkable shift is taking place in the relationship between "economy" and "society" through the possibilities of digital platforms, namely that an ever larger number of "normal consumers" are commodifying "space, skills, stuff and time" in certain areas of life and thus, to a certain extent, stepping out of their accustomed social role as consumers and partially professionalising selected elements of their living space. They thus become so-called "prosumers", a portmanteau (1980, 27) designed by Toffler.[23] Against this background, it is remarkable that Van Esterik's (1986) formulation "you are what you own" seems to have become "you are what you can access" in the digital age (Belk 2014). But as long as access really costs, the facts are actually the same, only that property rights are applied in a more differentiated way. It is precisely this differentiation of

[23] This term, of course, originated in a different context, is not a clearly defined term in economic science and should therefore be used with the appropriate caution in the present context. Toffler himself used it to refer both to individuals in the context of the pre-industrial economy and to those of the "third wave", while the term is also used in the context of the commons-based economy. However, it seems illustrative in the context of the various forms of the sharing economy, insofar as it reflects well the new form of hybrid position of the citizen as consumer/producer.

ownership and property rights that is possible on the basis of digitalisation that then leads to an expansion and dynamisation, the commodification described above by the World Economic Forum.

This shift from consumer to prosumer is clearly perceptible, but it does not affect everyone to the same extent. Hellwig et al. (2015) focus on the individual actors and differentiate among the four types of "idealists", "opponents", "pragmatists" and the "normative". Not everyone participates to the same extent in this form of economy. But in whatever form, what is "shared" is actually commodified, so it can be understood as an asset. Therefore all things can become assets because the platform creates the possibility to better utilise capacities that would not have been considered before because of too high transaction costs. This is at the heart of these platform models of the sharing economy, which is why it is at the heart of Munoz and Choen's (2017) definition, cited by Hussein (2023, 6) as particularly balanced. According to them, the sharing economy is a "socio-economic system enabling an intermediated set of exchanges of goods and services between individuals and organizations which aim to increase efficiency and optimization of sub-utilized resources in society" (Munoz and Cohen 2017, 21). The platform thus economically increases the "usefulness" (N'Guyen 2019, 83) of everything possible.

An obvious, fundamental economic policy question here would be how such assets are distributed. One can assume that a group of a few suppliers with large capacities is confronted with a group of many suppliers, each with small capacities. In the extreme case, the first group provides *asset hubs* accordingly. Such a distribution is nothing new at all, but in this context the indirect network effects and size effects that are important for the platforms must also be taken into account, which are relevant e.g. with regard to the revenues from advertising on such platforms. Via platforms such as Airbnb, a large number of suppliers with small capacities then link up. This can also be read as a Long Tail Effect, which was made prominent by Anderson (2006). Fernández-Macías (2018, 10) has described it as a particularly important effect of the use of digital technology that "long-tail markets" emerge at all, "(…) where the demand for low-market products and services can collectively exceed that of large mainstream goods". Thus, under the label of the sharing economy, there are only partially new markets, but many new participants and, as mentioned in the chapter on open markets, there lurks the danger of the winner-takes-it-all-effects.

From the perspective of competition policy, the latter problem is discussed as a problem of market power. The fact that something can be "shared" via a platform does not mean that the basic problem of market power is shared away. Before the age of the sharing economy, the market power problem was considered at the level of the supply side or the demand side in the markets for the goods and services that consumers want to consume or use. Now the problem of the market is at the level of the platform but vis-à-vis those who use it. This is illuminated, for example, by the fact that direct bookings are only considered to a very limited extent for the hotel industry, since overnight accommodation is almost exclusively sought and booked via platforms, not least because of the transaction cost advantages mentioned above. However, due to the decisive role of indirect network effects and economies of scale, in most cases only a few or only one platform remains in the market. And this also means that in certain markets participation in a platform becomes a barrier to entry for suppliers.

One does not even have to consider the forms of discrimination in terms of price[24] and quality and the privacy problem, which is also virulent here, to see that a tendency towards monopolisation can be observed here. There may be more than one platform for a given market, but rarely will many be worthwhile. Platforms in the sharing economy, just as shown in the chapter concerning open markets, can thus become so-called "gatekeepers" (see Geradin 2021). Multi-homing must be possible for the users (see with regard to the sharing economy Loginova et al. 2022; also already Gabszewicz and Wauthy 2004) to ensure that the platforms remain under the corresponding competitive pressure. This pressure should force all players to use possibilities for generating more market transparency as much as possible. It should foster them to outdo each other e.g. in the protection of privacy and not its illumination.

Furthermore, in the long term, the competitive pressure among the platforms will be decisive in bringing prices down. After all, the platform's business model does not inherently reduce the price, nor does it necessarily do so equally for all participants. Since the users of the platform are connected to each other via indirect network effects, the effect can also occur within the framework of such "sharing" models—similar to the example of the single bar in the chapter on open markets—that one group is cross-subsidised by the other (see Bakos and Halaburda 2020). Thus, one group may pay a price that is far above marginal costs. This is not atypical for sharing economy business models: "(…) pricing to one side below marginal cost is not a predatory behaviour but rather a common profit maximising strategy in two-sided markets" (Codagnone and Martens 2016, 8, footnote 9).

In this context, the question then arises again as to what conditions of use the platforms can impose on the suppliers operating there. Conditions of participation can, for example, make specific investments necessary in the form of quality requirements for the suppliers. Whether these lead to an increase in the quality expected by potential customers must be weighed up with reference to the problems mentioned above with the example of taxi services and also with the possibility that specific investments can also lead to anti-competitive lock-in effects. This results in a complex field of tension, as we have already observed in connection with the use of data in the previous chapter. Thus, competition policy, consumer protection and data protection are also challenged in the area addressed here.

The effects of the new sharing business models are thus quite ambiguous. Not only does "sharing" sound better than "owning", such models are also frequently discussed in connection with the topic of sustainability and the protection of the environment (see, for example, World Economic Forum 2013; DuPuis and Rainwater 2015, 2; Deloitte 2015). The basis of this positive slander is probably two facts. One is the confusion of terms described above, which simply confuses the new

[24] In this respect, differentiating studies for different markets are still lacking; for example, Gibbs et al. (2018) have shown in an empirical study that the private providers on platforms on the market for overnight stays make less use of price discrimination than is the case in the constellation business-to-consumer.

platform-based business models functioning under the label "sharing economy" with collaborative economy. It is not for nothing that Elinor Ostrom has left a lasting mark on the discourse on the use of natural resources. However, she did not have the business models in mind that we are talking about here, but rather the principles of the cooperative economy mentioned above.

The other issue is the assumption that existing resources are better used by more users, i.e. that there are efficiency gains (Hossein 2023, 2) and that an externality problem can therefore be reduced with regard to the use of environmental resources. On closer inspection, however, the question of whether this is true cannot be answered clearly without further ado.

To gain clarity, it is worth taking a look at the question of what is actually shared, i.e. what is actually exchanged on the two-sided markets. If we again take the optimistic quotation as a starting point—"space, skills, stuff and time"—then considerations on the topic of sustainability and the conservation of resources will probably refer primarily to "space" and "stuff". Immaterial goods, such as the time of a romantic rendezvous or the provision of services do have not necessarily have effect on the environment—unless a service that is associated with environmentally harmful effects is now demanded more frequently than before. If we stay with material goods, the quotation clearly demonstrates that among the various goods, only consumer goods can be "shared", i.e. they are used by more users. However, this does not mean that everyone would have bought such a good as an alternative, because this would have had to be paid for again; and the fact that the possibility of use by more users is now given does not mean that less of the corresponding good is then actually produced overall.

Meyer and Therl (2017, 87f.) offer five aspects with the aim of determining which goods are "shared" on such platforms and why, and which remain exclusively in the possession of individuals. Firstly, the *frequency* of use is decisive, because the more frequently a good is used, the more likely it is to be bought and not borrowed, *vulgo* "shared". Secondly, it matters how independent one can be in the use of the good, i.e. whether or not one has unrestricted *access* to it at all times. Thirdly, more or less *uncertainty* must be avoided in the case of different goods. Fourth, option utility and *availability* play a role; and fifth, *cost constraints*. One may simply not be able to afford a certain good. It is therefore not surprising that the more income people have, the less they make use of sharing options (Fremstad 2018). Also unsurprising are the agglomeration effects that are relevant in this context. Thus, sharing economy models are naturally much more widespread in cities than in rural regions, where, on the one hand, economies of scale can unfold less well, but on the other hand, distances unfold their transaction cost effect; sharing is an urban trend. Codagnone and Martens (2016, 6, footnote 5) have accordingly also noted this as the third essential common feature of the sharing economy phenomena not yet mentioned above: "(c) the participation of high cultural capital consumers rather than being limited to a survival mechanisms (sic) among the most disadvantaged".

Now, in an economy with free individuals, these restrictions already precede the decision whether they want to "share" something or not. In any case, the macroeconomic effect cannot be clearly determined. If a good, such as a car, tends to be "shared" more than before, i.e. its capacity is better utilised, then this effect would ultimately also have to be felt in the number of cars purchased, so sharing would first of all have a price effect on such goods that can also be "shared", but possibly also a negative effect on economic growth, because less of them would be produced overall.

However, as long as it is not a question of digital goods, wear and tear occurs for all consumer goods. The fact that goods are used via a sharing platform does not mean that less of such goods would therefore be produced. If even just as many such goods are produced, but they are more utilised, then there is more wear and tear overall and no resources are saved, on the contrary.

Thus, a similarly complex problem arises here as in the calculation of a realistic biological footprint. The resource consumption of an exclusive use of a good and a use in the form of sharing of the same good would have to be offset against each other; however, this will not be a trivial empirical task. As a proxy, the production quantity of a certain good and the quantity of scrapped units of the same good over a period could be compared. But in order to derive a meaningful statement from this, one would have to clarify, on the one hand, the question of the extent to which—precisely because platforms make two-sided markets possible—many more resources are not being commodified than before. And on the other hand, one would need solid knowledge about the respective product life cycle. This cannot be answered unequivocally.

However, to stay with well-known examples that are obvious, one could ask whether the existence of transportation services such as Uber might not mean that more kilometres are travelled by car than before. The fact that the sharing economy can also and especially cause externalities problems with regard to the conservation of natural resources is made quite clear by the example of Airbnb. On the one hand, the possibility of short-term commodification of private housing leads to short-term overnight stays without associated hotel services becoming relatively cheaper and homeowners earning extra money without much effort through the short-term commodification of their assets. However, this leads to rising rents, less available housing in inner cities and the decline of the quality of life of entire city districts (see, for example, Gold 2019). And whether the sharing of electric scooters provided by asset hubs in urban areas has helped save the planet? Probably even less convincingly (see also Fraiberger and Sundararajan, 2015, 7; similarly Horton and Zeckhauser 2016, 7).

Certainly, there are considerable differences with regard to the concrete design of the business models as well as with regard to the respective goods and resources made available. As far as the concrete design of the business models is concerned, the "bundles of rights" approach discussed above also helps, because of course the corresponding user contracts specify accordingly what consequences would occur if, for example, the rented flat were to be damaged or the electric scooter were to be deformed and then sold. As was already shown in the previous chapter, a differentiated view of property rights can also lead to further exploitation of the possibilities of the division of labour. In this context, it should be remembered that such models can also be used in the markets upstream of the consumer markets. In operations management, platforms are shared in order to generate efficiency gains that can then be passed on to the consumer. It was basically not an idea for which digitalisation would have been needed, and therefore it will not be discussed specifically here. However, it should be noted that digital technology can certainly be helpful in further exploiting existing forms of organisation in this area.

On this basis, it can certainly not be said that the new platform-based business models are bad per se, e.g. with regard to saving resources. This will have to be assessed differently from case to case. Open source software is a good example of how sharing can also lead to improvement. Of course, the low transaction costs of platform solutions, beyond the possibility of greater utilisation of existing assets, can also be an incentive for used goods to be sold rather than simply discarded, and in this respect it can be easier for appropriate secondary markets to emerge (see, for example, Fremstad 2017). In this respect, the argument of resource conservation would certainly hold water. However, it is important to keep this in mind when models of the sharing economy appear as elements of economic policy strategies—one could also think here of very specific questions of urban development.

All in all, to summarise the aspects mentioned, the business models of the sharing economy obviously do not mean a fundamental change in the economy in the sense that more is shared, less is consumed and more is cooperated. The term "sharing" is simply misleading. Nonetheless, the accompanying changes seem epoch-making and this on several levels.

Firstly, at the level of markets. Where up to the digital age different suppliers and demanders faced each other, today platform solutions take on an integrating role and platform markets emerge. This is accompanied by the problems that were dealt with in the chapter on the question of open markets. Because big data and AI have considerable potential for leveraging market power and facilitating abuse.

Secondly, at the level of goods, because those goods that were still consumer goods in the age before digitalisation are now partly becoming capital goods.

Thirdly, the position of people in the tense zone between economy and society is changing. On the basis of the platform models, the connectivity among people is indeed being expanded. But on the one hand, this connectivity happens essentially anonymously among those for whom the platform organises the matching, while the platform itself has an interest in knowing as much as possible about the actors involved in order to be more successful via AI. On the other hand, this connectivity comes about solely because and only as long as the operators of platforms, platform ecosystems and their components earn enough. Consumers becoming "prosumers" mean that commodification is further extended, digital technology leads to a "(…) massive expansion of markets" (Fernández-Macías 2018, 10). Parker et al. (2016) already pointed out in 2016 that the platform economy is leading to the commodification of more and more areas of life. In contrast, the long-term commitment that both ownership and non-anonymous interaction compel is being pushed back. The expansion of the economy may therefore come at the expense of social capital (see Gold 2019; Rogers 2017). This makes it clear once again that the elements of the central question of this book—"how to give the modern industrialised economy a functioning and humane order"—are now accompanied by new and much more complex conditions.

7.3.5 *Considerations on the Consequences for Citizens and the Regulator*

This section seeks to bring together the issues outlined above and consider what the implications are for citizens on the one hand and regulators on the other.

Do the new business models of the "sharing economy" require new regulation? Now, the sharing economy is not necessarily about new markets, but about an expansion of existing markets via new technological possibilities. Matching, which is cheaper in terms of transaction costs, expands the possibilities of commodification, creating new substitution relationships—so this is basically nothing new to begin with. However, the scope of this phenomenon in terms of the number of participants, in terms of the changes caused in markets with regard to market shares, market conduct and business models, and in terms of the observable dynamics also raises new questions. On the one hand with regard to the citizen, and on the other hand with regard to the state, which is obliged to its citizens. Several areas are addressed here. Let us start with general questions before looking at some partial aspects.

The questions arising in connection with the sharing economy are similar to those raised in the previous section in connection with the question of property in the digital age. In principle, it can therefore be said that it does not seem very useful to introduce general regulations, but rather to focus on where a market failure can actually be diagnosed (Peitz and Schwalbe, 2016, 245; see also the example of Airbnb given above). As outlined in the previous section, this affects in a novel field of tension the three areas of consumer protection, competition policy and data protection. As we have seen, however, these three areas are inextricably linked in the digital age. In the following, we will therefore only briefly outline the connections that are conspicuous for the phenomenon of the sharing economy.

First of all, the question of the extent to which new regulation is necessary in this area is answered differently. Basically, from an economic point of view, the question arises as to how the costs of regulatory measures relate to the costs of external effects or the procurement and/or provision of information by the existing suppliers or consumers. There is also the position that regulation could cause greater costs than the new market failure problems caused by the new business models or that the internet in particular could solve market failure problems such as that of Akerlof's "lemons" by itself (see for example Thierer et al. 2015).

The concerns that arise in this context essentially focus on the problem that the regulator is exposed to the danger of being influenced by the powerful addressees of the regulation, i.e. there can be a "regulatory capture" (Stigler 1971; on Dal Bó 2006, 204f.). Licensing of platforms, for example, could then also lead to the incumbent rather than the consumer being protected (Codagnone and Martens 2016, 21 with reference to Einav et al. 2015). That this danger is greater than the danger of monopolisation or market failure presupposes the assumption that regulation can be sufficiently replaced by the mechanisms for documenting reputation which can be realised on the platforms themselves. Accordingly, some call for complete deregulation (Deloitte 2015. Similarly Demary, 2015, 15.). The fact that the label "sharing" is used so demonstratively can be read as an expression of a "value and vision-loaded" discourse (Codognone and Mertes 2016, 18), but in this respect it can also be understood as the expression of a rhetorical protective positioning of the platform operators, which is sometimes reminiscent of mimicry.[25] In this context, too, the question of consumer protection in the sense that the parties involved are provided with adequate information is inextricably linked to the primarily economic problem of market failure.

Which solution one prefers with regard to information asymmetry, to remain with this central aspect, ultimately depends on how reliable one considers the corresponding instruments of screening or signalling to be. However, the problems involved have already been briefly mentioned above. It can never be said with certainty that the ratings of users are appropriate and correct, nor that the publicly available ratings are representative. There is also a problem with regard to signalling, because the presentation of different offers by the platform can have a distorting effect on consumer decisions.

Of course, new challenges arise for consumer protection beyond the information problem. In the context of the sharing economy, consumer protection also has the task "(…) to protect customers from fraud, liability, and practices that might endanger public health or safety" (Ranchordas 2015, 420). The focus varies depending on the sector. But even across industries, there is the challenge—similar to that described in the previous chapter—of sensibly balancing the necessary protective measures with the opportunities for innovation (see also Katz 2015). In order to react to the increased complexity of the business models of the sharing economy, more detailed governance regulations are also necessary here. This necessity has already become apparent in the previous chapter on the problem of data ownership. In a sense, this is the other side of the coin with regard to the phenomenon of the sharing economy.

The need for such smaller governance rules in response to increased complexity is evident in many areas in the digital age. This is particularly evident in the hybrid role of the "prosumer" mentioned above, which comes into focus with the sharing economy, and from which numerous new questions arise. For example, from the perspective of the taxation of income and corresponding depreciation options (e.g. Oei and Ring 2016); with regard to the need for social security contributions, labour protection, workers' rights (de Stefano 2016) and liability issues (e.g. McPeak 2016; Carder et al. 2017). The list could easily be continued. The heated and public debate about Uber's services also shows that existing business regulations can also come into conflict with innovative business models. Everywhere, new boundaries must be appropriately explored.

One of the difficulties for the regulator arises precisely from the fact that if new substitution relationships have come about in an existing market, the areas to be regulated can be different from the previous ones, such as those that have arisen

[25] See Newman (2018), who takes pains to debunk this position as "Silicon Valley rhetoric" and is quite thorough in doing so: "Uber scrupulously refers to itself as facilitating 'ridesharing'—by my count, more than seventy of its digital press releases include the term" (Newman 2018, 2).

through industries. This makes the search process to discover areas to be regulated and to design appropriate rules more complex and costly. One may argue that here, too, competition may be the best discovery procedure, but in doing so, one must also take into account the possibilities that arise from the interplay of, firstly, decisive economies of scale, secondly, indirect network effects and, thirdly, the possibilities of processing large amounts of data. For the sharing economy, this also means that the "pre-digital" discovery process of competition based on price signals is being pushed back in favour of an algorithm-based discovery process based on different types of data.

Now, the tendency towards monopolisation by platforms already described above will, of course, be extended to as many areas in which sharing models function. The conditions under which peer-to-peer and business-to-consumer models compete have already been mentioned above with reference to Einav et al. (2015). In terms of competition policy, the same questions arise here as with all other—non-sharing economy!—platform-based business models or digital ecosystems. The possibility of linking data even across several platforms—one possible constellation would be the condition of a platform to log in with a Facebook account (see Codagnone and Martens 2016, 22 with reference to Thierer et al. 2015)—then generates further business opportunities that go far beyond the original "sharing" of "prosumers" and offer the platform the possibility of leveraging its knowledge.

7.4 Concluding Considerations

This chapter draws some conclusions from the aspects of the sharing economy presented in the previous sections.

What conclusions can be drawn from what has been said in this chapter? In order to appropriately classify that property, i.e. ownership of the means of production is mentioned as a principle of the market economy, one must first remember that this had to be particularly emphasised in Eucken's original concept as the opposite of collective ownership—at that time a different concept to deal with problems of the role of the economy and the claims of the society. However, this private property can only become an effective factor of the market economy if the institutional conditions create corresponding incentives. It is therefore essential to combine it with freedom of contract and the liability of the actors.

This much can be implied after the problems highlighted in the previous sections that the economy under the conditions of digitalisation has gained considerably in complexity. The lynchpin of this is the ability of digital technology to collect, store and also process data.

The striking development that a lot of money can be made with data therefore served as an obvious starting point. It became clear that data is not some new commodity and common metaphors of data as new "oil" or "gold" are inappropriately simplistic. Rather, data is a highly context-specific product of interaction that can then be processed, stored and sold again, in further, different interactions and contexts—and so on. And in this respect, the question of who owns the data is simply not formulated in a complex enough way. In order to make it clear where the change of digitalisation actually comes in, one must also consider the two preconditions mentioned above, namely freedom of contract and responsibility. Then it might be more appropriate to ask not only who owns "the data", but who is allowed to know exactly what, about whom and/or what and for how long. Data and data processing are, as was already made clear in connection with the considerations on the price system, a form of *knowledge*, and knowledge is, as has been clear at least since Hayek's "competition as a discovery procedure", the actual basis of social coordination, including that of the economy.

If we think further, the same cross-context absorption process becomes clear here that was already described above with regard to data and the price system. In the age of digitalisation, property and freedom of contract have thus come under rather more complex conditions. If the economy is about payment or relevant non-payment, then it is logically necessary that everything that can serve as the basis of exchange for money is also defined in terms of property law in order to make exchange possible at all. Interestingly, digital technology, by making much of what was previously simply "known" by humans now more accurate, more extensive and tradable like a commodity, has now blurred the previous boundaries.

Overall, as the chapter on the sharing economy made clear, this leads to a tendency towards the commodification of all areas of life, which sometimes, but by no means everywhere, has something to do with "sharing" in the actual sense. The phenomenon of the sharing economy and its complexity may even best express the way in which digitalisation is changing the economy and affecting society as a whole. And, of course, this then also changes the behaviour of the individuals.

All this then leads to the degree of complexity that is explosive for concrete economic policy. As demonstrated in the chapter on the "bundles of rights", issues of data protection, property rights and competition policy are inextricably intertwined; neither are simple rules of principle possible, nor is the transferability of case-by-case solutions straightforward. This also tends to be at the expense of legal certainty, not unlike what has already been discussed in connection with the "more economic approach" in competition policy (see Schmidtchen 2007; Miceli 2017; Zalewska-Głogowska 2017). Furthermore, the critical trade-off constellations must be taken into account, which must be assessed differently depending on the economic situation or industrial policy agenda, etc.

Of course, even before digitalisation, economic policy was not without trade-offs. However, the possibilities for finding an appropriate legal and institutional framework for these processes are now necessarily more small-scale, more case-by-case and, in view of the developments, also more short-term. This also means that new transaction costs are accumulating with regard to an appropriate economic policy capacity to act, as the extent of necessary scientific, interdisciplinary staff work is growing. The need to explain economic policy action is growing likewise.

However, all this also means that the actors of economic policy are in danger of succumbing to an impression of a larger manoeuvring mass that arises from these piecemeal challenges that cannot be combined into one big, clear, unified line of argument. However, if one takes seriously that the understanding of details is becoming more necessary for appropriate decisions, then, with regard to the possibilities for action at given capacities, the opposite is the case.

References

Acquisti, Alessandro / Grossklags, Jens (2007): What can behavioural economics teach us about privacy? In: Acquisti, Alessandro Gritzalis, Stefanos / Costos Lambrinoudakis, Sabrina di Vimercati (eds): Digital Privacy: Theory, Technologies and Practices. New York: Auerbach Publications, 363–380.

Acquisti, Alessandro / Taylor, Curtis/ Wagman, Liad (2016): The Economics of Privacy. Journal of Economic Literature 54 (2), 442–492.

Akerlof, George A. (1970): The Market for "Lemons": Quality, Uncertainty and the Market Mechanism. The Quarterly Journal of Economics 84 (3), 488–500.

Anderson, Chris (2006): The Long Tail. Why the future of business is selling less of more. New York: Hyperion.

Bakos, Yannis / Halaburda, Hanna (2020): Platform Competition with Multi-homing on Both Sides: Subsidize or Not? Management Science 66 (12), 5599–5607.

Bardhi, Fleura / Eckhardt, Giana M. (2012): Access-Based Consumption: The Case of Car Sharing. Journal of Consumer Research 39 (4), 881–898.

Becker, Gary S. (1965): A theory of the allocation of time. The Economic Journal 75 (299), 493–517.

Belk, Russel (2014): You are what you can access: Sharing and collaborative consumption online. Journal of Business Research 67 (8), 1595–1600.

Benkler, Yochai (2004): Sharing nicely: on shareable goods and the emergence of sharing as a modality of economic production. Yale Law Journal, 114 (2), 273–358.

Besen, Stanley M. / Raskind, Leo J. (1991): An Introduction to the Law and Economics of Intellectual Property. Journal of Economic Perspectives 5 (1), 3–27.

Borgesius, Frederik J. Zuiderveen (2015): Behavioural Sciences and the Regulation on the Internet, in: Alemanno, Alberto / Sibony, Anne-Lise (eds): Nudge and the Law. A European Perspective. Oxford: Hart Publishing, 179–208.

Borgesius, Frederik J. Zuiderveen / Kruikemeier, Sanne / Boerman, Sophie C. / Helberger, Natalie (2017): Tracking Walls, Take-It-or-Leave-It-Choices, the GDPR, and the ePrivacy Regulation. Europan Data Protection Law Review 3 (3), 353–368.

Botsman, Rachel/Rogers, Roo (2010): What's Mine is Yours: The Rise of Collaborative Consumption. New York: HarperCollins.

Buchanan, James M. (1965): An economic theory of clubs. Economica, 32 (125), 1–14.

Carder, Casey / Edwards, Chase / Burns, Stephen (2017): Legal Ambiguity as a Competitive Advantage: Airbnb's Use of Technological Novelty to Avoid Liability. Real Estate Law Journal 46 (3), 352–381.

Chadhuri, Ananish (2021): Behavioural economics and experiments. London, New York: Routledge.

Choi, Jay Pil / Doh-Shin, Jeon / Kim, Byung-Cheol (2019): Privacy and personal data collection with information externalities. Journal of Public Economics 173, May, 113–124.

Coase, Ronald Harry (1960): The problem of social costs. Journal of Law and Economics 3, 1–44.

Codagnone, Cristiano / Martens, Bertin (2016): Scoping the Sharing Economy: Origins, Definitions, Impact and Regulatory Issues. Institute for Prospective Technological Studies. Digital Economy Working Paper 2016/01. JRC100369.

Codagnone, Cristiano / Biagi, Federico / Abadie, Fabienne (2016): The Passions and the Interests: Unpacking the 'Sharing Economy'. Institute for Prospective Technological Studies, JRC Science for Policy Report EUR 27914 EN.

Costa-Cabral, Fancisco / Lynskey, Orla (2017): Family Ties: The Intersection Between Data Protection and Competition in EU Law. Common Market Law Review 54 (1), 11–50.

Court of Justice of the European Union (2017): Press Release No. 136/17. The service provided by Uber connecting individuals with non-professional drivers is covered by services in the field of transport (Dec. 20).

Crémer, Jacques / de Montjoye, Yves-Alexandre / Schweitzer, Heike (2019): Competition policy for the digital era. Final Report. Brussels: European Commission, Directorate-General for Competition.

Dal Bó, Ernesto (2006): Regulatory capture: a review. Oxford Review of Economic Policy 22 (2), 203–225.

Dang N'Guyen, Godefroy (2019): The Collaborative Economy: What Are We Talking About? In: Chamoux, Jean-Pierre: The Digital Era 2. Political Economy Revisited. London, England, Hoboken, New Jersey, ISTE: Wiley, 81–100.

De Gregorio, Giovanni / Ranchordas, Sofia (2020): Breaking Down Information Silos with Big Data: A Legal Analysis of Data Sharing, in: Cannataci, Joe / Falce, Valeria / Pollicino, Oresto (eds): New Legal Challenges of Big Data. Cheltenham: Edward Elgar.

De Stefano, Valerio (2016): The rise of the "just-in-time workforce": on-demand work, crowdwork and labour protection in the "gig-economy". Conditions of work and employment series No. 71. Geneva: International Labour Office.

Deloitte (2015): The Sharing Economy: Share and Make Money: How Does Switzerland Compare? Online: https://www2.deloitte.com/content/dam/Deloitte/ch/Documents/consumer-business/ch-cb-shared-economy-share-and-make-money.pdf (last access: 11.3.2024).

Demary, Vera (2015): Competition in the Sharing Economy. Institut der deutschen Wirtschaft, IW Policy Paper No. 19/2015.

Demsetz, Harold (2002): Property rights, in: Palgrave Dictionary of Law and Economics, Vol. 3, 144–155.

Dewenter, Ralf (2006): Two-Sided Markets, in: MedienWirtschaft 3 (2), 57–62.

Douglas, Erika M. (2021a): The New Antitrust/Data Privacy Law Interface. The Yale Law Journal Forum 18, 647–684.

Douglas, Erika M. (2021b): Digital Crossroads: The Intersection of Competition Law and Data Privacy. Temple University Legal Studies Research Paper No. 2021–40. Available at ssrn: https://papers.ssrn.com/sol3/papers.cfm?abstract_id=3880737 (last access: 7.2.2024).

Dubois, Emilie A. / Schor, Juliet B., / Carfagna, Lindsey B. (2014): New Cultures of Connection in a Boston Time Bank. In: J. Schor & C. Thompson (eds): Practicing Plenitude. New Haven: Yale University Press.

DuPuis, Nicole / Rainwater, Brooks (2015): Shifting Perception of Collaborative Consumption: A National League of Cities Survey on the Sharing Economy. Washington.

Eckardt, Martina / Kerber, Wolfgang (2023): Property Rights Theory, Bundles of Rights on IoT Data, and the Data Act (February 26, 2023). Available at SSRN: https://ssrn.com/abstract=4376833 or https://doi.org/10.2139/ssrn.4376833 (last access: 7.3.2024)

Einav, Liran / Farronato, Chiara / Levin, Jonathan (2015): Peer-to-Peer Markets. National Bureau of Economic Research Working Paper Series No. 21496. Online: https://www.nber.org/papers/w21496 (last acces: 08.05.2023).

Elmer, Greg (2004): Profiling machines: mapping the personal information economy. Cambridge, Massachusetts: MIT Press.

Engels, Barabara (2016): Data portability among online platforms. Internet Policy Review 5 (2).

Esayas, Samson Y. (2015): The role of anonymization and pseudonymisation under the EU data privacy rules: beyond the 'all or nothing' approach. European Journal of Law and Technology 6 (2), 1–20.

European Commission (2016): Flash Eurobarometer 443. Report. e-Privacy.

European Commission (2020): The European data strategy. Shaping Europe's digital future. Online: https://ec.europa.eu/commission/presscorner/api/files/attachment/862109/European_data_strategy_en.pdf.pdf (last access: 7.3.2024).
Evans, David S. / Schmalensee, Richard (2007): The Industrial Organization of Markets with Two-Sided Platforms. Competition Policy International 3 (1), 150–179.
Ezrachi, Ariel / Robertson, Viktoria H.S.E. (2020): Competition, Market Power and Third-Party Tracking. World Competition 42 (1), 5–19.
Fernández-Macías, Enrique (2018): Automation, digitalisation and platforms: Implications for work and employment. Luxembourg: Eurofound, Publications Office of the European Union.
Fraiberger, Samuel P / Sundararajan, Arun (2015): Peer-to-Peer Rental Markets in the Sharing Economy. New York University – Center for Data Science. NYU Stern School of Business Research Paper.
Fremstad, Anders (2017): Does Craigslist Reduce Waste? Evidence from California and Florida. Ecological Economics 132, 135–143.
Fremstad, Anders (2018): Is there a future for sharing? A comparison of traditional and new institutions. Journal of Institutional Economics 14 (4), 595–616.
Fudenberg, Drew / Villas-Boas, J. Miguel (2012): Price Discrimination in the Digital Economy, in: Peitz, M. / Waldfogel, J. (Eds.): Oxford Handbook of the Digital Economy, 254–272.
Furubotn, Eirik G. / Pejovich, Svetozar (1972): Property rights and economic theory: A survey of recent literature. Journal of Economic Literature 10 (4), 1137–1162.
Gabszewicz, Jean J. and Wauthy, Xavier (2004): Two-Sided Markets and Price Competition With Multi-Homing (May 2004). CORE Discussion Paper No. 2004/30, Available at SSRN: https://ssrn.com/abstract=975897 or https://doi.org/10.2139/ssrn.975897 (last access: 7.3.2024).
Gal, Michal S. / Rubinfeld, Daniel (2019): Data Standardization. New York University Law Review 94, 737–770.
Geradin, Damien (2021): What Is a Digital Gatekeeper? Which Platforms Should Be Captured by the EC Proposal for a Digital Market Act? (February 18, 2021). Available at SSRN: https://papers.ssrn.com/sol3/papers.cfm?abstract_id=3788152 (last access: 10.06.2023).
Geradin, Damien / Katsifis, Dimitrios / Karanikioti, Theano (2020): Google as a de facto Privacy Regulator: Analyzing Chrome's Removal of Third-party Cookies from an Antitrust Perspective (November 25). TILEC Discussion Paper No. DP2020–034. Available at SSRN: https://ssrn.com/abstract=3738107 (last access: 10.06.2023).
Gibbs, Chris / Guttentag, Daniel / Gretzel, Ulrike / Yao, Lan / Morton, Jym (2018): Use of dynamic pricing strategies by Airbnb hosts. International Journal of Contemporary Hospitality Management 30 (1), 2–20.
Gold, Allyson (2019): Community Consequences of Airbnb. Washington Law Review 94 (4), 1577–1637.
Graef, Inge / Berlo, Sean van (2021): Towards Smarter Regulation in the Areas of Competition, Data Protection and Consumer Law: Why Greater Power Should Come with Greater Responsibility. European Journal of Risk Regulation 12, 674–698.
Graef, Inge / Clifford, Damian / Valcke, Peggy (2017): Fairness and enforcement. Bridging competition, consumer protection and consumer law. International Data Privacy Law 8 (3), 220–223.
Hacker, Philipp (2017): Personal data, exploitative contracts, and algorithmic fairness: autonomous vehicles meet the internet of things. International Data Privacy Law 7 (4), 266–286.
Hallinan, Dara (2021): The Essence of Data Protection: Essence as a Normative Pivot. European Journal of Law and Technology 12 (3). Online: https://www.ejlt.org/index.php/ejlt/article/view/767/1040 (last access: 10.06.2023).
Hayek, Friedrich August von (1945): The Use of Knowledge in Society. The American Economic Review 35 (4), 519–530.
Hayek, Friedrich August von (1968): Competition as a Discovery Procedure. Translated by Marcellus S. Snow from German of F.A. Hayek's "Der Wettbewerb als Entdeckungsverfahren," a 1968 lecture sponsored by the Institut für Weltwirtschaft at the University of Kiel, published

as No. 56 in the series Kieler Vorträge. The Quarterly Jornal of Austria Economics (3) (Fall 2002), 9–23.
Hellwig, Katharina / Morhart, Felicitas / Girardin, Florent / Hauser, Mirjam (2015): Exploring different types of sharing: A proposed segmentation of the market for "sharing" businesses. Psychology & Marketing, 32 (9), 891–906.
Horton, John J. / Zeckhauser, Richrad J. (2016): Owning, using, and renting: some simple economics oft he "sharing economy". NBER Working Paper 22029.
Hossein, Mokter (2023): Sharing Economy: A Comprehensive Literature Review. International Journal of Hospitality Management (forthcoming). Online: https://www.academia.edu/41938776/Sharing_Economy_A_Comprehensive_Literature_Review_International_Journal_of_Hospitality_Management_forthcoming (last access: 04.05.2023).
Katz, Vanessa (2015): Regulating the Sharing Economy. Berkley Technology Law Journal 30:385, 1067–1126.
Kemp, Katharine (2020): Concealed data practices and competition law: why privacy matters. European Competition Journal. Online: https://papers.ssrn.com/sol3/papers.cfm?abstract_id=3432769 (last access: 10.06.2023).
Kerber, Wolfgang (2019): Data-sharing in IoT Ecosystems and Competition Law: The Example of Connected Cars. Journal of Competition Law & Economics 15, 381–426.
Kerber, Wolfgang (2022a): Specifying and Assigning "Bundles of Rights" on Data: An Economic Perspective, forthcoming in: Hofmann, F. / Raue, B./Zech, H. (eds): Eigentum in der digitalen Gesellschaft. Tübingen: Mohr Siebeck, 151–176.
Kerber, Wolfgang (2022b): Taming Tech Giants: The Neglected Interplay Between Competition Law and Data Protection (Privacy) Law. The Antitrust Bulletin 67 (2), 280–300.
Koopman, Christopher / Mitchell, Matthew / Thierer, Adam (2015): The Sharing Economy: Issues Facing Platforms, Participants, and Regulators. Sharing Economy Workshop, Project No. P17–1200, Fairfax.
Krebs, David (2013): "Privacy by Design": nice-to-have or a necessary principle of data protection law? Journal of Intellectual Property, Information Technology and Electronic Commerce Law 2, 2–20.
Loginova, Oksana X. / Wang, Henry / Liu, Qihong (2022): The impact of multi-homing in a ride-sharing market. The Annals of Regional Science. Western Regional Science Association 69 (1), 239–254.
Mallard, Graham (2017): Behavioural Economics. Newcastle upon Tyne City: Agenda Publishing.
Mayya, Raveesh / Ye, Shun / Viswanathan, Siva / Agarwal, Rajshree (2023): Who Forgoes Screening in Online Markets and Why? Evidence from Airbnb (December 1, 2021). MIS Quarterly, available at SSRN: https://papers.ssrn.com/sol3/papers.cfm?abstract_id=3082018 (last access 10.06.2023).
McPeak, Agnieszka (2016): Sharing Tort Liability in the New Sharing Economy. Connecticut Law Review 49 (1), 171–225.
Meyer, Eric / Theurl, Theresia (2017): Neue Governance Strukturen für die Sharing Economy, in: Detlef Aufderheide et al. (ed): Digitale Wirtschaft und Sharing Economy. Wirtschaftsethische und moralökonomische Perspektiven. Volkswirtschaftliche Schriften 569. Berlin: Duncker & Humblot, 83–104.
Miceli, Thomas J. (2017): The Economic Approach to Law. Stanford: University Press.
Miller, Stephen R. (2016): First Principles for Regulating the Sharing Economy. Harvard Journal on Legislation 53, 147–202.
Munoz, Pablo / Cohen, Boyd (2017): Mapping out the sharing economy: A configurational approach to sharing business modeling. Technological Forecasting and Social Change 125, 21–37.
Musgrave Richard A. (1957): A multiple theory of budget determination. Finanzarchiv / Public Finance Analysis, New Series 17 (3), 333–343.
Nadeem, Shehzad / Schor, Juliet B. / Walker, Edward T. / Lee, C Caroline W. / Parigi, Paolo / Cook, Karen (2015): On the Sharing Economy. Contexts 14.

Newman, John M. (2018): Silicon Valley rhetoric: three myths debunked. CPI Antitrust Chronicle. May.

Norberg, Patricia A., / Horne, Daniel R. / Horne, David A. (2007): The Privacy Paradox: Personal Information Disclosure Intentions versus Behaviors. The Journal of Consumer Affairs 41 (1), 100–126.

OECD (2019): Enhancing access to and sharing of data: Reconciling risks and benefits for data re-use across societies. Paris: OECD Publishing.

OECD (2020a): Measuring the economic value of data and cross-border data flows. A business perspective. OECD Digital Economy papers 297, August.

OECD (2020b): Consumer Data Rights and Competition – Background Note by the Secretariat. 10–12 June.

Oei, Shu-Yi / Ring, Diane M. (2016): Can Sharing Be Taxed? Washington University Law Review 93 (4), 989–1069.

Ostrom, Elinor (1990): Governing the Commons. The Evolution of Institutions for Collective Action. Cambridge: Cambridge University Press.

Parker, Geoffrey G. / Van Alstyne, Marshall W. / Choudary, Sangeet Paul (2016): Platform Revolution. How Networked Markets are Transforming the Economy—and how to make them work for you. New York/London: W. W. Norton & Company.

PCAST (2014): Report to the president. Big data and privacy: a technological perspective. Executive Office of the President. President's Council of Advisors on Science and Technology. Washington, DC.

Petkova, Bilyna / Boehm, Franziska (2017): Profiling and the essence of the right to data protection, in: Poletsky, Jules / Tene, Omer / Selinger, Evan (eds): Cambridge Handbook of Consumer Privacy. Cambridge: University Press, forthcoming. Available at SSRN: https://papers.ssrn.com/sol3/papers.cfm?abstract_id=2911894 (last access: 10.06.2023).

Ranchordas, Sofia (2015): Does Sharing Mean Caring? Regulating Innovation in the Sharing Economy. Minnesota Journal of Law, Science & Technology 16 (1), 413–475.

Robertson, Viktoria H.S.E. (2020): Excessive data collection: Privacy considerations and abuse of dominant position in the era of big data. Common Market Law Review 57, 161–190.

Rochet, Jean-Charles / Tirole, Jean (2003): Platform Competition in Two-Sided Markets. Journal of the European Economic Association 1 (4), 990–1029.

Rogers, Brishen (2017): The Social Costs of Uber. University of Chicago Law Review Online 82 (1), 85–102.

Rutherford, Donald (1995): Routledge Dictionary of Economics. London and New York: Routledge.

Schmidtchen, Dieter (2007): The more economic approach to European competition law. Tübingen: Mohr Siebeck.

Schor, Juliet (2014): Debating the Sharing Economy. Essay. Great Transition Initiative. Online: https://greattransition.org/publication/debating-the-sharing-economy (last access: 06.05.2023).

Schwalbe, Ulrich / Peitz, Martin (2016): Kollaboratives Wirtschaften oder Turbokapitalismus? Perspektiven der Wirtschaftspolitik 17 (3), 232–252.

Selinger, Evan (2018): The Cambridge handbook of consumer privacy. Cambridge, United Kingdom: Cambridge University Press.

Shubladze, Sandro (2023): How To Make Use Of The New Gold: Data. Forbes. March 27, 2023, 07:15am EDT. Online: https://www.forbes.com/sites/forbestechcouncil/2023/03/27/how-to-make-use-of-the-new-gold-data/ (last access: 11.06.2023).

Sibony, Anne-Lise / Alemanno, Alberto (2015): The Emergence of Behavioural Policy-Making: A European Perspective, in: Alemanno, Alberto / Sibony, Anne-Lise (eds): Nudge and the Law. A European Perspective. Oxford: Hart Publishing, 1–26.

Smith, Adam (1762): Glasgow Edition of the Works and Correspondence Vol. 5, Lectures On Jurisprudence, edited by R. L. Meek, D. D. Raphael and P. G. Stein (Indianapolis: Liberty Fund, 1982). Accesible online by The Online Library of Liberty, a Project Of Liberty Fund, Inc.: https://competitionandappropriation.econ.ucla.edu/wp-content/uploads/sites/95/2017/04/LecturesOnJurisprudence.pdf (last access: 19.11.2022).

Solove, Daniel J. (2021): The Myth of the Privacy Paradox. 89 George Washington Law Review 1, GWU Legal Studies Research Paper No. 2020–10, Available at SSRN: https://papers.ssrn.com/sol3/papers.cfm?abstract_id=3536265 (last access: 10.06.2023).
Specht-Riemenschneider, Louisa / Kerber, Wolfgang (2022): Designing Data Trustees – A Purpose-Based Approach. Berlin: Konrad-Adenauer-Stiftung.
Spitko, E. Gary (2020): Reputation Systems Bias in the Platform Workplace. Brigham Young University Law Review 2019 (5), 1271–1332.
Stalla-Bourdillon, Sophie / Knight, Alison (2017): Anonymous data vs. personal data – A false debate: An EU perspective on anonymization, pseudonymization and personal data. Wisconsin International Law Journal, 284–322.
Statista (2023): Revenue of platform providers in the sharing economy worldwide in 2017 and 2022. Online: https://www.statista.com/statistics/878844/global-sharing-economy-revenue-platform-providers/ (last access: 14.08.2023).
Stigler, George J. (1971): The Theory of Economic Regulation. The Bell Journal of Economics and Management Science 2 (1), 3-21.
Stucke, Maurice E. (2018): Should We Be Concerned About Data-opolies? 2 Georgetown Law Technology Review 275, 275–324.
Sunstein, Cass R. / Thaler. Richard H. (2003): Libertarian Paternalism is not an Oxymoron. The University of Chicago Law Review 70, 1159–1202.
Suntum, Ulrich van / Böhm, Tobias / Oelgemöller, Jens / Ilgmann, Cordelius (2011): Walter Eucken's Principles of Economic Policy Today. CAWM Discussion Paper No. 49. Preliminary version. August.
Thaler, Richard H. / Sunstein. Cass R. (2009): Nudge: improving decisions about health, wealth, and happiness. New York: Penguin Books.
The Economic Times (2018): Data is the 21st century's oil, says Siemens CEO Joe Kaeser. ET Bureau. Last Updated: May 24, 2018, 08:50 AM IST. Online: https://economictimes.indiatimes.com/magazines/panache/data-is-the-21st-centurys-oil-says-siemens-ceo-joe-kaeser/articleshow/64298125.cms?from=mdr (last access: 11.06.2023).
The Economist (2017): The World's Most Valuable Resource Is No Longer Oil, but Data, print edition, 6th May.
Thierer, Adam / Koopman, Christopher / Hobson, Anne / Kuiper, Chris (2015): How the Internet, the Sharing Economy, and Reputational Feedback Mechanisms Solve the "Lemons Problem". Mercatus Working Paper. George Mason University Mercatus Center. Online: https://www.mercatus.org/media/60071/download (last access: 09.05.2023).
Toffler, Alvin (1980): The Third Wave. New York: William Morrow and Company.
Van Esterick, Penny (1986): Generating Status Symbols: You Are What You Own. Paper presented at Annual Conference of the Association for Consumer Research, Toronto, Ontario, Canada.
Wein, Thomas (2022): Data Protection, Cookie Consent, and Prices. Economies 10 (307). Institute of Economics, Leuphana University of Lueneburg.
Weitzmann, Martin L. (1986): The Share Economy. Conquering Stagflation. Cambridge, MA: Harvard University Press.
World Economic Forum (2013): Young Global Leaders Circular Economy Innovation & New Business Models Dialogue. Young Global Leaders Sharing Economy Dialogue Position Paper. Geneva: World Economic Forum.
Yates, Luke (2016): Sharing, households and sustainable consumption. Journal of Consumer Culture 39 (4), 881–98.
Zalewska-Głogowska, Marta (2017): The more economic approach under article 102 TFEU: a legal analysis and comparison with US antitrust law. Baden-Baden: Nomos.
Zervas, Georgius / Proserpio, Davide / Byers, John W. (2016): The Rise of the Sharing Economy: Estimating the Impact of AirBnB on the Hotel Industry. Boston University Working Paper.

Chapter 8
Labour and Incomes

> I regard it as the major domestic challenge, really, of the sixties, to maintain full employment at a time when automation, of course, is replacing men. (John F. Kennedy 1962)

8.1 The Perspective of This Chapter

This chapter focuses on the concrete impact of digitalisation on employees and labour markets, as well as on incomes. It focuses on the problems of individuals or specific groups of people in work.

The remainder of this chapter is structured as follows. Section 8.2 discusses the societal impact of technological change and briefly discusses the relevance of Eucken's approach.

Section 8.3 focuses on the impact of digitalisation on employment. It distinguishes between occupations and tasks and describes the characteristic field of tension between effects of hypercompensation and displacement effects. An own subsection is devoted to the qualitative aspects of the change in the labour market.

Section 8.4 looks at the effects of digitalisation on the distribution of incomes generated by human labour.

Section 8.5 summarises the arguments and draws some general consequences for policy by relating it to the normative demand of an efficient economy for a humane society.

© The Author(s), under exclusive license to Springer Nature Switzerland AG 2024
J. J. Dötsch, *Economic Policy in the Digital Age*, Contributions to Economics,
https://doi.org/10.1007/978-3-031-53047-0_8

8.2 Technological Change, Labour and Wealth

This chapter provides a short overview regarding the relevant background. It proceeds in two steps.

Section 8.2.1 sheds light on the social consequences of technological development and economic progress, which are extremely important for the purposes of these considerations.

Section 8.2.2 explains the most important parameters of the selected heuristic access structure and its particular relevance in times of digital change.

8.2.1 Social Impact

This section examines the significance of technological change for society and how the impact of digital technology differs from that of earlier technological achievements.

Technological change has always had an impact on economies, labour and labour markets.[1] So does the digital age actually bring anything new? The following chapter addresses the question of how the digital transformation is now causing specific forms of change for the working population and labour markets.

All major economic-social upheavals induced by technological change, whether one speaks of three (Rifkin 2011), four (Schwab 2017) or five (Freeman and Louçã 2001) industrial revolutions, can be associated with decisive processes of profound change both in labour markets (Mariniello 2022, 284) and with regard to the primary distribution of the wealth generated. In principle, such critical periods of major change are a basic phenomenon of the modern, industrialised economy, because the more extensively the work of an economy is mechanised and the more differentiated the division of labour, the more extensive the shift caused by technological innovations.

Just as in chemistry transformation processes generate heat, none of these shifts are without adjustment costs, that is to say, "transitions are costly, at least for some" (Mariniello 2022, 294f.). Polanyi's "Great Transformation" (2001, first published in 1944) is one of the most influential overall accounts of such processes in the context of industrialisation, showing well that such adjustment costs can be very painful on the one hand, and on the other that changes of this magnitude tend to be met with resistance. Is such resistance justified?

First of all, it is common for people to react to change with uncertainty and also fear, which can also be translated into resistance. Within economics, one aspect of

[1] The effect of technology on markets is not a one-way street, of course there are reciprocal effects. For the problem area targeted in this chapter, for example, the ageing of the population and the resulting shortage of skilled workers would be a motive for investing in digital technology to compensate for this shortage. Such connections were discussed in Sect. 2.1.3. Here we will now look at the extent to which the changes made possible by digital technology are specific.

this psychological predisposition became prominent by Kahnemann and Tversky (1979) as "loss aversion". With reference to economic transformation processes, the examples, such as the so-called Luddites of the age of industrialisation protesting against change (Caprettini and Voth 2020; Horn 2005), are legion (see Mokyr et al. 2015). The fact that this phenomenon seems to be booming again today (see Donelly 1986; Amies 2022) is a good symptom of the perceived scope of the current processes of change. It is widely associated with the fear of job loss through AI and robotisation, as illustrated by a fairly recent news article title, "A spectre is haunting…"—its name is "automation angst" (The Economist 2015; empirical on the topic Arntz et al. 2022).

So are the current, technically induced changes in the economy and society actually nothing new—or does digitalisation confront us with new challenges? Its potential for disruptive effects on the labour market has already attracted widespread attention (Brynjolfsson and McAfee 2014 or Ford 2015). However, assessments of the current changes differ. Some treat them as business as usual: "It may be reasonable to expect that this time, with the Fourth Industrial Revolution brought about by technological progress, is not going to be any different" (Marinielli 2022, 283). Or is it different this time, is the capacity of digital technology leading to robots and artificial intelligence becoming perfect substitutes for certain forms of labour?

Based on the previous considerations of what digitalisation means, this chapter takes the position that the current change has a new character. This is due to three reasons. Firstly, the current changes are *more complex than the previous ones.* Secondly—as was already pointed out in the chapter in the first part on digitalisation—the phenomenon of digitalisation has *a wider scope* than, for example, mechanisation, steam power or electricity. And thirdly, the age of digitalisation shows an outstandingly high *speed* of change or rather an *accelerating* effect on cross-sector developments.[2]

8.2.2 On the Perspective of Eucken's Principles

The following section illustrates the extent to which Eucken's principles represent an appropriate heuristic for understanding the impact of digital technology on the world of work and the distribution of income.

Eucken's principles come into a new light. As already explained in the introductory part and partly applied in the previous chapters, it makes sense from today's perspective to combine some of the principles and to additionally take into account contemporary insights.

With regard to the phenomenon of the threat to human labour by robots and AI, two of Eucken's four "regulative principles" are relevant, namely the *correction of*

[2] There is a separate discussion on the topic of such waves of development. However, the fact that the intervals are getting smaller seems to be a common, undisputed assumption of the type of waves diagnosed.

anomalous labour supply on the one hand and *income policy* on the other. What does this mean in this context?

The point of reference for Eucken's considerations is the model of perfect competition. In contrast to this, imbalances naturally arise in real economies. To take up an illustrative example for the subject area of this chapter from Eucken himself, such imbalances can arise in such a way that "(…) as a result of the increase in population (…) a wage pressure (can) set in in an area, which (can) intensify when, as a result of the wage pressure, more workers are forced onto the labour market" (Eucken 2004, 303, own translation).

Another example from Eucken could even apply specifically to the problem context of a potential substitution of human labour by digital technology considered here:

> (…) because of the implementation of technical improvements, redundancies occur on individual labour markets, which cause wages to slide. The establishment of a new equilibrium can be difficult due to the fact that the decline in wages gives rise to an increased supply of labour, i.e. not only the workers who were initially laid off, but also other workers seeking employment. (Eucken 2004, 303f., own translation)

Of course, digitalisation is not directly synonymous with this kind of redundancy. However, as already indicated above, technical change of course never takes place without changes in the employment structure of an economy and this then always has social effects. Eucken himself has also directly described this connection as an "economic and social policy problem" (Eucken 2004, 304, own translation). How is this to be understood?

Thus, with regard to labour, the labour market and the income earned from it, there are actually three dimensions that need to be considered in connection with the effects of technical change: firstly, the question of the *concrete forms of work* and the working place, of "(…) regulations on the length of the working day and other protective measures of workers, in particular of children and women" (Suntum et al. 2011, 8). Secondly, the dimension of the *labour market* in the narrower sense and the related challenge for policy as to how the formation of occurring imbalances can be cushioned. And thirdly, there is of course a, generally speaking, *social dimension*, because where there is only very poorly paid work or no work at all, precarious conditions arise. Whether and how well paid work can be is, of course, also a result of processes on the market.

These three dimensions influence each other. Obviously the first influences the second, and this in turn has an impact on the third dimension. Nevertheless, all three also have an effect independently of each other, each in light of how the institutional conditions change. Economic policy in this area is therefore, basically, faced with the challenge of to what extent technological change can be permitted, which is essential for positive effects on prosperity, but whose effects do not undermine the prerequisites for a sustainably stable social order and the legitimacy of its institutions (see Blix 2017, 9).

For this reason, too, it seems appropriate for the purposes of this book to deal with another of the regulating principles—that of *income policy* here at the same time. For even if the competitive order is better able to coordinate the distribution of economic output and income on the basis of price signals than central planning, it is by no means perfect in this respect. With regard to this problem, Eucken's remarks are by no means less relevant today than they were at the time they were written. For even if the coordination system of the market is used "(…) (this) distribution mechanism (…) also leaves questions open, and it needs correction. Significant differences in the distribution of purchasing power are formed, and the result is that production is directed towards the satisfaction of relatively insignificant needs, while urgent needs of other income earners are not satisfied yet. (…) The distribution, which takes place in the competitive order, requires correction" (Eucken 2004, 300, own translation). Eucken had concrete instruments in mind regarding the distribution problem and "(…) explicitly associated income policy with a progressive income tax which he favoured both for distributional and efficiency reasons" (Suntum et al. 2011, 8).

The considerations set out here cannot serve as an in-depth discussion of concrete instruments that can be used to mitigate the problems that arise in workplaces, labour markets or through the unequal distribution of income, but are aimed at a better understanding of *the extent to which digitalisation has a specific effect on labour markets and the distribution of income*, i.e. which groups are particularly affected and why.

To this end, the next sections elaborate the effects of digitalisation with regard to the three dimensions of *concrete forms of work*, the *labour market* and the *social dimension*. To make this overall context understandable, the next two chapters are structured as follows. Section 8.3 explains what is special about the current technological change and focuses on the role of digitalisation in terms of employment in developed economies. Section 8.4 then looks at the corresponding effects on distribution.

8.3 Digitalisation and Employment

The following paragraphs deal with the question of the extent to which digital technology effects the degree and structure of employment because it can potentially be a substitute for human labour. Therefore, the first thing to be clarified is the nature of the new technology in relation to human labour.

With regard to this question, there is a very broad discourse on what is meant by digitalisation and somewhat more specific terms as e.g. "artificial intelligence", "machine learning", "deep learning", "automation" or "robotisation", etc. in each case. To answer the question whether there is a substitutive relationship between human labour and these phenomena, a detailed differentiation of terms does not seem necessary here. For our purposes, "digital technology", "artificial intelligence" or "robotisation" will serve as pragmatic working terms and are hence often used synonymously in the following. Since—in contrast to the mechanisation or automation of all previous epochs of the industrial economy—for the first time ever it can be said that cognitive activity is being taken over by non-human entities, "artificial intelligence" is used preferentially. Where appropriate and with a view to answering sub-questions, the terms are explained in more detail or reference is made to the relevant discussion.

The rest of this chapter is structured as follows.

Section 8.3.1 introduces the problem of substituting human labour and differentiates between "tasks" and "occupations" with a view to the problems unfolding in the age of digitalisation.

Section 8.3.2 explains that the possibilities of job replacement should not be confused with a loss of jobs, but that digitalisation itself produces compensatory effects.

Section 8.3.3 focuses on the qualitative aspects that are decisive for the concrete effects of the specific impact of digitalisation.

Section 8.3.4 discusses the changes in working conditions made possible by digitalisation.

8.3.1 Occupations and Tasks

This section focuses on the question of where the effects of digitalisation unfold specifically with regard to the replacement of human labour.

Empirical studies show that many people are afraid that their labour will be replaced in the near future (see Arntz et al. 2022). Bizarre terms as "automation angst" (The Economist 2015, taken up accordingly by Arntz et al. 2022) or "automation scare" (Abott 2020, 37) are revealing expressions for this psychological phenomenon.

But what concrete effects can be identified with regard to the labour market? In order to be able to describe this situation adequately, it is first necessary to take a closer look at the nature of the new technology and the way in which human labour is used in modern industrial societies.

First of all, digital technology can digitally map, store and modify non-digital facts from a huge bandwidth of realms to an extremely high degree and can even do this independently by machine learning. It is hence probably appropriate that the technical phenomenon has been given the name artificial "intelligence".[3] But artificial intelligence is not only of a different nature than human intelligence.[4] For—at least

[3] Appropriate insofar as this technology has for some time been able to master specific tasks that could previously only be solved by human cognition, the complexity of the potential tasks to be mastered is growing dramatically. As shocking as the successes in chess or the Chinese board game "Go" were (Koch 2019), they now may seem downright boring in view of the achievements of even the free version of ChatGPT.

[4] It is not possible here to adequately reflect the relevant discussion on the extent to AI, for example, is similar to human cognitive processes or not; AI and machine learning are ultimately *simulations* of human intelligence, which, however, come about under both different conditions and function differently. AI forms an own research agenda within economics (see e.g. Agrawal et al. 2019), and we will concentrate here on the effects within the framework of the chosen principles. The author of this book took the liberty of asking the large language model-based ChatGPT the following, everyday

at present—on the one hand, humans have an extremely complex world knowledge[5] that cannot yet be absorbed and then reactivated to this extent by forms of digital storage and processing. On the other hand, individuals naturally also participate in different social systems,[6] e.g. they are also definitely employees, but in their role as employees they are not only supervisors, but also subordinates, colleagues, inventors and integrative figures at the same time—and also fathers, animal rights activists and so on. It is indisputable that all these aspects, by realising the integrity of employees, are relevant for the success of companies (see for example Ete et al. 2022). As intelligent as digital technology is and though it may already provide solutions, it is indisputable that artificial intelligence and human intelligence are by no means the same in the concrete world of work. This will be discussed again in the next chapter. To what extent then can humans or their intelligence be replaced by AI and robots?

For the sake of completeness, it must also be clarified what is commonly understood as a robot.[7] A clear boundary to the concept of automation, which "(…) may encompass machines that only partially substitute to human work" (Aghion et al. 2022, 9), cannot always be clearly drawn with regard to the labour market. If one wants to view digitalisation as a technical development process, then it is accordingly

language question: "Is Artificial Intelligence intelligent?" The answer was the following: "Artificial Intelligence (AI) refers to the field of computer science that deals with the development of intelligent machines or systems that can perform tasks that normally require human intelligence. However, it is important to note that AI in its current form does not have true human-like intelligence. (…) AI may have impressive capabilities, but they lack the broader understanding, reasoning and awareness associated with human intelligence. (…) They lack subjective experience, emotion and the ability to comprehend the world beyond their specific task or domain. (…) In summary, while AI can perform certain tasks with great efficiency and accuracy, it does not have the same level of general intelligence, awareness and understanding as humans" (OpenAI 2023). Well done, ChatGPT!

[5] Here, too, we are dealing with a somewhat problematic agglomerative term, which is already evident from the fact that the "makers" of the digital transformation differentiate the concept of and terms for knowledge differently and concretely in a problem-oriented way and, in order to capture more world complexity, naturally also strive for appropriate integration. See, for example, Wang et al. (2021), on "Linguistic Knowledge, World Knowledge and Common Sense Knowledge". For the purposes of this chapter, "world knowledge" will be used as a pragmatic working term, whose heuristic function is sufficiently evident from the above paragraph. Irrespective of this, it is of course quite clear that such world knowledge and—however accumulated—experience can also be increasingly absorbed by AI.

[6] At this point, this term refers to Luhmann's social systems theory (comprehensively Luhmann 1995; for an introduction, see recently Baraldi et al. 2021), with the help of which this problem area can be demonstrated quite vividly. From this theory's point of view, the phenomenon of "society" consists of communications which, differentiated by binary codes (see Luhmann 1982, 169f.), each form their own subsystems and maintain themselves. These few references must be left here; a discussion of systems theory approaches with regard to the subject matter of this presentation is simply not called for.

[7] The fact that the use of robots does not mean the disappearance of jobs will be discussed in detail. Irrespective of this, a robot is of course nothing other than "(…) a specific type of automation that is precisely designed to replace human work" (Aghion et al. 2022, 9), in other words "(…) any automatically operated machine that replaces human effort, though it may not resemble human beings in appearance or perform functions in a humanlike manner" (Moravec 2023), whereby the word "humanlike" is a good indication of the problems of knowledge and interaction mentioned above.

also not straightforward and clear how the degree of automation should actually be measured appropriately; not least, one robot can be smarter than another, just as a current version of AI used in any context can be smarter than the previous version, etc. Here, of course, appropriate proxies must be used in the context of the numerous empirical studies,[8] which must be taken into account when interpreting them.

This difference between the intelligence available in human persons and artificial intelligence, explained here using everyday examples, can accordingly be taken as an indication of the role of artificial intelligence with regard to employment and labour markets. AI and robots do not simply replace employees, but can initially take over *tasks* (see Acemoglu and Autor 2011). In many cases, they can certainly perform these tasks faster, better and more reliably than humans (see Fernández-Macías 2018, 16), but in individual cases this cannot be equated with an algorithm taking over an entire job.

8.3.2 Between Displacement and Hypercompensation

This section examines the extent to which the substitution of tasks by digital technology also holds the potential for employment growth.

Just as artificial intelligence is not the same as human intelligence, tasks are also different among occupations (see Fernández-Macías 2018, 7). Being able to have tasks done by digital technology does not mean that the workplace, the whole occupation, disappears (see also Brynjolfsson and Mitchell 2017).

However, jobs are made up of a bundle of tasks; the less complex they are, the less adaptation and learning they require, and the "smarter" the AI that can be used, the more tasks AI can absorb. Instead of the workplace disappearing, however, a *complementary division of labour* between humans and machines can emerge (see Autor 2015).

If one assumes that only certain tasks are taken over, then the employee who has fewer tasks to perform first gains correspondingly free capacities to use his or her skills and knowledge. Whether and to what extent the employee uses these capacities sensibly and/or creatively is one question. If so, whether he is willing to do so for the company that provided him with these capacities is another question.

The new complementary division of labour is particularly crucial insofar as productivity gains from digitalisation are only realised if they are "(…) combined with certain organisational and management practices, reflecting the synergies often found between different intangible assets" (McMahon et al. 2021, 15f, with reference to Haskel and Westlake 2018).

---

[8] Moreover, in order to gain insight into the extent of automation, artificial intelligence is used for text analysis. Publications often refer to data provided by the International Federation of Robotics (IFR), which also provides useful definitions (see World Robotics 2022, 27f.). For the purposes of this chapter, however, it is not necessary to work on such a fine-grained basis.

Only after a certain degree of absorption does substitutability arise, i.e. a competition between robots/AI and workers on factor markets. This is nothing new in principle, but such phenomena seem to be becoming more publicly perceptible as modern economies develop. A popular example is that of ATMs and how they made the jobs of bank tellers obsolete.[9]

In the relevant literature, the possibility of replacing human labour with digital solutions is discussed under the term *displacement effects*. Where is the degree of absorption of tasks, at which substitutability between humans and technology arises? What are the relevant assessments and what are the difficulties of its determination?

If one takes into account the diversity of industries and the well-developed (international) division of labour on the one hand, and the fundamental unpredictability of technical change on both a large and small scale on the other—also and especially with regard to the dynamic potential of digital technology—then it is not surprising that the assessments are very far apart. Mariniello (2022, 292) has summed up the problem quite well: "We cannot know what the future will bring, but we may guess what it will take away from us". In order to understand in which form displacement effects can occur, one must take a closer look at the mechanisms underlying these effects in the digital age.

As in earlier times, when a new technology led to a reduction in jobs, we can speak of *technological unemployment*: "This means unemployment due to our discovery of means of economising the use of labour outrunning the pace at which we can find new uses for labour" (Keynes 1930, 363). However, if one takes into account that digital technology is also introduced with the aim of increasing the productivity of the competitiveness of companies, then one can certainly expect compensatory effects. For example, if production technology is more efficient and productivity increases as a result (see Graetz and Michaels 2018), the goods produced can hence be offered at a lower price (see Aghion et al. 2020, 23).[10] This can then in turn also lead to an increase in demand, which leads to an expansion of production output and thus also to an increased demand for jobs (Aghion et al. 2022, 12). The same case can be assumed if the application of digital technologies leads to an international competitive advantage of the respective company and thus to internal company growth.

Even if certain jobs are saved through digital technology, this does not mean that these jobs will be missing from the labour market as a whole, as there can

[9] The optimistic Marininiello (2022, 284) points out, however, that "(…) instead, their job was transformed, with more time dedicated to direct personal advice and less cash handling". The fact that machines can replace jobs is of course not a problem as long as the people taking these jobs can then make themselves useful elsewhere and not at a significantly lower wage. The question is rather to what extent the known displacement effects of a technologised economy *has come under new conditions* as a result of digitalisation.

[10] A prerequisite for this argumentation to be successful is, of course, that all products can be sold and this also depends on a number of other factors. The cited study of Aghion et al. focuses on "evidence from France". They have referred to their own study again (Aghion et al. 2022, 10), in which they themselves state that "(w)hether it be the robot count or the patent measure, the aggregate measures of automation/robotization at the country or industry level provide inconclusive evidence". Accordingly, they also point to the study by Bonfiglioli et al. (2020), which relativises the possibility that lower prices are actually passed on to consumers.

also be a parallel surplus demand for the labour force (see Gregory et al. 2016). In principle, the so-called *reinstatement effects* can also be assumed, namely that the released capacity is channelled into other, more productive occupations (Acemoglu and Restrepo 2018; see Arntz et al. 2019, 10). But the investment itself must also be carried out by someone, e.g. specialised labour force or a specialised company, i.e. the introduction of digital technology may require the complementary use of new labour (see, for example, Arntz et al. 2019, 8; also Fernández-Macías 2018, 17). In the context considered here, the latter case means new jobs that did not exist before.

Overall, the assessments of which effects predominate diverge greatly. This has to do with the level of observation, the sector, the time period and also the nature of the data collected. Aghion et al. (2022, 3f.) have contrasted the direct effects of automation on labour demand as a "partial equilibrium effect" with the above-mentioned compensatory effects as "general equilibrium effects". In their comparison, they predominantly conclude that the effect is demand-dampening or, to a lesser extent, at best ambiguous. Acemoglu and Restrepo (2020) also come to the conclusion that the effect of job replacement dominates overall.

Another empirical approach to adequately depict the concrete adoption of tasks, i.e. not complete occupations, is the analysis of the texts of corresponding patent applications, as conducted by Webb (2020) or Mann and Püttmann (2023).[11] But even in this way, the results are by no means unambiguous.

It sometimes seems that the view guided by loss aversion only ever focuses on the losses due to automation and digitalisation. It is easy to lose sight of the fact that digital technology is also a driver of innovation and that innovations can create markets and thus new jobs (see European Central Bank 2021, 59). Looked at another way: If one country or region is relatively less innovative, cannot or will not absorb digital technology, it is not digital technology itself that is the cause of unemployment.[12] In an international context, it is accordingly also important to distinguish between the competitive relationship between AI/robots and workers in factor markets and the competition "(...) between countries in sector-specific product markets for inputs and outputs" (Artuc et al. 2018, 2). Accordingly, the "(...) relative production costs (driven by factor prices and technology) (...) determine country-specific robotization and trade patterns" (ibid.).[13]

[11] Independently of their research objective, their contribution also already provides a good indication for the considerations pursued here by documenting that the number and share of patents in this area increased strongly in their research period from 1976 to 2014.

[12] This statement is quite isolated in this form, since the technological absorption capacity in general, as well as that for digital technologies in particular, is tied to a whole series of important preconditions, such as those described very prominently by Acemoglu and Robinson (2012), focusing the institutional setting, but also to the given endowment with material- and immaterial resources, the degree of economic development as well as the position of a country in the international division of labour (see also the following footnote). In view of the generality of the present considerations, it is probably appropriate to point out that both scenarios, positive and negative, exist in principle.

[13] With a view to the international division of labour and the different levels of development of economies, these problems are discussed in detail by Carbonero et al. (2018), who also include trade aspects and "re-shoring", which is ultimately made easier by automation, in their analysis. These primarily international aspects cannot be discussed in detail here, but should be mentioned where appropriate.

Be that as it may, in any case, so much seems indisputable that as long as a competitive advantage can be achieved through the use of AI or robots, there will be a crowding-out effect vis-à-vis the less automated companies (see Aghion et al. 2022, 12), that is to say a pivotal point for the dynamics inherent in the age of digitalisation.

How the effects of robotisation are assessed also depends on whether the overall labour market or the company level is considered. For example, on the basis of their empirical studies, Acemoglu et al. (2020, 383) come to the conclusion that automation on the labour market as a whole and the "(...) firm-level adoption of robots coincides with declines in labour shares, increases in value added and productivity, and declines in the share of production workers. In contrast to the market-level effects, however, overall employment increases faster in firms adopting robots".

In view of the technically extremely dynamic development, no clear statements can be made at present as to what extent displacement effects or hypercompensation would predominate. Generally speaking, the wealth of research on the topic suggests that displacement effects can be, at least potentially, "(...) offset by productivity, growth, and innovation effects" (Mariniello 2022, 285). Admittedly, this is a very general perspective. And even if one can assume that there is at least agreement that these effects are present, the concrete assessments of the scope of this change are vigorously debated. A decade ago, for example, Frey and Osborne (2013, 1) estimated that in the United States about 47% of the American workforce could be replaced by computers by 2035.[14] Both Carbonero et al. (2018) and Arntz et al. (2016) arrive at a considerably lower estimate in their comparative studies, but their study is hardly less sobering in a long-term perspective.

If the potential compensatory effects mentioned above are taken into account, this does not mean that these people will no longer be employed. If one assumes that first tasks and then occupations (as bundles of tasks, similar to Arntz et al. 2019, 9) can be taken over by digital technology, then it can be assumed that first part-time employees will fall out of the labour market. Admittedly, this also depends on the level of qualification, cyclical phenomena in the value chain, etc. Such qualitative conditions will be discussed in more detail in the next sub-chapter. Either way, however, the transition phase is fraught with problems.

Transformation processes do not tend to take place without frictional heat and friction losses. For our perspective, it is crucial that if one decides to opt for a market economy, then this includes the decision for technological openness, so such upheavals are in principle pre-programmed. Making the instrument of the economy as a means of generating wealth as efficient as possible therefore means that the use of this instrument is in principle associated with inconveniences.

These inconveniences, if they are already unavoidable, raise two questions in principle. One is a *normative* question, namely to what extent such inconveniences are still "humane"? Based on the normative basis established for the present considerations, this is also a *pragmatic* question, namely how far the short-term frictions can

[14] This study is also often cited because the figures are so alarming. Methodologically, however, it should be taken into account that Frey/Osborne start at the level of *occupations*, whereas a reference to *tasks*, as Anrtz et al. do, leads to different results, if only because not all workers are the same, i.e. they can take on different tasks.

be mitigated[15] without destroying the functioning principle of the economy itself. In order to be able to do this, qualitative aspects must also be taken into account, which further differentiate the impact of the displacement effects and the compensation effects. The following paragraph is devoted to this.

8.3.3 Polarisation Effects

This section highlights the problem of how the absorption of human tasks, made possible by digital technology, leads to polarising effects on the labour markets in the long term and thus possibly also leads to further social problems.

The previous paragraph highlighted a difference between artificial and human intelligence and, on this basis, started from the distinction between tasks and occupations. At this level of observation, the displacement effects start with the tasks, i.e. jobs do not immediately disappear completely, but on the basis of the qualification of the workers on the one hand, and with a view to the differentiability and recombinability of tasks. There remains a scope for employment, which is estimated very differently and will of course also turn out differently depending on the sector or structure of an economy.

One limitation of this scope is, of course, the employees themselves, since not all tasks can be assigned to them, but they have different skills and qualifications that set limits to their ability to be deployed, i.e. to the demand for their labour. Therefore, despite the vagueness of the discussion, the question of which groups of employees are particularly affected by the digital transformation is urgent. This is the context in which technological progress in labour markets generates problems typical of change, as mentioned above, because of course not all skills are in demand to the same extent in principle, and in times of change the demand for certain, new skills grows while others become obsolete. Acemoglu (2002, 55), who has published authoritatively in this field, calls this phenomenon "skill-biased technical progress". This then leads to a mismatch between existing skills and those in demand, i.e. a form of structural unemployment. Can any special features be associated with the process of digitalisation in this respect?

Returning to the beginning of the last two sections, this question can be posed as the question of which tasks can be taken over by artificial intelligence or robots. In this regard, there is already a broad literature in which, in principle similar to the recognition of the effect of displacement and compensation effects, there is agreement at least in principle.

Services performed directly on people, such as in the field of care, cosmetics or even in the field of gastronomy, cannot simply be robotised away (see Fernández-Macías 2018, 17). On the one hand, this is the case because the tasks involved

---

[15] It could also be asked to what extent digital technology itself can be useful in mitigating frictions, for example by making better simulations available to political decision-makers. However, this raises a number of model-theoretical questions that cannot be dealt with here.

are too complex in terms of their physical execution, for example, in the case of a hairdresser, the appropriate execution of the cut. On the other hand, especially in the case of personal services, but also appropriate advice, quite simply, personal contact is elementary to these services. This is easy to understand from the previous examples, in addition to the latest gossip. Furthermore, the technical possibilities of robotisation in the service sector are currently reaching their cultural limits.[16] Common to those working in this field is a relatively low level of qualification, though accordingly good manual dexterity, the aforementioned knowledge of the world and personal appearance offer individual competitive advantages.

The best tasks to automate are routine tasks that, if they have to be physically performed, are not particularly complex—in production, for example, tightening screws precisely or drawing weld seams, etc.—and all other such activities that are repetitive, only slightly varied, make few demands on decision-making competence and do not require action competence in the event of unexpected changes in the situation. "Routine tasks are tasks which follow well-defined rules and can thus be automated on rule-based algorithms, using rapidly improving computers" (Arntz et al. 2019, 1). While automated production processes have long been the norm, it is now possible, with increasing speed, to perform all kinds of cognitively more demanding tasks (see Fernández-Macías 2018, 16), as long as they conform to the above characteristics in a certain, i.e. continuously increasing, bandwidth and as they are empirically traceable, e.g. in banks, insurance companies, everywhere in accounting or retail (see Blix 2017, 11). In developed industrial societies, it is primarily the population group that can be described as "middle class" that is affected with regard to the qualification profiles required for these tasks.[17]

What's more, if we assume a normal distribution of intelligence, skills and qualifications among the population of modern industrial societies, then sooner or later most "ordinary" people will have a problem: "it's not a great time to have only ordinary skills" (Bernstein and Raman 2015). Digitalisation thus leads to a so-called job- or employment polarisation to the disadvantage of the middle qualification levels (see Goos et al. 2014; Arntz et al. 2019, 1), which can be observed in all developed economies (European Central Bank 2021, 61f.). The socio-political and distributional implications will be discussed below. However, it cannot go unmentioned here that the said middle class is already affected by a process of erosion that has been

[16] Cultural limits are abstract, therefore cannot be rationalised away ad hoc and naturally vary considerably. Relatively well known in the context under consideration here is the very different acceptance of the use of robots in elderly care, which is relatively high in Japan, a country where on the one hand the threshold of shame is extremely high and on the other hand no one wants to be a burden to anyone else, while in European countries robots are not accepted as care workers. In gastronomy or show business, robotisation is sometimes encountered—see, for example, the bizarre "Robot Restaurant" in Tokyo, which is currently under maintenance—but rather to cause a sensation than to replace jobs. The same might apply to robotic brothels, which have been opening worldwide in the past few years (see Frank 2018; Spitznagel 2018) and naturally raise, above all other considerations, controversial ethical questions (see Hancock 2020; Johnson and Verdicchio 2020).

[17] Of course, this also means an important distribution problem. See the following sub-chapter.

going on for decades for other reasons not directly related to digitalisation (this is also emphasised by Mariniello 2022, 287).

8.3.4 Working Conditions and Employment Relationships

This section shows the extent to which digitalisation is not only changing the labour markets, but is also having a specific impact on both working conditions and employment relationships.

Digitalisation does not only affect the world of work in the sense of taking over tasks or entire occupations, but it also changes the *conditions* of work or the specific format of contract or *design* of working places. This aspect also eludes a clear evaluation, and the effects of digitalisation are ambivalent here as well. In the following, some aspects will be briefly discussed, without wanting to imply greater or lesser importance by the order.

Firstly, digitalisation makes it possible that a wide variety of tasks no longer have to be performed in person. In this way, the possibilities of digital technology in particular can help to mitigate effects of technological change that were previously relevant to the regional economy. For example, modern communication media can partially absorb the relevant effects in Eucken's example cited above, since one no longer necessarily has to be on site in person to fulfil one's tasks. Of course, this only applies to work that can be done at a desk, while the craftsman still has to take his hammer to the nail. But with regard to all others, and in developed economies this applies to broad strata, it is true that the physical location of service provision is increasingly irrelevant (Fernández-Macías 2018, 18). The various forms of remote working not only offer greater flexibility for employers in terms of the spatial distribution of the workforce, but also allow employees to be more flexible about their workload. In this sense, it is the same technology that triggers transformation processes that can mitigate the associated frictions. At the very least, flexible scheduling of working time is probably widely perceived by workers as a non-material welfare gain (see OECD 2022, 245).

The new form of remote working is spreading very rapidly and accounted for about one-third of all jobs during the Covid-19 pandemic (European Central Bank 2021, 58). Nevertheless, it must be taken into account that remote working also entails a whole series of problematic effects, which triggered an extremely broad discussion, especially in the course of the explosive spread of this form of work during the Corona pandemic. First and foremost, psychological and social problems should be mentioned in this context, as self-exploitation, extra work by using the time previously used for commuting as working time, loneliness and/or the destruction of the family balance due to the inadequate separation of the workplace and private space (see, for example, OECD 2022, 245; 256ff.). The dimension of this phenomenon, in that the flexibilisation of employment relationships and forms of work encompasses all possible occupational groups, is exceedingly large, and it is growing dynamically.

This is not the place to discuss in detail the wealth of research findings on this problem area, but it is undisputed that the advantage of flexibility buys disadvantages in other areas. For the economy of a society, this is of course only relevant when the working people can no longer sustainably provide the performance they would have been capable of under other conditions. Balancing costs and benefits here is a completely new task that can only be mastered in a long-term learning process.

Secondly, while digitalisation makes the use of personal labour more flexible, it also makes it possible to monitor it rigidly. Fernández-Macías (2018, 7) has highlighted this primarily with the densely networked sensory control in production processes, writing that "(…) the Internet of Things (…) promises a big leap in the efficiency of industrial processes, but it can also transform a factory into an invasive surveillance system".[18] It should be noted here that such monitoring can easily be extended beyond the factory, as far as an employee has a networkable device with him. "Remote sensors, cheaper and smaller cameras, and geo-localisation, make it easier than ever for firms to monitor work, whether inside or outside the boundaries of the firm" (OECD 2021, 220 with reference to Weil 2014). These new possibilities are also a driver for the trend towards a growing volume of outsourcing (OECD 2021, 211f.) and a correspondingly more differentiated division of labour.

Now, two aspects must be distinguished here. One is the ethical and at the same time legal aspect, namely how extensively a worker can actually be monitored and under what conditions. Digitalisation creates a new form of complexity in this respect as well, in which the employer's legitimate interest in optimisation must be weighed against the employee's legitimate interest in protecting his or her privacy, admittedly in compliance with the applicable law in each case. Independent of this balancing problem, employers, or more generally, the organisation, also face a kind of diminishing marginal utility of optimisation itself. What is meant by this?

Optimisation-driven monitoring can, in principle, become counterproductive in all value-creating, cooperative processes above a certain level. This connection is illuminated by a concept of Williamson, who contrasted the coordination of value creation on markets with that of organisation and attested to two different types of relations: On the one hand, "(…) market exchange tends predominantly to encourage calculative relations" (Williamson, 1975, 38). For transactions to be carried out optimally within an organisation, something else is needed. "(…) internal organisation, by contrast, is often better able to make allowance for quasi-moral involvements among the parties" (Williamson, 1975, 38). This difference means for the reality of the organisation that "(…) piecemeal calculativeness can easily be dysfunctional" (Williamson 1993, 480), i.e. it can no longer be used beyond a certain limit. In what area can we actually locate this limit, or, better asked, how and under what circumstances does this limit come about? Williamson has coined a term for this area in

[18] With this potential, Fernández-Macías identifies a problem area that cannot be dealt with in detail here. Zuboff (2019) has prominently discussed the fundamental problem of omnipresent surveillability through digital technology and offers an instructive overview of a new problem area, but takes a less comprehensive view than the title would lead one to expect (see critique by Johns 2020).

Markets and Hierarchies (1975) and The Economic Institutions of Capitalism (1985): "economics of atmosphere".[19]

The use of digital technology has made this question more topical than ever. This phenomenon touches on a whole range of questions of employee motivation. And in part it also refers back to the question posed at the beginning of the chapter on displacement effects. Namely, whether an employee who has gained new capacities due to digital technology is prepared to use them meaningfully and creatively for his or her company—or not. An optimal working environment would also mean ensuring the incentives to do so.

Thirdly, digitalisation is also changing the conditions for the design of contracts between the individual provider of labour services and the companies, because the *flexibilisation* discussed in the previous section is reflected in greater negotiating power for both sides. What does this mean in tangible terms? Seven aspects of the new, digital flexibility should be highlighted here.

(1) The flexibility mentioned above offers the advantage of cushioning technological change by reallocating labour. At the same time, however, the possibilities of digitalisation mean that the demand for labour is faced with a far larger pool of potential workers whose skills can also be scanned much more easily in advance than ever before. The reduction in transaction costs typical of digitalisation can therefore be observed here in the context of matching on labour markets (see, for example, European Central Bank 2021, 59). Depending on the occupational group or qualification in question, this opens up greater negotiating leeway for one side or the other.

(2) Flexibility is not only a possibility, it is also a new *condition* in the digital age. Employers will have greater incentives to keep labour commitments as low as possible, depending on the skills demanded. This can also be explained in terms of Coase's transaction cost theory. The existence of the firm as an arrangement of contracts with employees comes about if and only as long as this arrangement is cheaper than sourcing labour services not within the organisation but through the market. Blix (2017, 13) has correctly observed that "(w)ith gig platforms, the cost of hiring temporary staff on a needs-only basis is much smaller than in the past". It also seems a feasible assumption that the new flexibility made possible by digitalisation will exacerbate polarisation tendencies.

(3) The new flexibility leads, with or without national borders, to an erosion of the organised representation of employees, as was common for a long time, e.g. in the form of trade unions (see Fernández-Macías 2018, 19). For, not unlike the tendencies under the label of the "sharing economy", new non-standard

[19] Although Williamson coined this elegant term and conclusively drew attention to a phenomenon that is possibly more topical in the age of digitalisation than it was in his time, a theoretically consistent elaboration of this problem area is still open. Asked about it by Geoffrey Hodgson and David Gindis, three years before his Nobel Prize, Williamson replied, laconically, "(o)n the one hand it seemed an important concept and on the other it was hard to give a specific content" (Williamson, 2007, 378). That is where it has remained. Chassagnon (2021, 3), focusing on questions of organisation, points out that "Williamson's organisational atmosphere has barely been exploited in the economic literature".

forms of work typical of the digital age, such as "crowdworking" or "clickworking", mean that representation of common interests can no longer be organised cheaply enough. Overall, the labour market effects of digitalisation weaken the bargaining power of workers (see Blix 2017, 11; also OECD 2017, 165).

In general, it can be said that digitalisation, and primarily the existence of internet platforms, has led to a change in working patterns that, while varying widely by country, sector and skill, have so much in common that "(...) much work seems to be carried out in small units and irregularly" (OECD 2016, 19). It must be borne in mind that the platform markets belonging to the "sharing economy" only partially substitute for traditional forms of work and are rather to a large extent a supplement to regular income (see OECD 2016, 10). Of course, this flexibility can also be an opportunity for those who, for all sorts of reasons, are not available for regular full-time employment (OECD 2016, 21); another manifestation of the same situation would be that people have to engage in small-scale "multi-jobbing" without ever being able to be caught by the radar of labour protection. The OECD (2016, 22) has pointed out that this can also be at the expense of personal professional development in terms of expertise and networking, among other things. The latter two are then absorbed by the digital technology of the platform.

(4) The aforementioned reduction of transaction costs can lead to positive welfare effects overall. At the same time, however, it can also lead to a better depression of the wage level for certain jobs than before. The effects that occur in this context are discussed in more detail below with regard to their distributional relevance.

(5) The flexibility mentioned here is primarily due to the fact that, on the one hand, the term "workplace" no longer necessarily has to refer to physical characteristics and, on the other hand, it cannot be understood as a permanent integration of a person into an organisation, at least according to tendency. In the digital age, people, connected by the internet, perform certain services. Even if at first glance the eroding tendencies may predominate, it should not be forgotten that through digitalisation people who have not been able to participate in the labour market, e.g. due to disability, can now also be integrated, for example through the possibilities of augmented reality solutions.

(6) The possibility of close monitoring of work, also in the context of remote work, was mentioned above. For the employer or client, this ensures that the work is done as ordered and that the employees do not indulge in a little in-private pampering. At the same time, however, it will become more difficult to monitor whether workers are not working too many hours. "Working time is a crucial variable shaping the labour market and its adaptability to shocks. It can affect key labour market outcomes, such as workers' well-being, productivity, wages and employment" (OECD 2021, 274).

(7) Another new effect related to flexibilisation arises for the division of labour as a whole. Not only can tasks tend to be robotised away, but within the framework of the platform economy it has become incomparably easier to buy a wealth of work steps from the market due to lower information costs; this applies not

only to standard outsourcing solutions (see Frenández-Macías 2018, 10), but also to the possibility of contracting with individual contractors, worldwide. In principle, such contracts can range from a minimal "click-work" format to the contract for a design concept. This shifts the boundary of the enterprise, it is absorbed by the platforms, which now partly take over market functions by providing a medium in which suppliers and consumers meet, and on the other hand also functions of the enterprise, namely "(...) coordinating, monitoring and disciplining the supply of services through algorithms" (ibid.).

However, as can already be observed with other aspects, only very general tendencies can be identified so far, concrete effects cannot be predicted with precision, especially since different groups with different qualification levels in different sectors in different countries can be affected very differently.[20] Unfortunately, the responsible politicians will not be able to relax about the impossibility of reliable forecasts, because one thing is certain: "Labour markets now have much less time to adapt to a highly dynamic environment" (Marininiello 2022, 286).

8.4 Distributive Effects

This chapter deals with the question of the extent to which digitalisation causes changes with regard to income distribution. It is structured as follows.

Section 8.4.1 examines the level of the employees.

Section 8.4.2 focuses the level of companies in the sense of a heuristic supplement in order to more clearly illustrate the causes of the unfolding changes.

8.4.1 The Level of Employees

The following section is dedicated to the question to which extent the impact of digitalisation on the labour markets causes effects on the distribution of wealth.

Basically, it can be assumed that an improvement in technology will increase the productivity of the labour force.[21] In a market economy, the potential of a new

---

[20] Carbonero et al. (2018) provide a study focusing on the developing countries, which, as they specialise in production steps that require simpler activities within the international value chain, are of course particularly affected (ibid., 9). However, they attest that robotisation has "(...) a detriental effect on employment growth at the global level" (ibid., 1).

[21] Whether there is a new increase in productivity through digitalisation is by no means unambiguously answered. This may be due to the fact that the productivity effects affect different sectors or different sections of the value chains to different degrees. This phenomenon is also referred to as the "Solow paradox", because Solow said that one could "(...) see the computer age everywhere but in the productivity statistics" (Solow 1987, 2). See also Triplet (1999). In fact, since the 1970s, a stagnation of productivity has been observable in the developed countries, which, remarkably, has not been changed by the rapid spread of digital technology. The phenomenon is widely discussed

technology means corresponding incentives to invest more in this technology, at least as long as demand is enough or increases.

However, this means that as digitalisation progresses, more and more tasks can be successively replaced by capital. With regard to the problem of the distribution of the wealth generated, this means that if there are productivity gains, these tend to be captured by the owners of capital and are not necessarily reflected in the wages of the workforce. The use of AI and robots thus results in a redistribution effect in favour of capital owners, which is statistically verifiable (see Acemoglu and Restrepo 2020; Dauth et al. 2017) and has been discussed for some time. Brynjolfsson and McAfee (2015) address the "great decoupling" of productivity and wages.

Overall, this development leads to a "hollowing out of the middle class" (Autor et al. 2006), as already briefly mentioned in the previous chapter from the perspective of the qualification of workers.[22] In principle, it can be assumed that the more labour-intensive the sector, the greater the use of robots (see Carbonero et al. 2018, 2.7). Since, from the point of view of companies, it is ultimately less a question of which activities can be more easily replaced by digital technologies, but primarily of where a substitution of human labour is most profitable, they will most likely try to replace the middle, namely relatively expensive skill profiles (see Arntz et al. 2019, 7). This phenomenon is likely to intensify in the long run. Beyond the distribution of material wealth, however, the corresponding situation has further, important social implications, which Rifkin pointed out quite early on: "Barring an unforeseen blowback, much of the productive economic activity of society is going to be increasingly placed in the 'hands' of intelligent technology, supervised by small groups of highly skilled professional and technical workers as we journey further into the twenty-first century" (Rifkin 2014, 108).

As the advancing flexibilisation makes it difficult to organise the workers concerned, which would indeed be the traditional form of a trade union, the savings resulting from this flexibility will be realised on the account of the capital owner. The latter assumption is also underlined by the fact that the digital flexibilisation of labour has not led to real wage increases on the side of the employees yet.[23]

---

in the literature, and opinions differ. Brynjolfsson and Hit (1996) were quick to see the end of this paradox. Gordon (2015, 2012) attests only a minor impact of digitalisation on productivity and, although the USA in particular performed relatively well compared to other countries for the period around the turn of the millennium, he sees more of a secular stagnation for the USA. Gal et al. (2019), on the other hand, do attribute an increase in productivity at the company level to digitalisation. The European Central Bank (2021, 42) points out that after the industrial revolution was completed, substantial productivity were still realised, especially in the service sector.

[22] The phenomenon of polarisation to the disadvantage of the middle class is particularly explosive in the United States, although it can also be observed in other developed economies and also in developing countries. Certainly, the contribution by Autor et al. (2006) points to important causes to which the effects of digitalisation can be well connected. However, this phenomenon, which has been observable for some time, is also based on a whole bundle of causes. One key element is to be found in the Cantillon effect of inflation, see e.g. Sieroń (2019, 204f). This aspect is a specific phenomenon of the problem of monetary stability discussed in Chap. 5.

[23] *Nota bene*: This is a much-discussed finding. However, it seems plausible to assume that digital technology tends to promote this process rather than slow it down.

In order to differentiate the distribution effects of digitalisation with regard to different groups of employees, we refer to the problems shown in Sect. 8.3.3. It is primarily the middle skill levels that are affected by digitalisation, while the group of highly qualified, creative workers with management requirements on the one hand (see Dixon et al. 2019) and the group of those who perform customer-oriented services on the other form the two poles that cannot be easily robotised away. This so-called *skill-biased technological change* naturally has a corresponding, namely asymmetric distribution effect.

Job polarisation does not simultaneously mean that the two groups of (still) employed people can also benefit materially from the development. For example, the group of people providing services—often those close to clients such as the hairdresser in the chapter above—cannot benefit from the productivity gains made possible by technological development, which only benefit the group of highly qualified people who perform management tasks in complex organisations (see European Central Bank 2021, 61).

Moreover, it can be assumed that the long-term drop out of workers from the most affected middle skill level is most likely to strand them in the workforce providing physical services. "(…) (T)here's never been a worse time to be a worker with only 'ordinary' skills and abilities to offer, because computers, robots, and other digital technologies are acquiring these skills and abilities at an extraordinary rate" (Brynjolfsson and McAfee 2014).

This would mean that in this last group of service providers, unemployment would not initially spread, but wages would be depressed by a growing supply of labour (see Blix 2017, 11). The flexibility already mentioned in the sub-chapter on the qualitative aspects can cushion negative effects of digitalisation under certain circumstances, but together with the phenomenon of job polarisation it also leads to higher volatility of incomes and thus to greater uncertainty (see Blix 2017, 9).

The observed job polarisation, which is also expected to continue in the future, is therefore in favour of the group of highly qualified, creative workers with management tasks, while everyone else is worse-off. We can only speculate on the extent to which the innovations on the labour market mentioned in the previous sub-chapter have compensatory effects, but initially the scope of digital technology seems to indicate a relatively clear tendency, namely that both the overall level of employment and the wage level of the majority of those capable of working will fall.

8.4.2 Corporate Level

This section looks at the corporate level and focuses on the extent to which the opportunities offered by digitalisation are leading to concentration trends.

First of all, it can be assumed that the introduction of digital technology—one could also speak of an appropriate digital infrastructure—is a greater challenge for small and medium-sized enterprises than for large enterprises. On the one hand, it is more difficult for them to finance the necessary costs, and on the other hand, the costs incurred are distributed over smaller quantities of output. In this respect, it can be assumed that it is primarily the large companies that make up the bow wave of the digital transformation. This leads not only to a technological lead, but also to the fact that both the above-mentioned necessary complementary activities and the jobs requiring high qualifications and management skills are offered by the large companies first (see McMahon et al 2021, 15). This would accordingly lead to a segmenting effect on the labour market, with the large companies benefiting from the polarisation described above at the expense of the smaller and medium-sized ones.

Also the flexibilisation of work favours the large companies and, especially, the platforms. Blix (2017, 12) uses the term "gig work" "(…) to denote a situation whereby a worker performs tasks organised through the conduit of a digital platform, and whereby the platform owner does not take employer responsibilities, such as paying payroll taxes and value added tax (…)". In fact, "gig work" is spreading in many different professions and fields of activity. Only Upwork accounts for more than 18 million people with an account.

Empirically, it is not yet clear to what extent the flexibilisation of work formats, especially in connection with platforms, has special distribution effects. It has already been pointed out above that the contractual relationships that often come about in the context of platforms, which tend to be shorter term and smaller in scale, often represent a complement to other incomes. On the one hand, the empirical finding that the lower the other income, the higher the monetary value of this complement seems remarkable (OECD 2016, 20 with reference to Farrell and Greig 2017). On the other hand, it is an understandable effect of the dynamic development of non-standard work that "(…) non-regular employees are likely to earn less than full-time-permanent employees" (OECD 2016, 26).

Even if it cannot initially be said that this is a predominant phenomenon, the processes currently observable point in the direction that tendencies towards monopsony formation on labour markets are emerging. As indicated above, the Covid-19 pandemic represented a jolting change in the flexibility of work arrangements (see European Central Bank 2021, 60). It seems remarkable in this respect that one year of the pandemic alone caused a 10% increase in concentration in the labour markets of OECD countries (OECD 2022, 134). Of course, the lockdowns are in the background, so that empirically a normalisation is emerging, at least for the time being. This does not mean, however, that against the backdrop of flexibilisation on the one hand and the tendency towards an increase in the small-scale nature of the work contracts awarded on the other, one could not take a hint for a development trend from this. The OECD (2022) also mentions a regression analysis that "(…) suggests that labour market concentration tends to increase the use of flexible contracts" (ibid.).

Overall, it can be said that the segmentation processes resulting from different company sizes on the one hand and the role of technological advantage on the other also indicate segmentation processes at the company level, which reinforce the problems of employment polarisation and the erosion of the middle class mentioned in the previous sections with an overall declining wage level.

8.5 Conclusions and Policy Implications

This chapter takes the aspects discussed in the previous sections on labour and incomes as a starting point and draws some conclusions about the corresponding implications for policy.

From the perspective developed in the previous chapters, it seems obvious that the digital revolution is of a different nature than the industrial revolution. With regard to the problem area considered here, Bernstein and Raman (2015) have formulated quite aptly: "The Second Machine Age is playing out differently than the First Machine Age, continuing the long-term trend of material abundance but not of ever-greater labour demand". To what extent does policy now face new challenges in the area of labour markets and income distribution, what are the novel problems? Some general aspects can be identified.

First of all, the *speed* that can be observed in this area. And the cheaper robots and AI become, the more they will absorb tasks and thus also jobs. Not taken into account are other social factors such as the ageing population in developed economies, which will only accelerate this change (Blix 2017, 10; European Central Bank 2021, 58; 60), as the incentives are greater to automate certain jobs (ibid., 12). Digital technology is indisputably the most pervasive technology to date, unfolding exponentially. At the same time, it is important to emphasise that its use cannot be equated with the replacement of human labour, since, as shown above, complementary work may become necessary and different compensatory effects can unfold. Nevertheless, it would be naïve to underestimate the effects of displacement.

Since, as in all other areas of economic policy, there can be no one-size-fits-all recipe for the problem area under consideration here, one can only anticipate one thing, which is certainly the case: "Labour markets now have much less time to adapt to a highly dynamic environment" (Marininiello 2022, 286). Somewhat exaggeratedly formulated, one could claim that nothing actually changes in the known processes caused by the introduction of new technologies, but only their speed. Then, in the short term, it would essentially only be a matter of temporarily protecting those whose jobs have suddenly been robotised away.

Protective measures—as much can be explained in the context of the objective of this study—can be of very different types and scope. In principle, they begin with the call for an appropriate digital *infrastructure*, because only if this is in place can potential compensatory effects unfold at all. Another prerequisite for these effects to unfold is the existence of sufficient transparency so that job seekers and employers can quickly find each other at the moment when capacities are released. The question would have to be weighed up as to what extent a market solution via privately owned platforms or higher investment in the digital infrastructure of public employment services, e.g. as discussed by the OECD (2022, 102), would be an appropriate solution.

Apart from that, *education policy measures* are in general a commonly stressed issue in this context.[24] Irrespective of the fact that education policy has always been an important element of socio-political concepts and in recent decades, especially in Europe, has increasingly become the focus of economic policy considerations, it seems striking that very fundamental questions have to be asked in connection with the processes described here. For example, how the emerging job polarisation could be mitigated in the education sector. These considerations concern both the *structure* of the entire education system, the manner of participation in it—i.e. at school age as well as during lifelong learning—and the *content* of education itself. It is not possible here to give an adequate account of the relevant discussion in education economics. But at least this much is certain "(...) this time will be somehow more difficult for educational systems to adjust to the structural changes in the economy to equip workers with the necessary skills that future employers require" (Mariniello 2022, 286; see also Goldin and Katz 2009). Change is happening faster than ever, and, like all social change, it is open-ended.

However, regardless of the increased complexity, accelerated change adds up to greater adaptation costs within a single period. The extent to which these can be borne by the drivers of change, the companies, without putting them at a competitive disadvantage is still a balancing act that must rely on pattern predictions and, at the same time, also places a greater degree of risk on economic policy.

However, economic policy will have to get used to a greater degree of material inequality. Now, inequality is an inevitable result of economic and social freedom. To what extent it meets with acceptance is ultimately a cultural question. Either way, however, one of the core tasks of sustainable economic policy is to redistribute at least an acceptable amount of the wealth generated in such a way that its share across society is perceived to be fair and hence ensures the stability of that society as a whole. Today, this task is often referred to by the more fashionable term "social inclusion". However, one of the characteristic tendencies of digitalisation seems to be that it adds a new element to the inequality that has been growing in most OECD countries since the 1980s at the latest, especially through the job polarisation mentioned above. Several aspects are relevant here.

The long-term polarisation effect resulting from the absorption of tasks, the core of which is labour productivity, appears problematic. In principle, this raises the question of whether and in what way employees and employers can reach an agreement with regard to long-term, ultimate social goals, such as e.g. less working time

[24] The process of digitalisation is accompanied by a broad discourse on the necessary reform of education systems, the dominant element of which is the focus on competence instead of lexical knowledge. In the context considered here, even Mariniello (2022, 297) cannot refrain from repeating the usual nonsense: "So educational systems should shift from simply providing direct knowledge to students to providing the non-cognitive tools needed to acquire new knowledge autonomously". If these "tools" are "non-cognitive", what are they supposed to be? Haptic? Or rather olfactory? Even sniffing would require cognition. The dramatic impact of the mass use of digital media on the entire range of human cognitive and social abilities cannot be discussed here, but it is not too much to say that a digital downgrading of human abilities is taking place in the developed countries on such a scale that the boldest science fiction dystopian authors would not have dared to imagine it even a short time ago.

instead of more money due to higher productivity. Wage policy measures such as the widely discussed minimum wage (see for example Lübker and Schulten 2022; Burkhauser and Corinth 2021; with regard to the acceptance of higher incomes Fazio and Reggiani 2023) are thus also put in a new light: the higher the minimum wage, the greater the incentive to robotise away precisely the respective group of employees.

But it is not only the polarisation based on the demand for certain qualifications and skills that pose a problem, but also the forms of employment in which the new inequality is realised. For the possibility of a more small-scale distribution of tasks instead of the creation of regular long-term employment until the digital age tends to lead to a rat tail of micro-incomes in terms of distribution, which could also be called a long-tail effect in the sense of Andersen (see Fernández-Macías 2018, 10), that is to say, this is beneficial for employers, but problematic for employees. And therefore, the possibility of mitigating fragmenting tendencies faces two fundamental problems.

On the one hand, these employment relationships may be far more out of public reach than before, for example, because they are contractual relationships conducted through international platforms. Organising appropriate protective measures not only creates new, public organisational costs, but may not be enforceable at all. The new, flexible forms of work are not only completely coordinated past the traditional social partners and regulations of labour markets (see Fernández-Macías 2018, 10), but they also cross national borders. This means, among other things, that tax optimisation is easier for companies and also that the material basis for mitigating measures by the state is eroding. Especially since it is also precisely the levying of taxes that is an incentive specifically to robotise away jobs, because the majority of tax revenues are generated from labour income (see Abott 2020, 36f.).

Here, too, a new challenge arises. Namely, to balance the extent to which a "(...) combination of granting offsetting tax preferences for workers or reducing the tax benefits for using AI" (ibid., 46) could be designed sustainably, namely in the sense of "(...) to prevent the possible future automation of significant segments of the labour force from threatening both short- and long-term fiscal solvency" (ibid.) against the backdrop that companies, if necessary, can easily migrate together with their robots to more favourably taxed foreign countries.

On the other hand, the new masses of "informal workers" are united at best by the fact that they no longer have a collectively defensible status and identity to claim an appropriate commitment from the employer. "Subcontracting and outsourcing, even crowdsourcing, can result in less favourable conditions of employment for workers in terms of stability, income and working hours. By blurring company boundaries and disrupting union solidarity" (Fernández-Macías 2018, 19). Mårten Blix has summed up this explosive problem in a rather pointed way: "The risk of not responding to rising labour market uncertainty and income volatility is that disenfranchisement will continue to rise" (Blix 2017, 10).

Finally, the phenomenon of awarding small-scale, short-term tasks, which can be easily coordinated via platforms, clearly demonstrates that the corresponding policy is faced with a new type of complexity problem. This is because questions of privacy and competition, which have already been discussed in the corresponding chapters above, become relevant simultaneously across all sectors.

References

Abott, Ryan (2020): The Reasonable Robot. Artificial Intelligence and the Law. Cambridge: Cambridge University Press.
Acemoglu, Daron (2002): Technical Change, Inequality, and the Labor Market. Journal of Economic Literature 40 (1), 7–72.
Acemoglu, Daron / Autor, David (2011): Skills, Tasks and Technologies: Implications for Employment and Earnings. In: O. Ashenfelter and D. Card (eds): Handbook of Labor Economics, Elsevier, Vol. 4, Chapter 12, 1043–1171.
Acemoglu, Daron / Lelarge, Claire / Restrepo, Pascual (2020): Competing with Robots: Firm-Level Evidence from France. AEA Papers and Proceedings 110, 383–388.
Acemoglu, Daron / Restrepo, Pascual (2018): The Race between Man and Machine: Implications of Technology for Growth, Factor Shares, and Employment. American Economic Review 108 (6), 1488–1542.
Acemoglu, Daron / Restrepo, Pascual (2020): Robots and Jobs: Evidence from US Labor Markets. Journal of Political Economy 128 (6), 2188–2244.
Acemoglu, Daron / Robinson, James A. (2012): Why Nations Fail. The origins of power, prosperity, and poverty. New York: Penguin Random House LLC.
Aghion, Philippe / Antonin, Céline / Simon / Jaravel, Xavier (2020): What are the Labor and Product Market Effects of Automation? New Evidence from France. CEPR Discussion Paper 14443.
Aghion, Philippe / Antonin, Céline / Bunel, Simon / Jaravel, Xavier (2022): The effects of automation on labor demand: A survey of the recent literature. CEPR Discussion Paper 16868.
Agrawal, Ajay / Gans, Joshua / Goldfarb, Avi (2019): The economics of artificial intelligence: an agenda. Chicago and London: The University of Chicago Press.
Amies, Nick (2022): A growing movement is advocating the rejection of our digital society. The Brussels Times, Saturday, 31. December. Online: https://www.brusselstimes.com/343996/a-growing-movement-is-advocating-the-rejection-of-our-digital-society (last access: 16.05.2023).
Arntz, Melanie / Gregory, Terry / Zierahn, Ulrich (2016): The Risk of Automation for Jobs in OECD Countries: A Comparative Analysis, OECD Social, Employment and Migration Working Paper 189.
Arntz, Melanie / Gregory, Terry / Zierahn, Ulrich (2019): Digitalization and the future of work: Macroeconomic consequences. ZEW Discussion Papers 19-024.
Arntz, Melanie / Blesse, Sebastian / Doerrenberg, Philipp (2022): The End of Work is Near, Isn't It? Survey Evidence on Automation Angst. ZEW Discussion Paper 22-036.
Artuc, Erhan / Bastos, Paulo / Rijkers, Bob (2018): Robots, Tasks and Trade. World Bank Group. Development Economics Development Research Group. Policy Research Working Paper No. 8674.
Autor, David (2015): Why are there still so many jobs? The history and future of workplace automation. Journal of Economic Perspectives 29 (3), 3–30.
Autor, David H. / Katz, Lawrence F. / Melissa S. (2006): The Polarization of the U.S. Labor Market. American Economic Review 96 (2), 189–194.
Baraldi, Claudio / Corsi, Giancarlo / Esposito, Elena / Walker, Katherine (2021): Unlocking Luhmann. A keyword introduction to systems theory. Bielefeld: Bielefeld University Press.
Bernstein, Amy / Raman, Anand (2015): The Great Decoupling: An Interview with Erik Brynjolfsson and Andrew McAfee. Harvard Business Review. Online: https://hbr.org/2015/06/the-great-decoupling (last access: 01.06.2023).

Blix, Mårten (2017): The Effects of Digitalisation on Labour Market Polarisation and Tax Revenue. CESifo Forum. München: ifo Institut–Leibniz-Institut für Wirtschaftsforschung an der Universität München 18 (4), 9–14.

Bonfiglioli, Alessandra / Crinò, Rosario / Fadinger, Harald / Gancia, Gino (2020): Robot Imports and Firm-Level Outcomes. CESifo Working Paper 8741. Munich: CESifo.

Brynjolfsson, Erik / Hitt, Lorin (1996): Firm-Level Evidence on the Returns to Information Systems Spending. Management Science 42 (4), 541–558.

Brynjolfsson, Erik / McAfee, Andrew (2014): The Second Machine Age: Work, Progress, and Prosperity in a Time of Brilliant Technologies. London: W. W. Norton & Company.

Brynjolfsson, Erik / McAfee, Andrew (2015): The Great Decoupling. Harvard Business Review, June, 66–74.

Brynjolfsson, Erik / Mitchell, T. (2017): What can machine learning do? Workforce implications. Science 358 (6379), 1530–1534.

Burkhauser, Richard V. / Corinth, Kevin (2021): The minimum wage versus the earned income tax credit for reducing poverty. IZA World of Labor. Bonn: Institute of Labor Economics (IZA).

Caprettini, Bruno / Voth, Hans-Joachim (2020): Rage against the machines: Labor-saving technology and unrest in England, 1830–32. American Economic Review: Insights 2 (3), 305–320.

Carbonero, Francesco / Ernst, Ekkehard / Weber, Enzo (2018): Robots worldwide: The impact of automation on employment and trade. International Labour Office Research Department Working Paper 36.

Chassagnon, Virgile (2021): Atmosphere, private ordering, and industrial pluralism: Williamson's evolving science of organization. Journal of Institutional Economics 18 (2), 237–251.

Dauth, Wolfgang / Findeisen, Sebastian / Südekum, Jens / Wößner, Nicole (2017): German Robots—The Impact of Industrial Robots on Workers. IAB-Discussion Paper 30.

Dixon, Jay / Hong, Bryan / Wu, Lynn (2019): The Robot Revolution: Managerial and Employment Consequences for Firms. NYU Stern School of Business, Available at SSRN: https://ssrn.com/abstract=3422581 or http://dx.doi.org/10.2139/ssrn.3422581.

Donelly, F. K. (1986): Luddites Past and Present. Labour / Le Travail 18 (Fall), 217–221.

Ete, Ziya / Epitropaki, Olga / Zhou, Qin / Graham, Les (2022): Leader and Organizational Behavioral Integrity and Follower Behavioral Outcomes: The Role of Identifcation Processes. Journal of Business Ethics 176, 741–760.

Eucken, Walter (2004): Grundsätze der Wirtschaftspolitik. Herausgegeben von Edith Eucken und K. Paul Hensel. Tübingen: Mohr Siebeck.

European Central Bank (2021): Digitalisation: Channels, impacts and implications for monetary policy in the euro area, ECB Occasional Paper No. 266, 1, Frankfurt a. M.: European Central Bank.

Farrell, Diana / Greig, Fiona (2017): Paychecks, Paydays and te Online Platform Economy. Big Data on Income Volatility. JPMorgan Chase & Co. Institute.

Fazio, Andrea / Reggiani, Tomasso (2023): Minimum Wage and Tolerance for High Incomes. IZA Institute of Labour Economics Discussion Paper Series 16107.

Fernández-Macías, Enrique (2018): Automation, digitalisation and platforms: Implications for work and employment. Luxembourg: Eurofound, Publications Office of the European Union.

Ford, Martin (2015): The Rise of Robots. New York: Basic Books.

Frank, Lily (2018): The sex robots are here. Science 362 (6421), 1365.

Freeman, Chris / Louçã, Francisco (2001): As time goes by: From the industrial revolutions to the information revolution. Oxford, UK: Oxford University Press.

Frey, Carl Benedikt / Osborne Michael A. (2013): The Future of Employment: How Susceptible are Jobs to Computerisation? University of Oxford, Oxford Martin School Working Paper.

Gal, Peter / Nicoletti, Giuseppe / Renault, Theodore / Sorbe, Stéphane / Timiliotis, Christina (2019): Digitalisation and productivity: In search of the holy grail—Firm-level empirical evidence from EU countries. OECD Economics Department Working Papers No. 1533. Paris: OECD Publishing.

Goldin, Claudia / Katz, Lawrence F. (2009): The Race between Education and Technology. Cambridge, MA: Harvard University Press.

Goos, Maarten / Manning, Allen / Salomons, Anna (2014): Explaining Job Polarization: Routine-biased Technological Change and Offshoring. American Economic Review 104, 2509–2526.

Gordon, Robert J. (2012): Is US Economic Growth Over? Faltering Innovation Confronts the Six Headwinds. NBER Working Paper 18315.

Gordon, Robert J. (2015): Secular Stagnation: A Supply-Side View. American Economic Review, Papers and Proceedings 105 (5), 54–59.

Graetz, Georg / Michaels, Guy (2018): Robots at Work. The Review of Economics and Statistics 100 (5), 753–768.

Gregory, Terry / Salomons, Anna / Zierahn, Ulrich (2016): Racing With or Against the Machine? Evidence from Europe. ZEW Discussion Paper No. 16-053. Mannheim: Zentrum für Europäische Wirtschaftsforschung.

Hancock, Eleanor (2020): Should society accept sex robots? Changing my perspective on sex robots through researching the future of intimacy. Paladyn, Journal of Behavioral Robotics 11, 428–442.

Haskel, Jonathan / Westlake, Stian (2018): Capitalism without Capital. The Rise of the Intangible Economy. Princeton: Princeton University Press.

Horn, Jeff (2005): Machine-breaking in England and France during the Age of Revolution. Labour / Le Travail 55 (Spring), 143–166.

Johns, Fleur E. (2020): Surveillance Capitalism and the Angst of the Petit Sovereign. British Journal of Sociology 71 (5), 1049–1051.

Johnson, Deborah G. / Verdicchio, Mario (2020): Constructing the Meaning of Humanoid Sex Robots. International Journal of Social Robotics 12, 415–424.

Kahnemann, Daniel / Tversky, Amos (1979): Prospect Theory: An Analysis of Decision under Risk. Econometrica 47 (2), 263–292.

Kennedy, John F. (1962): The Presiden's News Conference. February 14, 1962. The American Presidency Project. Online: https://www.presidency.ucsb.edu/documents/the-presidents-news-conference-175 (last access: 03.06.2023).

Keynes, John Maynard (1930): Economic Possibilities for our Grandchildren. The Collected Writings of John Maynard Keynes. Royal Economic Society 1978, 321–332. Online via Cambridge University Press: https://www.cambridge.org/core/services/aop-cambridge-core/content/view/230A7959F87C44AC6E83E406DF126B97/9781139524162c25_p321-332_CBO.pdf/economic-possibilities-for-our-grandchildren-1930.pdf (last access: 01.06.2023).

Koch, Christoph (2019): How the Computer Beat the Go Master. Scientific American. March. Online: https://www.scientificamerican.com/article/how-the-computer-beat-the-go-master/ (last access: 29.05.2023).

Lübker, Malte / Schulten, Thorsten (2022): WSI Minimum Wage Report: Towards a new Minimum Wage Policy in Germany and Europe, WSI Report, No. 71e. Düsseldorf: Hans Böckler-Stiftung, Wirtschafts- und Sozialwissenschaftliches Institut (WSI).

Luhmann, Niklas (1982): The Differentiation of Society. Translated by Stephen Holmes and Charles Larmor. New York, NY: Columbia University Press.

Luhmann, Niklas (1995): Social Systems. Translated by John Bednarz, Jr., with Dirk Baecker. Foreword by Eva M. Knodt. Alexandria, VA: Alexander Street Press.

Mann, Katja / Püttmann, Lukas (2023): Benign Effects of Automation: New Evidence from patent Texts. The Review of Economics and Statistics 105 (3), 562–579.

Mariniello, Mario (2022): Digital Economic Policy. The Economics of Digital Markets from a European Union Perspective. Oxford: Oxford University Press.

McMahon, Michael / Calligaris, Sara / Doyle, Eleanor / Kinsella, Stephen (2021): Scale market power and competition in a digital world: Is bigger better? OECD Science, Technology and Industry Working Papers 2021/01.

Mokyr, Joel / Vickers, Chris / Ziebarth, Nicloas L. (2015): The history of technological anxiety and the future of economic growth: is this time different? Journal of Economic Perspectives 29 (3), 31–50.
Moravec, Hans Peter (2023): Robot, in: Encyclopedia Britannica. Online: https://www.britannica.com/technology/robot-technology (last access: 01.06.2023).
OECD (2016): New forms of work in the digital economy. 2016 ministerial meeting on the digital economy. Technical report. OECD digital economy papers 260.
OECD (2017): OECD Employment Outlook 2017. Paris: OECD Publishing.
OECD (2021): OECD Employment Outlook 2021: Navigating the COVID-19 Crisis and Recovery. Paris: OECD Publishing.
OECD (2022): OECD Employment Outlook 2022: Building Back More Inclusive Labour Markets. Paris: OECD Publishing.
OpenAI (2023): Is Artificial Intelligence intelligent? [Response to user query]. ChatGPT. https://chat.openai.com/ (30.05.2023, 17:34).
Rifkin, Jeremy (2011): The third industrial revolution: How lateral power is transforming energy, the economy, and the world. New York: Palgrave Macmillan.
Rifkin, Jeremy (2014): The zero marginal cost society. The internet of things, the collaborative commons, and the eclipse of capitalism. Houndmills, Basingstoke, Hampshire: Palgrave Macmillan.
Schwab, Klaus (2017): The fourth industrial revolution. New York: Crown Publishing.
Sieroń, Arkadiusz (2019): Money, Inflation and Business Cycles: The Cantillon Effect and the Economy. Abingdon: Routledge.
Solow, Robert (1987): We'd Better Watch Out. New York Times Book Review, July 12.
Spitznagel, Eric (2018): You Can Sleep With the Latest Sex Robots at This Brothel—But Only if They Say 'Yes'. Observer, 11.27. Online: https://observer.com/2018/11/sex-robots-hollywood-brothel-requires-consent-real-doll/ (last access: 29.05.2023).
Suntum, Ulrich van / Böhm, Tobias / Oelgemöller, Jens / Ilgmann, Cordelius (2011): Walter Eucken's Principles of Economic Policy Today. CAWM Discussion Paper No. 49. Preliminary version. August.
The Economist (2015): Automation angst. Three new papers examine fears that machines will put humans out of work. Online: https://www.economist.com/finance-and-economics/2015/08/13/automation-angst (last access: 10.06.2023).
Triplet, Jack E. (1999): The Solow Productivity Paradox: What do Computers do to Productivity? The Canadian Journal of Economics / Revue canadienne d'Economique 32 (2), Special Issue on Service Sector Productivity and the Productivity Paradox, 309–334.
Wang, Chenhao / Chen, Yubo / Xue, Zhipeng / Zhou, Yang / Zhao, Jun (2021): CogNet: Bridging Linguistic Knowledge, World Knowledge and Commonsense Knowledge. Proceedings of the AAAI Conference on Artificial Intelligence 35 (18), 16114–16116.
Webb, Michael (2020): The Impact of Artificial Intelligence on the Labor Market. Stanford University Working Paper. January.
Weil, David (2014): The fissured workplace: why work became so bad for so many and what can be done to improve it. Cambridge, MA: Harvard University Press.
Williamson, Oliver E. (1975): Markets and Hierarchies: Analysis and Antitrust Implications. New York: Free Press.
Williamson, Oliver E. (1985): The Economic Institutions of Capitalism: Firms, Markets, Relational Contracting. New York: Free Press.
Williamson, Oliver E. (1993): Calculativeness, Trust, and Economic Organization, in: Journal of Law and Economics 36 (1), Part 2, 453–486.
Williamson, Oliver E. (2007): An Interview with Oliver Williamson, Journal of Institutional Economics 3 (3), 373–386.
World Robotics (2022): Industrial Robots. Statistics Market Analysis, Forecasts, Case Studies. International Federation of Robotics, Statistical Department. Frankfurt a.M.: VDMA Services GmbH.
Zuboff, Shoshana (2019): Surveillance Capitalism. The fight for a human future at the new frontier of power. New York: Public Affairs.

Chapter 9
Concluding Remarks

What conclusions can be drawn from the observations made? Has the nature of our economy changed as a result of digitalisation—and does this create new challenges for economic policy?

The main chapters of this work endeavoured to trace the current transformation by shedding light on the extent to which certain principles of the market economy have come under new conditions in the digital age. And indeed, considerable changes have become apparent, which are interrelated in many respects. If we attempt the somewhat daring task of summarising the consequences of this, then it is useful to change perspective in order to view the interrelationships presented in a different light.

To this end, it makes sense to take up the idea of *instrumentality* formulated at the beginning of this book and relate it to the levels of social reality concerned here. Firstly, at the elementary level, this concerns technology in the narrower sense, i.e. digital technology. Secondly, the social subsystem of the economy which utilises technologies. Thirdly, economic policy forms a separate area that is committed to the prosperity of society as a whole, which we will not further segment and theorise here as a comprehensive system. So, what does the instrument of digital technology change on these levels?

Looking first at the subsystem of the economy, it can be said that the way in which business is conducted has not changed in principle. The markets follow market mechanisms. There is therefore no need for a new economic science. Accordingly, "diginomics" is not a new discipline, but a meaningful economic description of the effects of a technology on the reality of the economy. The fact that digital goods can be produced at practically zero marginal costs or the phenomenon that the platform economy has a new dynamic and brings with it problems such as the-winner-takes-it-all effects can, in principle, be captured well with the existing tools of economics. One could even argue that economics in particular offers a good approach to explaining the dynamics of current developments.

© The Author(s), under exclusive license to Springer Nature Switzerland AG 2024

J. J. Dötsch, *Economic Policy in the Digital Age*, Contributions to Economics,
https://doi.org/10.1007/978-3-031-53047-0_9

If we understand the economy as a social technique—in other words, an instrument—to solve the problem of scarcity, which should serve the society and its members, the situation is more complicated. Even if the economy itself continues to operate according to the same laws as before, this economy can use digital technology to encompass a rapidly growing number of other areas of society. The example of the "sharing economy" vividly demonstrates this process of a successive commoditisation, which was brought about by the transaction-cost-reducing effect of digital technology. However, this process of change goes beyond this commoditisation. The connectivity of the most diverse areas of life made possible by big data is causing the complexity of the economy to increase enormously. In terms of systems theory, one would say that the more the complexity of the world can be absorbed by the social subsystem "economy", the greater its own complexity. This is the core problem, which now confronts economic policy with new challenges. After all, it is the primary task of economic policy to ensure the sustainable instrumentality of the economy. However, greater complexity means more opportunities and, as always with markets, the results are often surprising.

The problem of this digital penetration and the associated increase in complexity was illustrated in all chapters, regarding the formation of prices, digital means of payment, the openness of markets, the question of ownership of the means of production and ultimately also with regard to the effects on labour itself. The general concept of digitalisation thus refers to the fact that the application of digital technology in certain areas of life has significantly complicated the question of the instrumentality of our actions and continues to do so. If Hayek (1979, 164) correctly claimed that we stumbled into our economic system because we were not clever enough to invent it, then in some areas we will have to admit that we have indeed invented digital technology, but that we are currently stumbling into digitalisation. Obviously, we are still facing a long-term learning process here.

As a result, economic policy now faces a multidimensional challenge. On the one hand, as has become clear everywhere, appropriate solutions require more detailed approaches. However, this means both greater effort and, due to the tendency to act on a case-by-case basis, an increased level of uncertainty for all parties involved. On the other hand, the options available give rise to a plethora of new and difficult balancing problems, as was particularly evident in the chapter on data. And last but not least, it is becoming increasingly recognisable that the challenges often go beyond the scope of national jurisdictions.

The extent to which the economy fulfils its instrumental character in the context of these developments is ultimately a normative question. It will not be possible to make an appropriate judgement on this question if one attempts to answer it from a purely economic perspective. For appropriate answers, and increasingly so, a vast number of other social questions will have to be taken into account. A system is needed to master this complexity and to reduce it. And this is precisely why an approach such as that of the Freiburg School, namely one that is open-ended yet guided by principles, is so topical. Hardly anyone has formulated this more succinctly than Friedrich August von Hayek: "Especially as far as economic policy is concerned, principles are practically all that we have to contribute" (Hayek 1963, 227).

References

Hayek, Friedrich August von (1963): The Economy, Science and Politics. The Collected Works of F.A. Hayek. Volume XV. Market and other Orders. Edited by Bruce Caldwell. Chicago, London (2014): The University of Chicago Press, 217–231.

Hayek, Friedrich August von (1979): Law, Legislation and Liberty, vol 3: The Political Order of a Free People. London: Routledge & Kegan Paul.

SPRINGER NATURE

GPSR Compliance

The European Union's (EU) General Product Safety Regulation (GPSR) is a set of rules that requires consumer products to be safe and our obligations to ensure this.

If you have any concerns about our products, you can contact us on ProductSafety@springernature.com

In case Publisher is established outside the EU, the EU authorized representative is:

Springer Nature Customer Service Center GmbH
Europaplatz 3
69115 Heidelberg, Germany

The manufacturer's authorised representative in the EU is Springer Nature Customer Service Centre GmbH, Europaplatz 3, 69115 Heidelberg, Germany. If you have any concerns regarding our products, please contact ProductSafety@springernature.com

Printed and bound by CPI Group (UK) Ltd, Croydon, CR0 4YY
01/10/2026
02225894-0019